THE
FINAL CALL

THE
FINAL CALL

HOCKEY STORIES FROM
A LEGEND IN STRIPES

KERRY FRASER

Fenn Publishing Company Ltd.

Fenn Publishing Company Ltd.

A Fenn Publishing Book / First Published in 2010
Copyright 2010 © Kerry Fraser

Library and Archives Canada Cataloguing in Publication

Fraser, Kerry, 1952–
        The final call: hockey stories from a legend in stripes / Kerry Fraser.

ISBN 978-1-55168-353-9

        1. Fraser, Kerry, 1952–. 2. Hockey referees—Biography.
3. National Hockey League—Biography. I. Title.

GV848.5.F73A3 2010   796.962092   C2010-903442-2

ONTARIO ARTS COUNCIL
CONSEIL DES ARTS DE L'ONTARIO

The publisher gratefully acknowledges the support of the Canada Council for the Arts and
the Ontario Arts Council for its publishing program. We acknowledge the support of the
Government of Ontario through the Ontario Media Development Corporation's Ontario
Book Initiative.

We acknowledge the financial support of the Government of Canada through the Canada
Book Fund (CBF) for our publishing activities.

Excerpt taken from *Playing with Fire*. Copyright © 2009 by Theoren Fleury and Kirstie
McLellan Day. Reprinted with permission of HarperCollins *Publishers Ltd.* All rights
reserved.

Fenn Publishing Company Ltd.
Bolton, Ontario, Canada
www.hbfenn.com

Text design and electronic formatting: Marijke Friesen
Printed and bound in Canada
10 11 12 13 14 5 4

To the most important people in my life, who at various times were the only ones I could count on:

My beloved wife, Kathy: soulmate, number-one fan, and best mother and grandmother a child could ever hope for . . .

Bursting with a father's pride for each of my exceptional children: Marcie, Ryan, Jessica, Matthew, Ian, Jaime, and Kara.

And finally for the little angels that they have blessed us with so far: Harrison, Brady, Madyn, Daryn, and Kiera.

CONTENTS

FOREWORD
by Wayne Gretzky

Every participant in a hockey game brings a unique perspective to the game. The players on the ice, the coaches behind the bench, and the fans in the arena all view the game differently and with different emotions. But there is another element in each game that is of great importance. The officials are actively involved in every minute of a hockey game. They are part of the action, and, like the players, they affect the outcome of the game. Kerry Fraser's new book gives us the insights of an NHL referee who worked 30 seasons and officiated in more games than any other ref. Kerry loves the game as much as anyone, but he has participated in a way that few of us have experienced. His book gives us a fascinating look at what professional hockey is like for an NHL referee.

Kerry began his career in the NHL one year after I did, so I spent nearly my entire career with him as a regular ref in our games. As any player does, I had a few run-ins with Kerry over those years. In fact, it was probably more than a few. I don't think he was always right, but I know I wasn't either. Players and refs often don't see things the same way in the middle of a game. But one thing Kerry always had from every player was respect. You would disagree with him, yell at him, maybe even say a few things under your breath that you wouldn't want him to hear, but in the end you always knew Kerry was being as fair as he could possibly be. In a 2005 poll of NHL players Kerry was voted "most consistent referee" by a wide margin. That shows you how highly the players regarded his officiating.

Hockey was Kerry's career and his passion, but he always kept things in perspective. His book makes clear that his family and faith were, and are, the most important and enduring things in his life. Sometimes a referee doesn't get much respect from anyone. The fans, the players, the coaches—all of us can be pretty hard on them. But everyone knows we need them. And we can all agree that they have an extremely tough job to do. I'm grateful for Kerry's enjoyable and fascinating look at his career and life. Since 1994 Kerry has worn number 2 on his jersey, but for myself and thousands of hockey fans around the world, Kerry will always be number 1!

HOLDING ON:
THE FINAL GAME

The relatively short walk along the rubber mat from the officials' dressing room to the ice at the Wachovia Center, home of the Philadelphia Flyers, seems longer today. The kind word and pat on the back I always receive from Louie, our dressing-room-door attendant, is softer than usual. It has the feel of an affectionate gesture, the kind extended when old friends part company, not knowing when (or if) they'll see each other again.

This is the final day of another regular season, my 30th in the National Hockey League and 34th as a contracted NHL referee. But it's not just another season; this will be my last!

Just two and a half hours from now, the 2009–10 season, and I will be swept out of the building along with the popcorn boxes, empty beer cups, and other refuse the patrons will have discarded. It is difficult for me to comprehend that time has passed so quickly. With each stride, I recall the tremendous excitement of my very first NHL game as a referee.

Thoughts of that night—October 17, 1980, in Denver, as the Colorado Rockies hosted the Minnesota North Stars—fuse with the bittersweet emotion I now feel. My mind spins out of control as I try to connect the dots of all the games between my first and last. I'm overwhelmed for a moment, then reality takes hold and the analytical part of my brain tells me to check these thoughts along with the rising wave of emotion.

The shrill whistle from the lips of John Malandra, the NHL's security representative, clears the way past the Zamboni, where the ice crew and ushers have formed a sort of receiving line or honour guard. Stepping onto the polished floor of my office for the 1,904th time (an NHL record), I feel the buzz of the capacity crowd of 19,536. They are at the ready, poised to erupt in unison when their heroes take to the ice from either dressing room. Competition between the rival groups of partisans had already begun in the pre-game warm-up, the chants of "Let's go, Rangers" being drowned out by the sheer numbers of vocal cords countering with "Let's go, Flyers." So far, it appears that no fights have taken place in the stands. This afternoon's game has assumed the magnitude of a Game Seven, as the winners will capture the final Eastern Conference playoff spot while the losers will break out their golf clubs earlier than expected.

Depending on the tone that the game takes, I suspect that violence between fans will be a foregone conclusion. (Fortunately, we on-ice officials won't be called on to break it up.) The passion the fans from these two cities feel for their respective teams, and the animosity they demonstrate for each other, whether on the football field, the baseball diamond, or in the hockey arena, runs deep. And hockey fans are a special breed, one that takes team loyalty to a whole different level, especially when it comes to the Flyers and the Rangers.

When this type of energy is generated by the hockey faithful, it spurs athletes and officials alike to reach their peak of performance. I feel the juice running through my soon-to-be-58-year-old-body (considered ancient in this occupation) as I take my first turn around the Wachovia ice. The first lap is always the litmus test as to how my body feels and will respond to the demands that

I am about to make on it. Over the course of my career, I've learned to utilize my internal thermometer to gauge the physical and emotional signals my body sends me. When necessary, I use positive self-talk to overcome any deficiencies that I detect, whether it is a lack of energy, heavy legs, aches, pains, or a need for heightened awareness and mental focus. The brain is the strongest muscle I have packed into my diminutive frame. Today, mission control tells me that all systems are go. My blades glide effortlessly over the ice as I fly around the 200-by-85-foot surface with the enthusiasm of a rookie.

Looking at the excited faces on the other side of the glass, I recognize many that are familiar. There are no lingering gazes today, however, as I quickly scan past the masses to find the box where my wife, Kathy, our children, grandchildren, and other family members are located. I catch a glimpse of them standing and waving, cheering on their hero. A tear forms in my eye as I consider the love and pride I feel for each of them—and them for me.

I'm transported back to a magical evening spent last night at our home with Kathy, all of our seven children and their spouses, five grandchildren and other extended family. We are joined by my fellow officials for this game: referee Kelly Sutherland, linesmen Don Henderson and Darren Gibbs, and their wives. It was a casual and relaxed evening, sharing a barbecue, but the love that our family feels for one another was clearly demonstrated and visible to our first-time guests. Throughout the evening, we shared stories and laughter. From time to time, each of the officials would remark on the magnitude of this game and the opportunity we were being given in this final moment of my career. I was presented with beautiful, heartfelt gifts from my family and friends, and I was deeply touched by all the love our home held.

The evening ended at a reasonable hour, all of us knowing full well the importance of the game at three o'clock the next afternoon. The NY Rangers had beaten the Flyers the night before at

Madison Square Garden creating a tie for the final playoff spot
between the two rival franchises. The entire regular season boiled
down to this one last game and had all the makings of a Cinder-
ella story.

Our house overflowed with laughter and music as my brother
Rick and our sons Ryan and Matthew played their guitars and
sang well past midnight, though by then I had long since retired
for the evening. I would sleep restlessly, but my final thought as I
dozed off was how blessed I was, not only to have had this mag-
nificent career, but more importantly, the love and devotion of a
very special family.

When I awoke, in the still-dark room, on Sunday morning, I
realized I had guests with me, ones who hadn't been formally invited yet are always welcome. They came from another place and
a previous time in my life. Now that I think of it, they've always
been there to guide me.

My father was the first of them, followed by John McCauley,
my mentor, former colleague, and NHL director of officiating.
They were joined by Chief Dennis Ryan, the NHL's former security representative for the New York Rangers—I knew who he'd
be cheering for—and his son-in-law Mikey O'Laughlin, a former
security representative for the New Jersey Devils who had succumbed to an horrendous form of cancer, leaving his wife, Mary
Katherine, and their young children behind. I felt their presence,
and I recognized them. I was startled by it all; I also had the sense
that, while their visit was supportive and friendly, it was stirring
up emotions that I couldn't allow to carry me away. I had to focus
on the task at hand: the game. I pushed them aside in my thoughts
and extended an invitation to visit another time.

Then I heard two of our granddaughters, Madyn and baby
Daryn, enjoying the morning excitement of waking up in Mama
and Papa's house for the first time. It made me smile, but it also
reminded me that, as I had been forced to do when I sent the

visitors away, I needed to insulate myself from all distractions until after the game. I quickly showered and dressed and told Kathy I was heading off, alone, to Mass—the Feast of Divine Mercy—and that I would see her after the game.

My equipment bag had been packed the night before, and it sat waiting for me at the back door, as did a second duffle bag containing the nine number-two jerseys I would wear that day. I wanted my kids to be able to share this moment with me forever, so I planned on changing in the penalty box during every commercial time out so that I could give each a game-worn jersey. My waiting bags were a common sight for the Fraser family, but on this solemn morning I grabbed them to leave one last time and waved goodbye to Kathy and the kids. At that moment, they stopped what they were doing amid the usual bustle of a weekend morning, their heads popping out from various rooms and activities to wish me good luck. I turned and met the teary eyes of each of them; their sadness began to materialize for me, too. But I had to hold back that flood, so I quickly exited the house.

I went by myself to church, followed by breakfast alone at a local diner, and then off to the rink. As I pulled into the players' parking lot, my phone beeped with a text message that had been sent at 11:34 a.m. It read: "Congratulations to u and your family on an outstanding career! U without question made the game better! Best wishes to u on the next step of life! 99." The peace I had gained at morning Mass was immediately replaced with an adrenaline rush, thanks to that message from Wayne Gretzky.

Rolling my equipment bag toward the entrance, I noticed some loyal Flyers fans had already assembled along the fence above the parking lot to offer support as their heroes entered the bowels of the arena. Several of them called down to me, wishing me luck in retirement and to have a great last game. Once inside, I was greeted by the familiar and always friendly faces of the Wachovia Center staff, standing at their posts by the door and in the corridor.

On this game day I arrived 45 minutes earlier than normal and two hours prior to the opening faceoff. I wanted to savour all the day had to offer as well as fulfill media requests. I met with Michael Newall, a reporter with the *Philadelphia Inquirer*, at one o'clock to conclude a feature on my retirement game. At 1:30 I taped a television interview, to be aired during the second intermission, with my good friend Steve Coates, a Flyers colour analyst. Coatsie is a former player from the Broad Street Bullies days and he brings lots of energy to the Flyers' broadcast while reporting from ice level between the benches.

My colleagues arrived in our dressing room just after I finished up with Coatsie. We revisited the wonderful evening we'd spent at our home last night as their equipment was unpacked and laid out. I stepped into the hall outside our dressing room and was greeted by Mark Messier, whose trademark smile lit up the hallway as he stopped by to congratulate me on a great career and wish me the very best in retirement. Mess was not only one of the greatest players—and leaders—in the history of the game but a special individual as well. I felt extremely privileged and humbled to have him visit. Mark graciously accepted my invitation into the officials' room to say hello to my colleagues. I knew it would mean a great deal to them as well. Added to the text I had received from Gretz, I felt I was being touched by greatness a second time.

Now, though, it was time to put on my game face. Hanging up my light grey pinstripe suit, I put on my work clothes and stepped back into the hall with my exercise bands. Darren Gibbs and I broke a sweat as we performed a stretch-and-resistance routine with the bands. While working out in the hall I also got a chance to say hi to Glen Sather, the Rangers' president and general manager; Jim Schoenfeld, their assistant GM; and Peter Luukko, president and chief operating officer of Comcast-Spectacor, the owners of the Flyers, as they passed by.

After the teams completed their on-ice warm-up, it was time

for us to return to our dressing room to suit up and go over any last-minute details on our mental checklist for the game. I had been in this situation countless times over my 2,164 games, but I didn't want to leave any stone unturned in this, my last one, so I took a leading role in the discussion. The guys I was sharing the room with this day had been hand-picked, not just because they were loyal friends, but because they were also great officials. They didn't need a Knute Rockne speech at this point in their career.

I stressed that every decision we made had the potential to impact the game and the season for either team. There could be no guessing on a play, and if one of us didn't have the best sightline to make a call, the others needed to step up in a supporting role. Finally, I told Kelly, "Let's make sure that every penalty we call will stand the test of any form of scrutiny." We all knew what was expected of us, and as we left the dressing room I was confident that the Rangers and Flyers would decide their own fates that day and that we would not have a negative impact on either.

I was the first one through the door. It was now time to take that short walk along the rubber mat to start a game for the very last time.

The sound of my name on the public address system jolts me back to the present. The announcer informs the crowd that this will be Kerry Fraser's final game in the NHL. A three-minute highlight video, prepared by my daughter Jessica, is shown on the video screens, prompting a standing ovation from the sellout crowd. Both the video and the crowd's reception are unprecedented for a referee and are tremendously humbling.

What would Fred Shero, the legendary coach of the Broad Street Bullies, have thought as the Philadelphia faithful—and the Ranger fans who had infiltrated the sea of orange and black—recognized a ref in such kindly fashion?

My two grandsons, eight-year-old Harrison and six-year-old Brady, were skated over by one of the Flyers Ice Girls to join me for a ceremonial faceoff between captains Mike Richards of the Flyers and Chris Drury of the Rangers. Each youngster wore an actual jersey of mine from the 1993 Stanley Cup final between Montreal and Los Angeles, which took place following "The Missed Call" (more on that later). Across the back of each sweater, the name FRASER was proudly embroidered. The boys stood beside me and my colleagues at centre ice as Lauren Hart, daughter of the late Flyers broadcaster Gene Hart, started her rendition of "God Bless America."

I often think of Gene, the Flyers' original play-by-play voice who helped the City of Brotherly Love fall head over heels in love with the team. I recall the chance meeting my wife and I had with Gene one morning during breakfast at Olga's Diner in Marlton, New Jersey, just a couple of weeks before Gene passed away in 1999. The entire conversation focused on his talented young daughter (Lauren), whom he was helping to become a professional singer. I consider how proud Gene must be of Lauren, a cancer survivor, right now as he looks down from his heavenly press box.

My knees buckle as Lauren is joined from a higher place by Kate Smith, whose image and voice now appear and boom out from the big screens over my head. This mirage from the days of the Broad Street Bullies transports me across the parking lot to the Spectrum, and back in time to 1985. For a moment I am poised to drop the puck between Mark Messier of the Edmonton Oilers and Dave Poulin of the Flyers to begin my very first Stanley Cup final. As I stand at centre ice today, my heart pounds with such ferocity that I can hear it above the decibels generated by Lauren's and Kate's powerful vocal cords.

In this moment, I take refuge in the silent bunker of internal solitude. Suddenly, the delirious crowd is hushed. I am left to complete my final pre-game ritual by talking privately with God as I offer thanks and adoration for all that He has blessed me with. I have so much to be thankful for, and without Him none of it would be possible.

The anthem is complete, my prayers have been said, my little grandsons have been ushered off the ice, and our team of officials comes together at centre ice. Each of us touches one hand to our shoulder, then to our heart, and then brings our fists together in the middle to show solidarity as a crew and to honour our fallen colleague Stéphane Provost, who was killed in a motorcycle accident during the lockout season. We carry his memory with us every game. With this gesture complete, my colleagues assume their starting positions.

The Wachovia Center seems quiet, almost serene, in this moment before all hell breaks loose. As I hold the puck in my left hand, I put my right hand upon my chest and briefly speak to the opposing centremen, Jeff Carter of the Flyers and Artem Anisimov of the Rangers, just before dropping the puck.

"Boys," I say, referencing Herb Brooks's speech to the 1980 U.S. hockey team that carried out the Miracle on Ice at the Winter Olympics in Lake Placid. "This isn't about me; this game is about you. And this is your time, not mine."

They both nod slightly.

I look down at my right hand, which now holds the puck with a firm grip. Just as I have done 2,164 times before (between regular season and Stanley Cup playoff games), I ask the two centres to please put their sticks down on the ice—a request I always make politely and which has never been denied. It is now that I normally drop the puck between the waiting sticks, but I find myself hesitating this time. I can't seem to let go. The muscles in my hand squeeze the puck in a viselike grip for what seems like an entire career.

The players hunger for the black disc, but I don't want to release it. If I drop the puck, it will bring me one second closer to the end. It remains in my hand; I am frozen in time.

IN THE
BEGINNING

I learned to skate practically as soon as I was able to take my first steps. I was 15 months old and somehow my dad found a pair of skates the size of a baby shoe. He was playing minor professional hockey in the IHL at the time. The team trainer laced up my skates and I pushed a chair around the ice before the players practiced. I cut my teeth in hockey dressing rooms and I was seldom seen without a little hockey stick in my hands, slapping around a puck or a ball. My great-grandfather on my mom's side, Rawcliffe, lived with us, and used his walking cane as a goal stick during our games played in the kitchen. When one got past him I raised my stick in the air and celebrated by shouting, "He scores!"

My father, Hilt, went on to coach me to a high level of amateur hockey and instilled in me a "never quit" attitude along with unwavering courage to fight the good fight. I am reminded of the countless hours spent skating on the backyard rink Dad made for my brother, Rick, and me. Many nights our game of shinny was halted and we were carried into the kitchen to wolf down the dinner that Mom had prepared. Our skates dripped melting snow onto the newspapers that were placed beneath our chairs. After dinner was hastily consumed, we were lifted back out to our fantasy

Maple Leaf Gardens, taking on the names of our favourite NHL players until the floodlights flickered. That was our signal that the game was over and bedtime was soon to follow. Fatigued from a long day of child's play, I was lulled to sleep with the memorable sound already etched into my young mind of the nasal voice of legendary Leafs broadcaster Foster Hewitt, saying, "Goodnight, hockey fans across Canada and the United States from the gondola high above Maple Leaf Gardens."

I even got to skate with the big kids once in a while. Pat "Whitey" Stapleton, who lived up the street before moving on to star with the Boston Bruins and Chicago Blackhawks, had a great rink which he would let my dad play on. In addition to high boards and chicken-wire fencing, to keep the pucks in play without having to dig them out of a snow bank, Whitey even had a shed with a pot-bellied stove that became a dressing room every winter. As a five-year-old, I felt like I had made it to the big time whenever I got to play on his rink! Pat Stapleton was, and still is, a hero of mine.

I would never have considered a career in officiating if it weren't for Ted Garvin. Ted was a lifelong family friend who played in the International Hockey League with my dad and suggested to me that I should get into officiating following my final season playing junior hockey. Ted was coaching the Port Huron Flags of the IHL at the time, prior to moving on to coach the Detroit Red Wings for a brief period. He felt that the game needed officials who had played to at least the junior level and understood the game from a player's perspective. Ted was a good judge of talent and knew that I would never play at the NHL level; rather than see me kick around in the minor pro leagues, he felt my best avenue to the NHL was as a referee.

Ted's antics from behind the bench were legendary when it came to referee-baiting. He would throw a towel out onto the ice to protest a call and would be handed an automatic bench penalty under the rules for throwing articles on the ice. To circumvent the rule Ted tied a string to the towel. At the opportune moment, the towel was fired high into the air and over the boards in view of the official. As the referee started to snap his arm up to signal a penalty, Ted would jerk on the string to retrieve the towel before it ever hit the ice, causing the ref to scratch his head. Legendary IHL referee and dear friend Sam Sisco finally put a stop to the fishing-line towel when he told Ted, "When I see that towel go up you better have the power to suspend it in the air, because if it comes down anywhere you are getting a bench penalty!"

"Terrible Ted" was responsible for more than one rule change in the book. One time, a penalty shot was called against his team; rather than have his goalie, Gaye Coolie, between the pipes for the free shot, Ted put monster defenceman Gerry "Kong" Korab in goal. Ted instructed Kong to charge the unsuspecting shooter as soon as he crossed the blue line and flatten him with a bodycheck. The move proved successful and quickly caught the attention of Roger Neilson. After Roger used the tactic in an NHL game, a rule was instituted that only a goalie could defend against a penalty shot.

Given these antics I thought Ted was just looking for a familiar face in stripes to play his tricks on, but nonetheless I filled out the application that Ted gave me and attended the Haliburton Referee School in late August of 1972. The camp administrator was Bill Beagan, commissioner of the IHL at the time, who had fined and suspended Garvin on multiple occasions. Bill's instructors at the five-day camp included Vern Buffey, Bill Friday, Bruce Hood, Ron Wicks, John D'Amico, John McCauley, and other experienced professional officials. The World Hockey Association came into being that summer, and opportunity knocked when the NHL lost several officials to the upstart league.

On the evening of the second-to-last day of school, I was assigned to referee 10 minutes of a summer league game. The instructors would supervise our work and offer a critique. Also in attendance was Frank Udvari, a retired referee (and Hockey Hall of Fame inductee) and assistant to the NHL's referee-in-chief, Ian "Scotty" Morrison. After my 10-minute stint, Mr. Udvari met me in the officials' room. He said he liked what he'd seen of my work and wanted to invite me to the NHL officials' training camp in Toronto two days later. Since it was so soon, Frank said he would have to check with Scotty to make sure they could accommodate me.

"If I can bring you to camp," he added, "there is one thing that I must ask of you."

"Anything, Mr. Udvari. What is it?"

He looked at my then-stylish Beatle cut that hung to the bottom of my ears and quipped, "You've got to get a haircut!"

Even now it is hard for me to fathom how I could have embarked on this ambitious career path so quickly. I was only 20 years old and had virtually no officiating experience beyond helping my father drop pucks as a 12–14-year-old in an Industrial league just to get in some extra skating when I wasn't playing a game. Here I was, after completing a five-day referee school, joining the regular NHL officials at their training camp. I was either in the right place at the right time, living a charmed life, or had a guardian angel sitting on my shoulder. Looking back, I believe it was all of the above. My wife Kathy often says that with my God-given talent for this job I was simply born to referee; the Wayne Gretzky of officiating!

I got home late Friday evening from Haliburton Referee School and was awakened early the next morning to a phone call from Mr. Udvari. Frank said he was pleased to confirm my invitation to the NHL officials' training camp and told me to report to the Toronto Airport Hilton hotel by five the next day. He advised me the camp would last a total of 10 days and told me what to bring. I was so excited I hardly heard anything he said—including the part about what time to report. I rushed off to get a haircut and tell my mom and dad the good news. Dad immediately pulled out one of his old scrapbooks and showed me an article from the 1948–49 season, when, as a tough defenceman for the Sarnia Sailors of the OHA Senior B loop, he was suspended for one game and fined $5 (at the time a loaf of bread cost five cents) for punching referee Frank Udvari during a game! I thought it prudent to keep that information filed away in my "scrapbook" until now!

The next day, I got up in the wee hours, leaving Sarnia at 2:00 a.m. so I could check in by the designated time. I sure didn't want to be late. I approached the front desk at 4:45 a.m., gave my name and stated proudly that I was part of the NHL officials group. The clerk said, "Gee, you're awful early, we don't have a room ready. We were told you guys weren't checking in until five o'clock this evening." At least I had gotten the five o'clock part right. It was at that moment that I learned you'll never get in trouble for being early—just for not listening properly! As soon as my room was ready, I caught up on some badly needed rest prior to a scheduled reception to kick off training camp.

It was at that reception where I first met Scotty Morrison, the NHL's referee-in-chief. Mr. Morrison was small in stature (even shorter than I was) but carried himself like a giant. I remember noticing the presence he commanded just by walking into a room. While his demeanour could be intimidating, especially to a 20-year-old aspiring official, I also saw a warmth about him as he moved around the room, joking with his staff, particularly his veteran core of officials: Art Skov, Lloyd Gilmour, Wally Harris, Bruce Hood, Ron Wicks, John D'Amico, Matt Pavelich, and Neil Armstrong. I caught a glimpse of a "fatherly" side of Scotty as he greeted his next generation of "go-to" guys: Dave Newell, Bob Myers, John McCauley, Andy Van Hellemond, Bryan Lewis, Ron

Hoggarth, and Ray Scapinello, among others. It made me feel much more at ease, especially when, after Frank Udvari introduced me to the "boss," I felt Mr. Morrison's genuine warmth and sincerity as he welcomed me to camp for the very first time. I instantly felt more relaxed, even though I made a point of wiping my sweaty palm before shaking Scotty's outstretched hand.

Once the meeting began, I sat at the back and off to the side with the other invitees and absorbed everything that was said as if I was a sponge trying to drain the ocean. That's just how little I knew, compared to how much I hoped to learn.

I'll acknowledge that I brought with me to camp an abundance of confidence, along with an aggressive nature that was, in part, a by-product of my Type-A personality and the Little Man Syndrome I had acquired. Both, on occasion, had served me relatively well as a player. If not held in check, however, I would quickly cross the line into cockiness and arrogance. But I recognized that God gave us two ears and one mouth for a reason: to listen at least twice as much as we spoke. So much could be absorbed and learned just by listening to the experiences of officials who knew more. In my particular case, that was everyone!

Medical examinations took place the next morning, and we stood in line, military style, to fill out paperwork and receive our labelled urine-specimen bottles and blood vials. The urine bottle was easy to fill for most, as a large amount of liquid had been consumed during the reception the night before. Blood collection, on the other hand, was not always so easy. Dave Newell was the first guy I saw go down. I'm not talking about just knees buckling; he literally passed out and needed to be revived after the first prick of the needle. Newelly got somewhat better with it over the years, but the docs always stood by with a towel to absorb his sweat and smelling salts to revive him. (Today, Dave has to check his blood sugar throughout the day and has no problem with pinpricks, although he's still not real fussy on needles.)

Once the medicals were out of the way, we could get down to the real business of training camp. The operative word in those days was "training," as players and officials alike had to work for two weeks to get into the required physical shape after an extensive, largely idle, off-season. Training habits and methods would improve drastically after Team Canada faced the Soviet Union in the 1972 Summit Series, and NHLers got their first exposure to such finely conditioned athletes as the Russians.

While we worked hard in training camp, we played even harder. Each day, we trained at Centennial Park in Etobicoke, not far from Pearson International Airport. Aside from twin ice rinks, the complex had a soccer/football field surrounded by an all-weather track, a ski hill, and chalet that was used for lunch and classroom/meeting purposes. Two-a-day sessions on the ice were always followed by discussions about rules and administrative matters. One of those on-ice sessions would be spent playing hockey. I had just finished playing junior hockey a few months earlier, but some of these scrimmages were more brutal than any league game I had ever experienced. In one game, veteran referee Lloyd Gilmour chopped linesman Ron "Huck" Finn so hard with his stick I thought the benches would clear! All was forgotten that night, though, when the action was relived into the early-morning hours.

We went through the rule book from cover to cover during camp and arduously analyzed every rule—the history of each, and the "what-ifs" that always came up. In the late afternoon, the sun would blaze through the chalet windows so intensely that some guys would nod off, looking like turtles basking on a rock. For me, the rules discussions were fascinating—to hear the actual circumstances under which various rules came to be written into the book, as a result of calls made by such legends as King Clancy, Red Storey, and George Hayes. I felt privileged to gain these insights; they were a valuable education, one that gave me cause not only to see the game from a different perspective but to feel the depth of passion that the game stirred within me. This sharing of knowledge enabled each official to enforce the rules with a common-sense approach that does not seem so common today.

The rule book has expanded extensively since 1972, and as time passed I was able to pass along the historical background I had gained in those early years. While some of the group seemed to care, the reality was that many didn't.

On the evening of the fourth day of training camp, Scotty organized a squash tournament at the Skyline Hotel on Dixon Road, with a reception to follow. It was part of the agenda, so attendance was mandatory. While it was designed under the guise of keeping the group together and letting them enjoy a "few" beers in a social setting, I think Scotty's real goal was to control and limit the amount of socializing that took place on a nightly basis. I made an appearance and also a conscious effort to maintain a low profile by having two beers away from the main crowd that had gathered in the room. I was about to leave the party when Dave Newell approached me and introduced himself.

Dave began the conversation by complimenting my skating ability, saying that he wished he could skate as well as me. Next, he asked if I had any plans for the rest of the evening because, as he put it, "some of the veterans have been observing you since the start of training camp and we really like the way that you carry yourself. We would like you to join us tonight for a few beers if you don't have any plans." I felt humbled and privileged by the invitation to join the upper echelon of the officiating fraternity, even if only for one night.

In addition to Newell, the core members of this "welcome wagon" comprised Art Skov, Lloyd Gilmour, Bob Myers, John McCauley, Ron Hoggarth, and linesman Jim Christison. Even though I socialized to the fullest extent that my tolerance would allow, I remained true to my "two ears, one mouth" philosophy and soaked up as much as I could from my newly acquired mentors.

A couple of days later, I would feel the genuine warmth that came from being fully accepted—initiated—by the number-one referee in the world, Art Skov. I was standing in the shower after an on-ice session when I felt a warm spray against the back of my leg—and it wasn't coming from the shower nozzle. Turning around, I saw Art with his "hose" in hand, urinating on my leg. I was now fully vested into the officiating fraternity! In that moment, I learned it is much better to be pissed *on* than pissed off. I knew that if I succeeded in my quest to make it to the NHL as a referee, I would join an elite group of about a dozen men in the world. And I knew I still had an awful long way to go.

After training camp I was assigned a number of pre-season games as a linesman. The first game I worked was with Neil Armstrong, who is in the Hockey Hall of Fame as a linesman and is a fellow Sarnia resident. Once the season began, Frank Udvari placed me in the American Hockey League as a part-time linesman. There, I would gain experience and be exposed to the highest level of professional hockey below the NHL. The AHL paid me $85 per game, plus expenses—but no benefits. I got another part-time job, in the display department at Sears, dressing mannequins and hanging decorations. The guy I worked for, Bill Foubister, was fantastic. He allowed me the flexibility to get away whenever I had games.

There wasn't a city I could drive to from Sarnia, so I experienced air travel for the first time. Usually, I'd fly out of Detroit, unless I was assigned to a game in Halifax, Montreal's farm team, in which case I'd fly from home. I worked 58 games that season, so you do the math! Clearly, I was a long way from "The Show." One of the benefits, however, was that I got see how the referees under NHL supervision called and controlled the games. Of course, that was part of Frank Udvari's educational plan for me. I was learning the ropes from guys like John McCauley, Bryan Lewis, Ron Hoggarth, Alf LeJeune, Greg Madill, Dave Shewchyk (the father of current NHL linesman Mark Shewchyk), and Bob Kilger. Some of them became successful NHL referees; others found success elsewhere. Kilger, for example, went on to bigger and better things as a member of Parliament, moving quickly up through the ranks to become chief government whip and deputy speaker when Jean Chrétien was prime minister. Bob's son Chad played more than 700 games in the NHL, with Anaheim, Winnipeg/Phoenix, Chicago, Edmonton, Montreal, and Toronto. Bob was a wonderful guy and an excellent role model. Before our pre-game lunches, he would take me on a walk that would inevitably lead us to a Catholic church in time for noon Mass or just to stop in and say a few prayers, as he put it. I wasn't a Catholic, or even particularly spiritual at the time, but I always went in with him. It might have been an early "call" to me from above, which I finally answered in 1995.

John McCauley and Bryan Lewis (after John's unfortunate passing in 1989) both held the position as NHL referee-in-chief, thereby becoming my boss. I truly loved John. He was such a great guy to travel with during that first year, and with his relaxed demeanour he instantly became a wonderful mentor to me right up until his death. I have had the pleasure of working with John's son, Wes, many times since he joined the NHL officiating staff. (I'll speak more about the McCauley family a bit later.)

In September of 1973, I returned to training camp, and Scotty offered me my first NHL contract, to work as a minor-league referee. I quickly signed and returned the contract before he could change his mind! My base salary was $6,500 with a $1,000 bonus for working a prescribed number of games (which I achieved) in the American and Central Professional leagues. The NHL also had a working relationship with the International Hockey League, the Western Canada Hockey League (now the WHL), and the Midwest Junior Hockey League based out of Minneapolis (Paul Holmgren played for the St. Paul Vulcans of that league). All I can say is that the $7,500 sure beat the $85 a game from the previous year. I even had health care and pension benefits to boot! I thought I was really on my way up—that is, until I got my first assignment after the pre-season games had concluded.

I was sent to the WCHL for eight games in 10 days. The first was in Flin Flon, Manitoba. No offence to Bobby Clarke, Reggie Leach, and all the other great players who have come out of that "rock pile," but when the little 12-passenger plane I took from Winnipeg landed, I thought I had touched down on the moon! The terminal looked like a shack without the tar paper. "Old Joe," the baggage handler, took the luggage off the plane, put it on a cart, and wheeled it inside the shack. Taking my bags off the cart, I noticed that Joe had hung his baggage handler's cap on a hook and immediately replaced it with one bearing a limousine company logo. Then he loudly inquired, "Anyone for transportation into town?" (I was the only passenger that remained. Everyone else had been picked up by family or friends!)

I jumped aboard Joe's stagecoach—actually, a Suburban—and we bounced into town over what seemed like an old-fashioned corduroy road. I checked into the Flin Flon Hotel on Main Street—complete with wooden sidewalks. Heading down to the dining room, "Miss Kitty" served me a wonderful home-cooked meal, after which I walked along Main Street to get a feel for what the entire town had to offer—after all, I had two games here, with a day off sandwiched between them. Five minutes later, I was back at the hotel and in bed for a pre-game nap prior to being picked up by the local linesman for the game that night.

As I sat in the lobby, waiting for my ride and feeling pretty detached from the rest of the world, let alone the NHL, a little old lady with bluish-white hair shouted from the octopus-like phone switchboard beside the front desk, "Is there a Kerry Freezer here?"

I raised my hand and said, "Right here, madam."

"You got a call from New York City. I'll patch it through to the house phone." It was Frank Udvari. He was almost apologetic for sending me to Flin Flon and seemed to read my mind when he said, "I know it must seem like you're a long way from the NHL, but I just wanted you to know that I'm behind you and want to wish you luck in your first game."

I can't tell you how much that call lifted my spirits. What I didn't know at the time was that Frank had also called Ed Chynoweth, president of the WCHL, to say he was sending him a kid who was really green and asking him to hang in there with me because he thought I could be a good one over time.

The Saskatoon Blades were the visiting team, and Pat Price, a highly touted defenceman, was their star player. I didn't realize that visiting teams often developed the "Flin Flon flu" in epidemic proportions at the very thought of the physical abuse they would endure at the hands of both the players and their fans. I would soon find out if I was immune to the dreaded disease. In that first game, I threw out the coach, the legendary Patty Ginnell; their captain and tough guy, Cam Connor (who played for Montreal, Edmonton, and the Rangers); and two other monsters, Jerry Rollins and Kim Clackson (who went on to play for Pittsburgh and Quebec). Throughout the third period, I was skating up and down the middle of the ice to maintain a safe distance from the fans. And if that weren't enough, not only would I have to do this all over again in two nights, but I would get to spend a Saturday night in Flin Flon, hangin' out with the locals! Needless to say, Saskatoon won that first game and their players felt somewhat protected as they entered the game on Sunday.

The writer from the Saskatoon Star Phoenix who covered the team wrote an article the next day about this little referee who had been the star of the game by taking control of it and not being intimidated by the "goonery" of Ginnell and his gladiators. Ed Chynoweth told me later that he called Frank Udvari immediately after reading the newspaper report and said, "Frank, what did you send me?" Frank started to apologize and reminded Ed that he had cautioned him to be patient with me. "No, Frank," Chynoweth said, "you didn't tell me you were sending me a superstar!"

Years later the three of us had a laugh together about my debut in the WCHL. It sure was a great training ground, and if something didn't happen at that level, you wouldn't have to worry about it because it would never happen anywhere else.

I spent so much time alone on the road in the minors. That's because I would most often work with part-time linesmen who went home to their families after the game. And very seldom did we have supervision at that level. You had to try and figure everything out as you went along. I quickly learned that if I was going to get better, I needed to be my strongest critic. After each game, I would reflect on what I did and didn't do right. I tried to be blatantly honest with myself and think of ways I could have achieved a better end result. Not only was I a student of the game; more important, I was a student of officiating.

Every chance I got in the minors, I would observe the unique styles and personalities that each NHL referee brought to his game. If I had a night off, I would ride a bus or stay in an NHL city to take in a game and hang with the crew of officials to listen and learn. I had so much respect for each of them; they were where I wanted to be. I recall watching Art Skov work in Boston one night. Afterward, "Popsy" invited me to join him and the linesmen for a beer at Sansones, across the street from the old Madison Hotel, where we stayed. The Madison was attached to North Station and Boston Garden. The rooms were so small you had to back out, and it often felt as if the trains passed right through on the way to NY Penn Station!

I owe so much to men like Art Skov, Wally Harris, and many others who helped in my development and ultimate success as an official. There are none, however, who had a greater impact on my growth as a referee and as a person than Dave Newell. While there was a brief period in the middle of our relationship when we didn't necessarily see eye to eye, I always admired the unparalleled courage and integrity that Dave displayed, both as a referee on the ice and as president of the NHL Officials' Association for many years.

One night, I watched a Flyers–Leafs playoff game on TV from Maple Leaf Gardens that turned into a war. One of the Flyers was even accused of clubbing an usherette behind the bench. As the Flyers ganged up on Darryl Sittler and Borje Salming, there was Dave in the middle of it all, trying to help protect the players and restore order. In the aftermath, Dave was seen holding a clipboard in his blood-drenched hands, transcribing the penalties for time-keeper "Banana Joe" Lamantia. I recently did a radio show with Bill Clement, the former Flyer who is now an outstanding broadcaster. Years after the fact, his eyes widened as he told me he once saw Bob Clarke spear Dave in the groin during a scrum. Those were intimidating times, and Dave never wavered.

On that night, I learned as much or more about Dave the man as I did about how to referee. In 1973, he had a night off in Minneapolis prior to a North Stars game. I had a game in the Midwest Junior league that night, an hour-and-a-half drive from the city. Dave asked if he could come and watch me work the game and critique my performance. Later, when I was in the same position that Dave had been in, I reflected on the personal sacrifice he made that night for a young referee. That's the kind of guy Dave Newell is.

Once he retired from the ice in 1990, Dave took a management position with the league under the various titles of supervisor, officiating manager, and assistant director of officiating—always with the aim of helping make an official the best he could be. His ability to communicate the vast officiating knowledge he acquired has launched many a career. Several past and current officials will admit that Dave Newell was the very best officiating coach they ever had.

And that list would include the guy who fired him. Unfortunately for the game and the development of young officials, Dave Newell was fired by Stephen Walkom in August of 2006, one year after Walkom took over as the NHL's senior vice-president of officiating. While Walkom has since returned to the ice, much damage was inflicted during his short tenure.

GETTING IN SHAPE

It's always rewarding when the final buzzer sounds to bring another long grind of a hockey season to an end.

My beaten-down body is usually a good indicator as to just how many miles I have travelled and how demanding the 73 games or more that I officiated over the course of the season were.

While the regular season usually begins the first week of October, hockey season in the Fraser household really starts around the end of July, the first week of August at the latest. That's historically when I, Papa Bear, come out of hibernation with a gnawing hunger that won't be satisfied until I've successfully completed the demanding fitness test and weigh-in administered by Dave Smith, the fitness and medical director at the NHL officials' training camp, sometime after Labour Day.

It has taken tremendous dedication and sacrifice to excel as an NHL official for all these years. Unfortunately, far too often my family's sacrifice has been, at the very least, equal to mine. While July and August are supposed to be our off-season vacation time, spent at the Jersey Shore, Kathy and the kids have reluctantly accepted that Dad spends that time obsessing over weight, body fat, and cardio conditioning.

Sometimes, I've tried to combine family activities with training. In late August of 1989, our first summer in New Jersey after our move from Sarnia, Kathy rented a house in Avalon, by the Shore, for a week. We bought one of those big storage pods that strapped to the top of the minivan. I felt like Jimmy Stewart in the classic movie *Mr. Hobbs Goes on Vacation*. I had that sucker loaded with lawn chairs, boogie boards, and even a portable gas grill. The van was jammed so tight with kids (we "only" had six then—Kara was born in 1990) and luggage that we almost had to leave the family dog, Tinker, at home. I ran along the beach all week, chasing kids and fishing them out of the surf when it got rough. I would inline-skate at least 10 miles a day before everyone got up or after the gang went to bed.

Being close to the water is something my family enjoys very much. I grew up playing in the clear, blue water of Lake Huron. My hometown of Sarnia, known primarily for its petrochemical industry and shipping, is near the mouth of the lake, where it joins the St. Clair River, which flows 60 miles south to Detroit. Across the river is Port Huron, Michigan. The entire region is known as Bluewater Land, and the cities (and countries) are connected by the Bluewater Bridge.

After training camp in 1988, Kathy and I loaded the kids and Tinker into the minivan and drove 600 miles to our new home in southern New Jersey, near Philadelphia. Two hours into the drive, just past Toledo, everyone's initial excitement for the move gave way to every kid's number-one question: "Are we there yet?" At that point, we only had 10 more hours of drive time ahead of us.

Finally, we reached Philadelphia and were crossing into New Jersey over the Walt Whitman Bridge. Looking down at the water below, our daughter Jaime, who was six years old and was then the baby of the family, asked with total innocence if this bridge was named the Greenwater Bridge.

Quality of family time has always been a priority for Kathy and me, in spite of this little bump in the calendar caused by my obsessive training-camp preparations. In fact, my goal of cutting down on travel and having more family time at home during the season was at the top of the list of reasons we moved from Sarnia. We were looking for an NHL market that was easy to travel to and from, and with five teams within 150 miles of Philadelphia, I could work a game in that region and be home before midnight. Just ask any player who has been traded to the Flyers from the Western Conference, and they will tell you how much easier their travel became. In Sarnia, the only venue where I could work the game and be guaranteed to sleep in my own bed afterward was Detroit, 60 miles away. One can never depend on the winter weather in southern Ontario, so Toronto and Buffalo games often resulted in a hotel stay.

Our research told us that former players who had been traded away from Philadelphia often returned to the area when their careers were done, while players who retired as Flyers tended to stay there. It was a great endorsement of the way the local fan base has embraced the hockey community, which in turn is a by-product of the passion and class the organization has demonstrated, from owner Ed Snider on down. Joe Kadlec, the team's travelling secretary and one of the finest men I had the good fortune to know within the game, was extremely helpful with all kinds of information about the area.

Once we decided on Philadelphia, the question became where, exactly, to put down stakes. The majority of the Flyers lived in Voorhees, New Jersey, not far from the team's practice facility. The public school system there was ranked in the top 10 in the nation, and there was easy access to major highways, turnpikes, and the airport.

There happened to be a great two-story house on the market that was perfect for our needs, and the seller was very highly motivated. Mike Keenan had been let go as coach of the Flyers at the end of a disappointing season. He would not be out of work for long, as the Chicago Blackhawks quickly snapped him up. Iron Mike had already purchased a home in Chicago, and wasn't excited about owning homes in two cities. When you think about it, if he'd held onto property in every NHL city where he has coached, he might have been the wealthiest real estate baron in the league!

Kathy and I fell in love with the house as soon as we walked into the foyer. We went back to the hotel that evening, determined to do whatever we could to eliminate the obstacles that stood between us and owning the house.

But buying a home anywhere would have been a risky proposition that summer. The NHL Officials Association was involved in protracted contract negotiations with the league. We faced the prospect of being locked out or on strike as of September 1. For the sake of the children, we wanted to be settled into a new house (and country, for that matter) before the school year started, but because Kathy would be unable to work in the U.S., the financial burden rested entirely on my shoulders. Until the new contract was ratified, we weren't certain whether we'd be able to afford the payments. We didn't even know how much I was going to be paid under a new contract.

It was a pretty gutsy move, but we were able to negotiate a tricky lease-to-purchase agreement through Mike's real estate agent. Even then, it wasn't until a few days before training camp that a new collective bargaining agreement was reached and we could load up the moving van. In the meantime, there were many details to attend to. After all, we weren't just moving around the corner. We had a home and a rental property to dispose of, as well as immigration paperwork, and the kids' school year was drawing closer. Fortunately, Kathy was a top sales agent with ReMax. She was a champ at listing and selling the two properties, and negotiated closing dates that coincided with our move to the United States.

When I got to training camp and saw the terms of the new contract, I started to doubt our ability to keep up with the mortgage payments on the $42,000 base pay I was due to receive that season. But a bizarre wrinkle took some of the pressure off. The new collective bargaining agreement contained language the league insisted on, called a discretionary bonus clause or "C-clause." Basically, the league put money into a fund, which each official could negotiate individually with the NHL for a share of. This contravenes the whole premise of collective bargaining.

It was called "discretionary" because it was totally up to the league's discretion as to how much of it each official would get. It could have also been called the Kerry Fraser Clause, since it was, in reality, an equalization fund to compensate those who were paid less based upon their years of service, yet were outperforming—in the league's view—others at the top of the pay scale. As an example, I worked the Stanley Cup final in 1985, becoming the youngest referee to do so at the time. My base pay was $32,500, while the top of the scale was $65,000. Some of those earning the top salary had not been selected by the officiating department to work in the playoffs.

During training camp, each of us had to meet with John Mc-Cauley, a.k.a. "The Master," to discuss how much of a bonus we'd get. The league's senior VP of hockey operations, Jim Gregory (the former GM of the Toronto Maple Leafs) would sit in.

My respect and affection for both of these fine men is unparalleled. Not only did I lose a great friend and mentor when John passed after the 1989 Stanley Cup final, but the officiating department has not yet fully recovered from this loss. The NHL will also lose one of the most respected hockey minds and historians when Uncle Jim, as some of the officials affectionately call him, leaves his post.

I knew what I needed to bring in for our home purchase, and I sold The Master on the difference between my value and my years of service. My position boiled down to this: "John, look what I've done for you lately—comparatively speaking, of course." I threw a ridiculous figure at him—$15,000—that seemed to catch him off guard. He countered with $5,500. I dropped to $12,000. The numbers started flying back and forth at such a rapid pace that I felt like a contestant on *Let's Make a Deal* with Monty Hall. When John fired back a counter-offer of $8,800, I shouted, "Done! We got a deal." Jim Gregory looked at The Master and said, "John, I think you've just been had."

Without batting an eye or losing momentum, I said I needed a $10,000 loan—interest free—from the league to help with the down payment on Mike's house. I promised to pay it back at the end of the season from my playoff money.

I felt like I had just jumped out of an airplane and was in free fall, and I hoped that the 'chute would open before I hit the ground!

I held my breath as John looked at Jim and asked, "Can we do that?" I could have jumped across the table and given Gregory a big kiss when, after some thought, he said, "Yeah, I think we can do that." I shook their hands to cement the deal, and after extending my sincere thanks I rushed off to call Kathy with the good news. I felt like we'd just struck the mother lode.

That wasn't the end of it, though. We were just getting settled in when I got a telephone call from John Ziegler, president of the NHL. It had taken about a month for the particulars of my arrangement with McCauley and Gregory to make it to the top of the chain of command.

The tone of Mr. Ziegler's voice clearly demonstrated that he was not calling to welcome me to the neighbourhood: "Kerry, how the hell can you even afford to buy a coach's house?" While he acknowledged the fine judgment I demonstrated on the ice, he chastised me for exercising extremely poor judgment in buying a coach's house in the first place, let alone turning to the league to lend me money for it. Was it the only house on the market? he asked.

I bit my tongue, as I did not want to throw John McCauley under the bus by telling Mr. Ziegler that it was John who had told me to look at Keenan's house.

The interest-free part of the loan really got him going because, as he put it, "I don't even get an interest-free loan from the league!" (I could have suggested he needed a better negotiator, but again thought better of it.) The final edict he handed down was that I was to make full disclosure, in writing, of all the particulars of the purchase, and a budget outlining how I expected to pay for the home. I was to send this to Ken Sawyer, the league's senior VP of finance, within the next couple of business days. (Ken is a brilliant guy who, for the past number of years, has been the chief financial officer of the Pittsburgh Penguins under Mario Lemieux.)

Armed with the new CBA, including my C-Pool bonus, substantial salary increases for years worked after the first season, my track record (albeit a short one at that time) of Stanley Cup playoff compensation, and some smoke and mirrors, I was able to convince Sawyer (and even myself) that we were in great financial shape to purchase Keenan's house. After receiving the material, Ken called and said it was obvious to him I would have no problems keeping up the payments. Fortunately, Ken was proven correct.

Over the years, I've employed some creative methods to minimize the degree to which my training infringed on our summer family time. In 1994, I realized a dream of mine when Kathy and I bought a new 34-foot sailboat (of course, it had to sleep seven down below) and named her, appropriately, *The Search Is Over*.

This was truly a family project. Kathy and the children had to listen to me pining over boats I had seen during trips to Marina del Rey when I was in Los Angeles to work Kings games, and watch as I daydreamed and wore out the pages of the sailing magazines I subscribed to. I came home from one West Coast trip to find a shoebox decorated with sailboat cutouts and a sign that read, "DAD'S SAILBOAT FUND."

I was so touched that the kids were kicking in their change and money from odd jobs. At one point, the shoebox fund was up to $54. But the next time I came home, it was down to $33!

The boat was delivered during the second round of the Stanley Cup playoffs to a yacht club on the Sassafras River, just off Chesapeake Bay in Georgetown, Maryland. We pretty much lived aboard *The Search Is Over* for most of that summer and the three that followed, cruising and exploring historic Chesapeake Bay. Wonderful experiences and lasting memories were created there for all. One downside, however, was that I didn't have access to a gym, so I was forced to improvise when the need to resume training hit me quicker than a Chesapeake Bay thunderstorm. At the time, Kara, our youngest, was four years old. (She is now in her sophomore year as an English Lit major at Mount St. Mary's University in Emmitsburg, Maryland.)

When we weren't sailing, we were swimming in the pool or the bay for hours. I found swimming to be a great cross-training activity. As I improved at swimming distances, I looked to add some resistance. I would tether a five-gallon pail to my safety harness and drag it behind me as I swam. With September approaching, I felt the need to turn it up a notch, and little Kara, in her life jacket, fit perfectly in the pail, providing me with the extra resistance to push me over the top. After training with Kara in tow, my body fat registered below 10 per cent at training camp.

Officials are no different than players in that we're just as suscep-tible to injury. I certainly have had my share over the years. As a young hockey player, I learned from my father that a champion never gives in to injury or the pain associated with it. You never let them know you're hurt. Basically, Dad said that if the bone hasn't broken through the skin, don't come off the ice; and if you do, make sure your team has the puck! He schooled me well from his experience not only as a hockey player but as a semi-professional boxer as well.

In 1982, Edmonton Oiler defenceman Paul Coffey intercepted a pass in the neutral zone just 10 minutes into the first period and tried to pound a slapshot back into the attacking zone. The prob-lem was, I had been chasing the play out of the zone and was 20 feet away—and in the direct line of Paul's slapper. The puck struck me directly on the ankle and caromed off the end of my fibula, ex-iting the playing surface and stopping play.

Paul apologized for not having seen me, the linesman got another puck, and we played on. I knew the damned thing was fractured because the pain intensified and extended up to the knee joint as the game wore on. Since we had only one referee on the ice in those days and Dad's rule (the bone hadn't broken the skin) held true, I finished the game. Between periods I kept my skate laced tightly and walked around instead of sitting down in an attempt to keep some mobility in the joint. Once the game was over and I finally removed the boot, my foot instantly blew up as if it had been inflated by an air compressor. One of the linesmen in that game, Wayne Forsey, was living in Edmonton. I had made plans to stay at his apartment because he, Swede Knox, and I were driving to Calgary for a game the next day.

Since I didn't need an X-ray to tell me the ankle was broken, and didn't want to spend the rest of my Friday night in the emergency room of the Edmonton hospital, I hobbled out of Northlands Coliseum, supported by a broken hockey stick with a towel taped to the end, which I placed under my arm as a crutch. We went straight to Forsey's apartment, where I immediately self-medicated with a bottle of Scotch. I had a sound sleep that night, but Forsey said my loud moaning from the spare bedroom kept him awake all night. I called referee-in-chief Scotty Morrison first thing the next morning and informed him that my ankle was broken. Since we didn't have an overabundance of officials at that time, and it wasn't easy moving people around the West, I had taken the liberty of looking over the assignment sheets to see who might be available to fill in for me.

Dan Marouelli was an Edmonton fireman who was also working as an NHL trainee referee in the American Hockey League. I saw that he was home, so I suggested that Scotty could use him to work the game on an emergency basis. Scotty assigned Dan as a linesman, and turned to Swede, a highly respected veteran linesman, to act as referee. The boys dropped me off at the Calgary hospital on the way to the hotel, and I spent the next five hours being attended to.

While X-rays confirmed the obvious (broken fibula), the ankle was far too swollen to put in a cast. It would take a week and a half before the swelling had subsided enough to allow for a fibreglass cast to be applied, and seven weeks before I returned to action, in time for the final month of the regular season. In place of a cast, the ankle was wrapped with a Tensor bandage, and the broken hockey stick I'd hobbled into the hospital on was replaced with a pair of crutches. I went to the Flames game that evening and watched from the press box. Sitting beside me was my dear friend, and the head of Calgary's off-ice officials crew, Don Young. Don became my "male nurse" and porter the next morning, showing up at the hotel to get me out of bed, dressed, and to the airport on time.

On board the flight to Toronto, I had the good fortune to sit beside the next prime minister of Canada, John Turner. We had a delightful conversation throughout the duration of our flight, which helped me forget about my throbbing ankle. Mr. Turner was a charming seatmate, and I regret not taking him up on his kind invitation to hunt grouse with him at his Connecticut estate once my ankle healed.

Dan Marouelli, subsequently joined the staff as a full-time referee and had an outstanding career. He also retired at the end of the 2009–10 season.

Despite my decision not to wear a helmet until it became mandatory under our collective-bargaining agreement, which came during my final three seasons in the NHL, I only had three facial cuts and one in the back of my head that required stitches. Not a bad batting average over all those years and games. Either I was so bloody short that the pucks generally went over my perfectly coiffed hair or I had developed a keen, laser-like sense of awareness for incoming projectiles. I like to think the latter is true.

One recurring problem I have to deal with involves both knees. When I was 15 years old and playing Midget AAA hockey in the All-Ontario semifinals against the Toronto Young Nationals, the blade of my left skate got stuck in a rut where the Zamboni door opened. An opponent hit me from in front, causing my body to twist—a full rotation—in the direction of contact. With my left skate locked, my left leg from the knee down didn't follow the rest of my body. I ripped the anterior cruciate ligament (ACL) clean through and tore the medial meniscus as well. To this day, I have never experienced pain like that. For 10 or 15 seconds, it was excruciating; then it just stopped.

I was on crutches for a week and watched the final game of the series from behind the bench in Toronto as my teammates and future NHL stars Wayne Merrick (four Stanley Cups with the NY Islanders) and Bob Neely (Toronto Maple Leafs) put us in into the Ontario championship against Copper Cliff the following weekend. I was back in the lineup taking a regular shift and was able to play two out of three games in the championship series. The first of four surgeries to my left knee was scheduled for the end of the following season, my first in junior hockey. Back then, they didn't repair the ACL.

A big cut on the inside of my knee allowed the surgeon to clean out the torn meniscus, resulting in a lengthy rehabilitation process. In 1972, I finished playing as captain of the Sarnia Bees of the Southern Ontario Junior A League. In spite of several scholarship offers to top Division 1 college programs, I realized I had come to the end of the line as far as my playing aspirations were concerned. It was time to find a job, preferably one within the game that I so dearly loved. Little did I realize just how quickly a door of opportunity would become unlocked when Ted Garvin introduced me to officiating.

In preparation for my final season I started training earlier than I ever had before. When I was younger, I could ramp it up with two-a-day workouts after enjoying the off-season to the fullest. With age and injuries, I had to avoid letting my baseline fitness level get too far off track. Had I not been dedicated to a healthy lifestyle and pushed myself to maintain a high level of fitness, there would have been no way I could have worked at this level just short of my 58th birthday.

How does a 57-year-old man prepare his minuscule, well-used, sometimes abused body to enter into an arena filled with youthful, athletic gladiators whose chiselled physiques look like granite statues?

Well, if you want to walk in someone else's shoes, you'd better shop at the same shoe store as they do. Not only did I find that shoe store just 20 miles from my home, but more important, I connected with the master shoemaker himself. Jimmy McCrossin has been the Philadelphia Flyers' athletic therapist and strength and conditioning coach for the past 15 years. He and I are about the same height, about the same age (he's only 52, but anything over 50 puts us all in the same category), and, like me, has a pretty serious knee problem. That's about where the comparison ends. Jim leads by example as he competes hard in all of the components of the conditioning programs he designs for his athletes. They are challenged to keep up with him as he continually raises the bar.

My first extended interaction with Jim occurred after I herniated two discs in my back in 1995. The outstanding care I received from him and the specialists he put me in touch with allowed me to return to action in time for the playoffs. Jim McCrossin has always extended his time, talent, and rehabilitation facility to get me back on the ice through numerous injuries including knee surgeries in two successive off-seasons (2006 and 2007), a shattered big toe I suffered two days prior to training camp in 2006, and a partial thickness tear in my left shoulder that resulted from a blindside hit from behind I took in a game in Los Angeles in March of 2009.

(I shattered the toe when I fell down the stairs carrying Jaime's television on her return home from a summer job, before she entered Rutgers Law School. I missed the second step, and as I flew down the stairs, I cradled the TV in outstretched arms in a pose reminiscent of a football wide receiver. I jammed my right foot down—as if looking for the sidelines—and the joint in my big toe exploded. I am happy to report the television escaped injury.)

On the third Friday of June 2009, I outlined my personal objectives for injury rehab and ongoing maintenance: stabilizing my core, increasing my lean-muscle mass and adding strength, increasing my cardio capacity, and getting my body fat level below 10 per cent. Short of bronzing me and putting me beside the statue of Rocky at the Philadelphia Museum of Art, I knew it was a tall order to fill, even for someone of Jim's ability. But he simply said, "We can do that. Just follow the same program I have set out five days a week for my players. When do you want to start?" I loved his confidence. The following Monday, I went to work. I embarked on the routine Jim had designed for the players, along with some specific exercises he'd added for knee and shoulder maintenance. Four hours each day, five days a week, and boy, did it pay dividends.

On Saturday mornings, I would ride with my son-in-law Harry Dumas III and the Pro Pedals Bike Club based out of Hammonton, New Jersey. We rode 50 miles at an average speed of between 21 and 23 miles per hour just before breakfast. I took the Sundays off and dedicated them to Kathy and the family.

I've developed a love for road biking over the past few years. I ride in charity events such as a 95-mile ride for ALS and the 50-mile ride from Philadelphia to the Jersey Shore, which is a cancer fundraiser. Some days, when Jimmy Mac had an upper-body workout scheduled for me, I would ride my hybrid bike the 20 miles to the Flyers Skate Zone, complete my workout, and ride the 20 miles back.

I got hooked on road biking by accident. Just two days prior to a scheduled knee surgery in June 2006 (to be performed by outstanding orthopaedic surgeon Dr. Peter DeLuca of the Rothman Institute, who works for the Philadelphia Flyers, NBA 76ers and the NFL Eagles), Harry and his father, Harry II, convinced me to participate in the 50-mile ride for cancer. While I hadn't trained for the event, I thought, how hard can it be? The guys took it easy on me and we only averaged 16 to 18 miles per hour. It was so much fun. I was immediately sold. Two days later, Dr. DeLuca scoped my knee, cleaned out some debris, and told me to take it easy for a while. Truth is, I couldn't wait to get back on the bike with the Saturday-morning Pro Pedals group.

One Christmas, my family surprised me with a beautiful (and very expensive) Cervélo racing bike. I had been riding my hybrid, which has wider tires and is heavier than a racing bike, with the bike club.

Biking protocol, I learned early, is that you ride along in a line and the leader "pulls" the team along (breaking wind and setting the pace) for a period, then he bumps out to the left, falls to the back of the line, and it's the next guy in line's turn to lead. Everyone else drafts close behind the rear tire of the guy in front. When it came to my turn, the guy ahead of me had set a pretty good pace, so I continued on. Not wanting to wimp out among this new bunch of guys, I took a little longer turn in the lead than others had. I really gutted it out. The young guy behind me cruised up alongside on his lightweight racer and said, "Pops, that fucking mountain bike you're on shouldn't be going that fast!" I said, "You're kiddin' me; nobody told me." I didn't know the difference, but I came to learn that there are bike snobs who check out your bike before even looking at the rider. With their Christmas gift, my family provided me with a bike most of them drool over!

Between Jim McCrossin's training program and my extra effort with the bike club, I felt like I had just been through two months of boot camp. I went to my final training camp in fantastic condition.

The primary objective of officials' camp is to have some fun playing hockey against one another, refresh our knowledge of the rules as well as any new directions we are asked to implement, and above all, leave camp healthy for the start of the season. While I aced Dave Smith's medical and fitness tests on the first day of camp, I didn't realize that boot camp wasn't quite over yet. We were transported from Toronto to the Blue Mountain resort in Collingwood, Ontario. I was returning home, in a sense, as I played my first year of junior hockey with the Collingwood Blues of the OHA Central Junior B league as a 16-year-old.

Camp was moving along nicely, I felt good on my skates, my team was in first place going into the championship game, and I had been contributing. On the next-to-last day of camp, we played two games and sat through two administrative classroom sessions. During the latter, your body tends to tighten up from sitting. The agenda called for a "secret" late-afternoon field trip. We didn't know what we would be doing or where we were going. The only instruction was to wear long pants, a long-sleeved shirt, and bring hiking boots. There was speculation that we might take a nice hike through the woods or into the hills along the shores of beautiful Georgian Bay. During our lunch break, beer was purchased so that each guy could have a couple of cold ones on the bus ride. It was a beautiful, hot, sunny day, and it sure seemed like a good idea at the time.

We boarded the yellow school buses, downed a couple of beers, and enjoyed the noise and merriment on the bus. We drove for some time in the direction of Owen Sound, and someone with some knowledge of the area exclaimed, "Holy shit, I think they're taking us to the military training base in Meaford!" Our visions of a leisurely hike evaporated as the bus pulled up in front of Land Force Central Area Training Centre Meaford, which conducts year-round courses for regular personnel in the Canadian Forces, and a master drill sergeant herded us grunts off the bus and started yelling at us to move it.

We were divided according to our hockey teams on the parade grounds behind the centre, and the ranking officer addressed our "shabby group" of "recruits" in a tone that left no doubt as to who was in charge. He spelled out the rules we would play by for the duration of our time at the camp. We were told we would be put through the same training course that the troops go through before heading off to Afghanistan, and that some of the drill sergeants were battle-hardened soldiers who had recently returned from multiple tours in that country.

"This is a very dangerous facility, and we don't want any of you to get injured and not be able to start your season," he said, "unless your name is Kerry Fraser!"

He continued: "We also realize that some of you might be nursing injuries from your training camp or from previous game-related injuries and pre-existing conditions. I want you to advise my master drill sergeants, positioned behind me, of anything you might have that would prevent you from doing an exercise that we ask of you or might cause you additional pain and suffering— *unless* your name is Kerry Fraser!" There were a couple more protocol instructions that singled me out, but I think you get the picture. I realized after the very first order was issued, and after taking note of the cold stares I was receiving from the drill sergeants, that these guys were all Leafs fans—I was doomed! I didn't know whether to ask for the last rites or a blindfold.

My team was ordered off to the bayonet range first. It was about a quarter of a mile, and we were not allowed to simply walk—we were to jog, or preferably, double-time it on a dead run. Ever since I blew my knee out, I'd been confined to low-impact exercises—bike, elliptical glider, and so forth. On this day, I returned to jogging. If need be, I'd have had the damned thing drained afterward.

We were lined up in front of 75 pounds of battle gear, ordered to put it on, and instructed in the art of gutting the "enemy"—a stuffed dummy hanging on a hook. If you struck him in the right spot, with deadly force, he fell of the hook and "died." The master drill sergeant was scary; our team lucked out and got the trained assassin, recently returned from a fifth tour. There was no doubt in any of our minds that this soldier enjoyed what he did for a living. (I'd use his name, but I fear he'd hunt me down!)

When the order to "kill" was issued, I lunged at the enemy, catching him off centre and causing him to spin on the hook, drawing the wrath of the sergeant, who yelled, "Fraser, are you having fun?"

"Yes, Master Sergeant."

"Then hit the fucking thing, and don't tickle it!"

"Yes, Master Sergeant!" We were never to address him as "sir." That was our very first mistake as a group, and it sent him into a profanity-laced tirade that he'd earned his rank on the effin' field of effin' battle and not through some effin' school or effin' academy like an effin' pussy. Well, I just wanted to kill my dummy and move on to the next exercise.

As luck would have it, the rope climb was just next door—a short jog through a ditch. The thick rope was attached to a large wooden beam 20 feet off the ground. We watched a soldier go up that thing like a monkey, hand over hand—and usually, they do it in full battle gear. We were allowed to use our legs as well as our hands and arms. The team scored a point every time one of us climbed the rope and slapped the beam at the top. We had a set time in which to complete the drill. I went up and down the rope four times. While it may not sound like much, some of our really strong linesmen were unable to make it to the top even once because their legs were so large and heavy. I was only pulling 156 pounds!

By this time, I was feeling pretty good about myself and was ready for the obstacle course. That's where my luck ran out. One of the obstacles was a rope swing over a ditch, on the other side of which was a retaining wall of planks. My arms were still heavy from the rope climb, and when I jumped for the rope to catch it, I got it too low and slammed right into the bloody wall and snapped my ankle back and to the side.

The drill sergeant saw what I'd done to the ankle, and for a fleeting second, I think, he almost felt some of my pain. Then: "Fraser, get your ass moving!" I made it on the second attempt, then finished up the rest of the course on adrenaline. As our team toured the barracks and visited with recruits, my deep respect and appreciation for what our military men and women do to keep us safe and free hit an all-time high. None of us can ever imagine just how demanding the training is, let alone the sacrifices (sometimes, the ultimate sacrifice) these brave men and women make for us. God bless you all, and thank you for your service.

For me, camp was over. My ankle blew up before we left the base, and by the time the school bus rolled up to our hotel at Blue Mountain, I couldn't put any weight on it. It wasn't all that bad because it was on the same side as my bad knee, which had also blown up due to the running I had done, so I was able to keep my weight off both injuries. Camp broke the next day, and Dave Smith arranged for me to visit Dr. Mike Clarfield's clinic in downtown Toronto. I'd be good to go in a couple of weeks—or, as they might say on the bayonet range, "It's only an effin' flesh wound, you effin' pussy, Fraser!"

Leaving camp, I was determined not to take any shortcuts—it just isn't within my makeup to do so. I wanted to be sure I left the game having given everything I had to give. Because of my competitive spirit, I wanted to prove to management that I was an asset to the game, one that would be sorely missed.

One goal I had set was to work deep into the playoffs, and ultimately, the Stanley Cup final. I remain faithful to the belief that superior talent and hard work should be rewarded with selection to perform on that stage. Although players around the league, polled independently by ESPN, chose Kerry Fraser once again as the best referee in the game, I knew full well that all I could control was the way I worked and not the way anyone evaluated me. Still, in case the opportunity arose and I was deemed worthy, I wanted to be ready. Sadly I came up short of my goal, due to the subjective selection process employed by the Officiating Department and Hockey Operations. The Stanley Cup final would, from this point forward, only occur for me on ESPN Classics.

THE MISSED CALL:
TORONTO MAPLE LEAFS

Most hockey officials look forward to the beginning of the season far more than the end. Skates and equipment have been packed away for three months, and cabin fever has reached epidemic proportions throughout the fraternity. We have endured a month of hell in the form of crash diets and (almost full) days spent in conditioning, just to get ready for training camp and the tune-up of pre-season games that follows. The rust built up over the summer months has been shaken free. As opening night nears, the yearning to get back on the road to work is overwhelming—and that's just how the wives feel! Truly, though, each of us involved on the ice is anxious to reconnect with the game in a meaningful way.

Opening night found me working a game between Ottawa and Toronto, teams that built up a fierce rivalry through four playoff meetings in five years between 2000 and 2004—all of them won by the Leafs. But there was something missing—a certain intensity that I'd come to expect when these two teams had met in previous years. The difference appeared to be in the personnel: while Daniel Alfredsson, Chris Neil, Chris Phillips, and Mike Fisher were still in their familiar Ottawa jerseys, the Leafs had never made up for the loss of the likes of Darcy Tucker, Gary Roberts, or Mats Sundin. Toronto hadn't even made the playoffs since 2004.

Nonetheless, it was somehow fitting that I would begin my final season in Toronto.

For the players, no matter how old they are or how long they've been in the game, a youthful enthusiasm grabs hold prior to that opening night. Events of the previous season—slumps, injuries, missing the playoffs—are long forgotten, and players and fans alike look forward to the new year with renewed confidence that this will be their year. And a win in that first game takes on added importance because it can put them atop the standings, even if only for a day.

The officials have a similar motivation, as we look to improve upon our rankings within our peer group. The eternal optimists hold out hope that the slate has been wiped clean, pre-existing conditions apply only to health insurance, and everyone starts the season on an equal footing. That is, until the first puck is dropped, at which point it becomes clear that—whether we're talking about players or officials—some are created more equal than others.

For the fans, opening night is just as special. While "hockey talk" never completely dies down in the major Canadian cities, things really seem to kick into gear as early as August. A buzz can be heard in the streets, in the coffee shops, and on sports-talk radio. Fans retrieve their hockey jackets from the neighbourhood dry cleaners in anticipation of an early cold snap. And Leafs fans are, without a doubt, a breed unto themselves. Nobody knows that better than I do! Not just because I have incurred their wrath for the past 17 years like no other referee in the history of the game, but because, perhaps to your surprise, I used to be one.

As a kid growing up in Sarnia, 180 miles west of Toronto, my brother Rick and I watched the Leafs every Saturday night while wearing our "team uniforms": Leafs pyjamas complete with attached foot covers and, in the early going, a "trap door" on the backside. I guess that would qualify me as a "Baby Leaf"! Saturday nights with the Leafs became an extended-family tradition, as most of the clan gathered at Grandma and Grandpa Fraser's, up the street from our house. Prior to Foster Hewitt calling the Leafs game at eight o'clock, we would enjoy Gram's homemade spaghetti and meatballs. After dinner the house came alive with music and song performed by Grandpa on the fiddle, Uncle Bob on guitar (and eventually his son Bobby), and my dad, Hilt, on guitar and vocals.

They played right up until the opening faceoff, at which point the only sounds you heard were Foster Hewitt's voice and the groans from the living room whenever the Leafs missed a scoring chance or were scored on. Dad and Uncle Bob had played with Allan Stanley growing up in Timmins, and I felt as though he was part of the family, given the stories they told of their youth. I was mesmerized by the size and skill of Frank Mahovlich, the speed and tenacity of Dave Keon and Ron Ellis, the gentlemanly leadership of the captain, George Armstrong, and the entertaining antics of Eddie Shack. (Dad also played against Randy Ellis, Ron's father, in the Scottish International Hockey League in the late 1940s and said the senior Mr. Ellis was a great player in his day.)

Whether we were skating on the outdoor rink in the winter or playing street hockey in the summer months, I always took the name of one of my Leafs heroes and tried to emulate his every move. While I concede that wearing Leafs pyjamas with little feet on them (and let's not forget the trap door) doesn't necessarily qualify me as a card-carrying member of Joe Bowen's Leafs fan club, I have to tell you they were my favourite team. (I think Joe might still wear those pyjamas on cold nights.)

Today, as I enter retirement and throw open the closet door with this shocking admission of my Leafs loyalty, I have no doubt that every Leafs fan reading this will undoubtedly ask, "So why did you screw us in '93?"

So, let's talk about that, finally!

While this won't be the first time that I have openly discussed the details and answered questions about the infamous "missed call" in Game Six of the 1993 Campbell (now Western) Conference final between the Leafs and Los Angeles Kings, hopefully it will be my last.

Let me preface by saying I can understand the frustration Leafs fans feel. I watched with you as a 15-year-old in 1967, and celebrated the Leafs' Stanley Cup victory as George Armstrong paraded the Cup around Maple Leaf Gardens before passing it off to the hands of his waiting teammates. It was, without question, my favourite moment as a hockey fan growing up.

Had I not joined the fraternity of officials, which demands complete impartiality, I could very well have been cheering right alongside you in 1993. But the career path I set out on as a 20-year-old prevented that from happening.

Maybe I'm a glutton for punishment, or perhaps I feel the need to seek absolution from Leafs fans for committing the grave sin of missing "The Call" on May 27, 1993, but my many attempts in the confessional have never been private, and on any of those occasions the chief priest, usually a member of the media, has yet to bless me and tell me my sin is forgiven and to go forth and sin no more. In fact, not only have many cast the first stone, they have continually gone back to the quarry to reload.

Anyway, I invite you to take a lap in my skates on that fateful night in the Great Western Forum.

The Leafs were one game away from appearing in the Stanley Cup final for the first time in 26 years. I say "one game away," but in the minds of most of their fans, to this day, they were one *call* away. After eliminating Detroit and St. Louis in a series that went the full seven games, the Leafs drew Wayne Gretzky and the Los Angeles Kings. After falling behind two games to one, they had rallied to a 3–2 lead in the series. The Montreal Canadiens, having already defeated the New York Islanders for the Wales Conference championship, were waiting, and Toronto fans were buzzing about the potential for a classic matchup between the NHL's two oldest franchises.

Game Six was in overtime, tied at four, and the Leafs were down a man with Glenn Anderson serving a boarding penalty. About a minute into overtime, Kings defenceman Rob Blake, at the right point, passed the puck forward along the boards to Wayne Gretzky. Gretzky's shot from the top of the faceoff circle was blocked by defenceman Jamie Macoun. Gretzky and Leafs centre Doug "Killer" Gilmour both went after the loose puck, and Gilmour fell to the ice, injured.

As a referee, the biggest fear I've always had is that when I blink, something could occur in that fraction of a second that I will miss. It's also uncomfortable when a player simply passes in front of your line of vision—you worry something fateful might occur.

Was this one such moment? There was an aching in the pit of my gut, a feeling of helplessness, a sensation so awful I wanted to throw up. The only thing to do in a case like this was to seek out help, like an investigator collecting facts before deciding whether to make an arrest and that's just what I did. First I approached Gilmour, and I could see as he touched his chin that there was blood, although it wasn't oozing. My initial thought was that some old scar tissue had been scraped off. God knows, Killer had enough of that on his face.

Next, I asked him what happened. Doug said, "Wayne took a shot and the follow-through struck me on the chin." To which I responded, "If that's the case, a normal follow-through of a shot is not a penalty," because contact made when a shooter is following through is exempt from a penalty for high-sticking.

Doug said, "Okay." He accepted that no penalty was warranted.

I then noticed that Gretzky had drifted away from "the scene of the crime"; unusual for him, since he was normally right there to provide input when necessary. Upon reflection, that might have been an admission of guilt on Wayne's part, a sign he thought he was about to receive a four-minute double-minor for high-sticking.

My next course of action was to appeal to both linesmen and hope that, from one of their vantage points, they could give me accurate information about what had happened. I gathered Ron Finn, who had been at the opposite-side blue line, and Kevin Collins, who had conducted the end-zone faceoff and was retreating to his position on the same side of the ice where the incident had occurred.

With an intensity and urgency in my voice, I asked for their help, if there was any to be had. Both linesmen answered they hadn't had a sightline that could definitively determine what had happened.

It was at this moment that I came to understand clearly that in hockey officiating, it's not always black and white.

And now that aching in the pit of my stomach only intensified, and my mouth went dry. It's the most helpless feeling that I've ever had in any of the 2,165 NHL games that I refereed.

For most of my career, video review of plays wasn't even technically feasible, and even today, it is not allowed for a penalty call. The play was over and gone, lost to that split second of time and space that seemed like an eternity once Doug's blood started to drip.

All Gilmour could do was go in for repairs, and all that was left for the officials to do was drop the puck and hope that, if a high-sticking call had in fact been missed, there would not be a consequence that would affect the game's outcome.

Big gulp here.

Seconds later, Gretzky scored the game-winner and the series was tied. Game Seven would be played two nights later, in Toronto.

Leafs fans watching on television, as well as the *Hockey Night in Canada* team of Bob Cole and Harry Neale, had the advantage over those of us on the ice. Even so, Cole's first impulse was to suggest Gilmour had been hurt while blocking Gretzky's initial shot. Neale was quick to guess that Gretzky had high-sticked Gilmour, but it wasn't until a replay, from a different camera angle, was shown that he was able to definitively make "The Call" from the broadcast booth.

It's important to mention that even after Gretzky scored the overtime winner, I wasn't chased off the ice. Neither the Leafs players, nor coach Pat Burns, harangued me for missing the call. The only dissenter was Anderson, who was still pleading his case over the boarding call that caused him to watch from the penalty box as the game was decided.

In the dressing room afterward, director of officiating Bryan Lewis informed us that it had been reported, but not confirmed, that *Hockey Night in Canada* had a replay that detected Gretzky clipping Gilmour in the face with his stick. But he said we had followed the proper procedure in trying to determine whether an infraction had been committed.

I went to bed, and the next morning caught a flight home to Philadelphia. The next day at about 6 p.m. I spoke to my parents at their home in Sarnia. That's when I heard that my father had been awakened between 4 and 5 a.m. to the sound of one car hitting another in his driveway. Looking out the window, he saw a vehicle continually backing up and ramming into the trailer hitch of his mini-motorhome parked in the driveway. Clad only in his tightie whities, he grabbed an axe from next to the back door and chased the motorist up the street.

I was livid. I was furious that someone would take out their hostility on my family. The next call I made was to NHL security, who investigated and later informed me that the vandal was a Leafs fan from Kitchener-Waterloo, who had made the 90-mile drive to the Fraser family homestead. My parents also received obscene crank calls; this prompted my mother to answer the phone with a referee's whistle poised at the ready to shatter the eardrums of anyone who dared invade their privacy.

(After Dad passed on, Mom still kept the whistle hanging by the telephone. It's time for her to retire her whistle as well!)

In the seventh game, Gretzky scored a hat trick and added two assists as the Kings won, 5–4. Gretzky has called it "the best game I ever played."

The misplaced hostility and aggression were not limited to the days and weeks after the Leafs lost the series. Following a game I worked at the Air Canada Centre in 2008, I joined Wes McCauley and the officials who'd worked the game with me at the Irish Embassy, a pub on Yonge Street, near both the ACC and the Hockey Hall of Fame. NHL security representative Paul Hendricks had a table reserved for us. As I entered the establishment, I noticed that many of the male patrons were wearing vintage Leafs jerseys. Most of them were probably teenagers back in 1993.

I passed one table, where a fellow with his back to me was wearing a jersey with the name and number (29) of Félix Potvin, the goalie of that '93 team. I heard someone at his table say, "There's Fraser." I made my way past a partition, only to be confronted by the same fan, who stood there with a beer in his hand and said, "Fraser, you're a fucking asshole!"

Under normal circumstances, when I come face to face with an angry fan I offer my hand and a friendly smile and open myself up to entertaining any questions he or she might have. In this situation, I quickly determined that the man in the Potvin jersey was neither open nor receptive to any dialogue.

So I assumed a defensive posture. With my right hand, I grabbed him by the bicep of the arm that held his beer and applied pressure until I had control of him. I took half a step back so that I was off his back shoulder blade rather than beside him. He looked at the beer in his hand, to which I responded, "Don't even think about it. I will knock you out." And I squeezed harder. In the defining moment, our eyes met. He knew that he was vulnerable and that I meant business. This would not be a negotiation.

At this moment, a friendly barmaid danced around the corner and asked, "Mr. Fraser, can I get you anything?" To which I responded, "Please get this guy away from me, because I'm going to hurt him."

She aggressively shooed him back to his table and told him to stay there. As my colleagues joined me, they found me sitting with my back to the wall at our reserved table. I informed them of my confrontation and said that if I happened to lunge across the table, they should stay out of the way.

Although I kept an ever-watchful eye on the corner from which the Potvin fan had materialized, we had an enjoyable evening. At about midnight, "Potvin" returned for one last verbal assault. While he hadn't appeared drunk earlier, he seemed to have consumed enough liquid courage in the interim to face the table.

He stopped across the table from me and shouted, "Fraser, you fucked us in '93!" and then gave me a two-finger salute—and not the two thumbs-up that Don Cherry has made famous.

I started to get up. He started to backtrack. Paul Hendricks shouted at him, and the guy took off for the door with Hendricks in pursuit. Shortly thereafter, Paul returned, dusting off his hands and saying, "We won't have to worry about that guy again; he missed the last three steps on the way out."

I have never avoided answering questions about the incident, but there are only so many ways a person can say "I missed the call" or, in stronger terms if it makes you feel any better, "I *blew* the call!"

Seventeen years later, the incident still haunts the Leaf Nation faithful as viscerally as though Gilmour's cut is fresh and his chin is still bleeding. The media loved to play it up around the anniversary date of the incident or whenever I worked a game involving the Leafs. Since the latter won't happen again, I propose that after this full and honest disclosure we bury the hatchet and move on— or, as Killer said in Mike Zeisberger's *Toronto Sun* column on March 27, 2010, the date of my last game at the Air Canada Centre, "Please let it go. It's over. The man's retiring. For the sake of his sanity, let it go."

SIDNEY AND MARIO:
PITTSBURGH PENGUINS

My final visit to Mellon Arena—for a game in which the Penguins beat the Bruins 6–5—brought back memories of my earliest stops in Pittsburgh. In the early 1980s, the Pens were not a very good team. In fact, they were a laughingstock. Not surprisingly, they had a comedian: toothless Gary Rissling. Nobody in the game has ever made me laugh more.

Rizz had the unique ability to practically swallow his face. When the national anthem was being sung, he'd be in his familiar location at the end of the bench. He would make sure I caught his eye, at which point he would contort his face to look like a 100-year-old smoker. I lost any pretense of solemnity during the national anthem whenever I looked over at Rissling and had to stifle a laugh.

Things changed for Pittsburgh in 1984, when they landed the prize catch of the amateur draft, Mario Lemieux, amid more than strong suspicion they had tanked the final game of the season to acquire the coveted first-overall pick. The Penguins had finished dead last in the NHL with 16 wins and 38 points in 80 games, three behind the New Jersey Devils. Both teams seemed incapable of winning during the last couple of weeks of the season.

In 1984–85, Mario's rookie year, they improved to 24 wins and 53 points. Mario had 100 points, but didn't appear among the top 10 scorers. That's what hockey was like in the '80s. As a sophomore, Mario catapulted to second, behind only Wayne Gretzky, with 48 goals and 93 assists for 141 points. And the Penguins improved in the win column to 34, with 76 points, just two shy of a playoff spot.

Mario was beyond the real deal; he was the saviour of the franchise—as it would turn out, on more than one occasion. His immediate impact as a player was felt on the ice, at the gate, and in the buzz he created throughout the hockey community.

He was a giant of a man who was unique in that he had the hands of a surgeon, the wingspan of an albatross, and he always knew where the net was. Much like Mike Bossy, he always knew where to shoot the puck and could thread a needle with his passes.

Mario arrived as a proud French Canadian with a relatively poor grasp of the English language, a skill he quickly polished. He also brought with him a reputation for being independent-minded and perhaps a bit high-maintenance. In his final year of junior, he refused to play for Canada in the World Junior Championships, and at the draft he refused to go to the Penguins' table and pose for photos in a team jersey with the team's front-office staff.

What I'm saying here is that he had it all. With the exception of one thing: maturity.

He was under a lot of pressure to lead his team out of the wilderness. And the team put added pressure on him by requiring that he be a team leader by naming him captain in 1986–87. Management worked to help him in both departments by building a supporting cast. For example, they brought in Paul Coffey in November of 1987 in a blockbuster trade with Edmonton to stabilize their porous defence and provide leadership both in the locker room and on the ice. The Penguins now had two of the game's greatest impact players on their roster.

As an extremely skilled player, Mario was way ahead of the curve. And he didn't have much patience for the clutch-and-grab style that prevailed at that time. And why should he? People pay to see skill and grace, especially the type that Mario—and few other players of the time—possessed. The problem was that years of expansion had brought with it an influx of unskilled players. They survived by doing whatever they could get away with to neutralize the stars. We officials let them get away with "checking" tactics that pushed the envelope, and the more we allowed, the more universally accepted the interference and obstruction became. The true artists of the game were stifled and frustrated.

Lemieux was a target, of course. Whenever Mario was on the attack or the forecheck, it was common to hear coaches and players alike call out, "Hold him up." That was the signal to reach out, latch on, and go for a ride. Often, it resembled waterskiing on ice. It was hard for a player with Mario's presence to hide, so he had to be creative, in a way no player has been before or since, to find open ice and shake whatever player had been assigned to be his Siamese twin for the night. Mario was the first player I ever saw skate into a pack of players to draw his checking assignment into an area of heavy traffic. He would use those players as pylons to shake his confused dance partner and come out free on the other side of the pack.

All of that "special attention," along with the clutching and grabbing in general, was frustrating for Mario. Understandably so. But it was apparent to me that he expected to be afforded preferential treatment. The problem was that neither the rules nor the standard of enforcement could be altered in favour of Mario, Wayne, Denis Savard, or Marcel Dionne.

During Lemieux's second year as captain, I recall that he and I locked horns one night. Throughout the game, whenever he felt he was being illegally handcuffed, he gave me an earful. Finally, he'd had enough and decided to take matters into his own hands, delivering a retaliatory two-handed slash to an opponent's leg. Hooks and holds are one thing; a vicious slash is another. My arm went up immediately and I sent him off.

On the way to the penalty box, Mario chastised me for not calling the original penalty. He let me know in no uncertain terms that he had had enough, not only of the obstruction, but of me. For the duration of his penalty, he stared daggers at me from the box. A power-play goal was scored against the Penguins, and instead of skating to the bench for a line change he headed directly to centre ice, where I stood waiting to conduct the faceoff. He tapped his stick on the ice at my feet in a mocking form of applause and said, "Nice call."

At this point, I'd had enough of Mario as well, and I unloaded on him verbally.

"You're supposed to be the captain of this team, and you don't know how to be a captain yet. Your teammates don't follow you and if you want to know how to be a leader, take a look at that guy." I pointed to his teammate Paul Coffey. "He's a leader, he's a captain." Mario lowered his stick, as well as his head, and I dropped the puck.

A couple of days later, I had a game on Long Island. The Penguins were the visitors. At the end of the first period, a scrum gathered. I blew my whistle loudly and instructed the players to break it up and go to their dressing rooms. They didn't respond, so I blew the whistle a second time, louder, and told them more stridently to break it up and get off the ice.

They still weren't budging. At this point, Mario skated in, looked down at me, and told his teammates, "C'mon, boys, let's go." They immediately obeyed the captain's command. As I stood there, I brushed away a feather from the side of my mouth from the crow I had just been fed by the captain of the Pittsburgh Penguins. In that moment, Mario was clearly in charge of his team, but more important, he let me know it.

Over the next seven years, there was a relaxing of tensions between us, as I worked the All-Star Game in Pittsburgh in 1990 and the Stanley Cup final in 1991, in which the Penguins beat the Minnesota North Stars. It seemed to me that I had developed a professional working relationship with Mario.

There wasn't a confrontation of any magnitude between us until April 5, 1994, when the Penguins were hosting the Tampa Bay Lightning. The season before, Mario had left hockey for two months for cancer treatment, only to return and still win the scoring title by 12 points over Pat LaFontaine. He then had surgery to repair a herniated disc in his back in July 1993, and missed 58 games in 1993–94 because of recurring back issues.

Against Tampa, he was stripped of the puck and felt he'd been hooked. I deemed it stick-to-stick contact. In frustration, Mario brought his elbow and stick up high into the Lightning player who had trailed him. I raised my arm and called a high-sticking penalty. Once in the box, Mario flipped his stick over the glass and onto the ice in protest. I cruised by the penalty box and gave him a misconduct penalty. Mario immediately charged out of the penalty box in an effort to get at me. Fortunately for both of us, he was restrained by Kevin Stevens, Ron Francis, and others.

This incident occurred just prior to the Stanley Cup playoffs, and a special hearing was held by Brian Burke, the NHL's senior VP of hockey operations, to investigate and determine what suspension, if any, would be applied. I was not required to attend the hearing; I had filed a report at the end of the game that had gone directly to Burke. Later, Burke asked me about a feud Mario had mentioned in the hearing, one that dated back to when he first became the captain in Pittsburgh.

If anything good came out of this incident, it was that Mario, a bona fide superstar and the face of the game, now had a platform and had gotten the attention of the keepers of the game in an attempt to effect change and eliminate the trapping and obstruction at the height of their use.

While several failed attempts were made to crack down on obstruction, real change wouldn't occur until 2005–06, the first season after the lockout, and Mario's last in the NHL.

In retrospect, given the amazing accomplishments of this special athlete and the adversity he overcame, I have nothing but respect and admiration for Mario Lemieux as a player and as a man. I deeply regret the dressing-down I gave him in his early years, for which he may have harboured resentment toward me until it all rushed out of the penalty box that night in the Igloo in 1994.

After his playing career, he was called upon again to save the franchise, this time as the owner, and then to acquire the next-generation superstar, the next saviour of the Penguins and the new face of the game: Sidney Crosby.

I attended the USA Hockey national tournament at the Ice House in Hackensack, New Jersey, in 2008 as the guest of my friend and former colleague Pat Dapuzzo. While there I enjoyed the company of Mario, who was coaching his son's team in the tournament. What I noticed most about him in retirement is that he carries himself with the same grace and class that we witnessed while he was on the ice.

To a lesser degree, there is still growth taking place for Crosby, most recently the hero of the Canadian Olympic gold-medal victory in Vancouver.

Sidney brings intensity to every game, has a tremendous work ethic, and competes hard night in and night out. He's a leader.

He and I experienced some initial growing pains as we tried to build a working relationship, not unlike my experience with his boss and landlord (Sidney moved into Mario's house with his family when he arrived as a rookie in 2005).

Sid the Kid came into the league with a little bit of an edge to him. For budding superstars like Sidney, their celebrity status is thrust upon them at a very early age. Some are mustangs who don't want to be saddled, while others are thoroughbreds willing to race to the finish line under a jockey's direction. Sidney came in as the wild mustang. My aim was not to break him of it; I just sought a measure of respect that I believe I'd earned and the game deserved.

We had moments of confrontation during his rookie season, usually over his whining. When he continued to direct negative energy toward officials in his sophomore year, I thought it was imperative that he focus more on his game and less on us. But unlike my improper reaction to Mario when he was a young captain, I tried to take a more fatherly approach to the Nova Scotia native.

One night in Toronto, he felt he had been fouled and he retaliated with a slash to the ankle of a Leafs player. I whistled him for the infraction, and on the way to the penalty box he gave me the kind of grief that I deemed inappropriate.

At the time, he was in a neck-and-neck battle with teammate Evgeni Malkin for the league scoring lead. While Crosby was in the penalty box, Malkin scored a short-handed goal. A referee knows he's living right when that happens. It's as close to winning as we ever get. You call a penalty, and the penalized team scores a shorthanded goal. This usually alleviates the frustration (or in some cases, even anger) a penalized player might feel.

The Pens went on to kill Sidney's penalty, and at the first stoppage after he got out of the penalty box, he again revisited his upset over the slashing penalty.

This didn't make any sense to me. I said to him, "Wait, I have to understand something. Are you still upset with the obvious slashing penalty your team just killed off, or are you now more upset that Malkin scored and got a point while you were sitting there watching him?"

He gave me a dirty look and skated off in a huff. Although I was frustrated with Sidney, I had to admire the way he challenged himself. That's why he's such a great competitor. He wants to win and won't settle for second best.

At the next commercial break, I decided we needed to have a "father-son" chat. I asked his permission to talk, which he granted. We huddled near the penalty box, and I told him: "You are the face of the game. You are a superstar."

To which he responded, "No, I'm not." Perhaps he thought I was chiding him.

"No, I'm serious," I said. "You are the new face of the NHL. And I say that with the utmost respect for your skill and ability. With that comes huge responsibility, and I'd just like you to be aware of the impression you will leave on youngsters who are watching your every move, and that they will turn around and emulate everything you do. So I recommend that you use that responsibility wisely."

He seemed to get it, seemed receptive to what I had to say; perhaps equally important was the way the message was delivered.

He nodded, and I said, "Let's go play."

He took the faceoff and played on.

There was a game the next season in Philadelphia when he approached me after a play on which he thought he might have been fouled. Now the captain, he skated over with a different, more kindly demeanour and said, "I know you're not my number-one fan. I just want you to know the guy brought his stick up and caught me."

"I really am a fan," I assured him. "I've always been a fan of excellence. Concerning your question, I didn't think the stick had contacted you. If it did, I apologize. I missed it."

He said, "Okay, no problem," and skated away.

Over the years, I've been blessed to watch at close hand some of the greatest players the game has ever seen. Mario and Sidney, bookend superstars for the Pittsburgh Penguins, certainly fall into that category.

On this night, in my final game in the Igloo, Sidney—returning from an injury—scored a goal and two assists to help beat the Boston Bruins. He was chosen first star, took over the game, and ignited the crowd and his team just like his boss had done so many times not all that long ago. This Pittsburgh Penguins franchise is clearly on a strong footing both off and on the ice for years to come.

MONDAY-NIGHT MIRACLE: ST. LOUIS BLUES

It only seemed fitting that I would travel from a spiritual retreat directly to a city named after a saint to work my final two games there. It also seemed fitting that I checked into the Marriott Hotel at the old Union Station, where, according to a sign at the front desk, spirits have been seen prowling the halls, walking through walls, and slamming doors.

My previous game, four days earlier, had been in Chicago. From there, I travelled to Malibu, California, at the request of my good friend Ray McKenna, a lawyer from Arlington, Virginia, who founded a faith-based organization called Catholic Athletes for Christ. I was invited to make a presentation at Major League Baseball's annual retreat, which was attended by such stars as Mike Piazza, Mike Sweeney, Jeff Suppan, and Bobby Keppel.

It was inspiring and refreshing for me to leave behind the madness that sometimes occurs in the NHL and join this grace-filled, humble, and grounded group of men for a couple of days in the beautiful setting of the Serra Retreat Center. The facility sits high atop a hill, and the prayer gardens and chapel offer panoramic views of the Pacific Ocean. From there, it was easy to let go of the noise and stress and "stuff" I'd brought with me.

One of the highlights for me was to be able to sit beside "Jesus" at morning Mass. Of course, I mean Jim Caviezel, the actor and devout Catholic who portrayed Jesus in Mel Gibson's blockbuster movie *The Passion of the Christ*.

After two and a half glorious days, I was now back in my everyday world of NHL officiating. I prayed the inner peace I'd found in Malibu would sustain me and keep me in the "light," even if a call I made (or missed) should come under attack from a "darker" place.

I became a daily communicant at Mass after responding to a calling in 1995 that was very mystical in nature. I know miracles happen every day, and I could tell you of many that I have seen and experienced personally. I am far from alone in this belief.

On Monday, May 12, 1986, perhaps some new believers joined the flock from among the 17,801 in attendance as the Blues, on the verge of elimination at the hands of the Calgary Flames, overcame a three-goal deficit with just 12 minutes remaining to force overtime. Seven and a half minutes into overtime, Doug Wickenheiser scored the game winner, sending the series back to Calgary for the final game, the winner of which would compete for the Stanley Cup. Blues fans still refer to Game Six of the 1986 Campbell Conference final as the Monday-Night Miracle.

At the end of the second period of that game, however, there was at least one soul waiting in the shadows for the opportunity to strike—and his intended target was me!

I arrived in St. Louis early in the afternoon the day before the game to prepare physically and mentally for what would be an important match. I was in my sixth season in the NHL, and this was only the second time I'd been assigned to work beyond the second round of playoffs. The previous year, I'd moved to the uppermost rung on the ladder, getting the nod—along with Andy Van Hellemond and Bryan Lewis—to officiate in my first Stanley

Cup final series. The Oilers triumphed over the Flyers to win their second Stanley Cup.

For this game between the Blues and the Flames, I was to be accompanied on the ice by two outstanding linesmen, Ron "Huck" Finn and future Hall of Famer Ray Scapinello. Their experience, as well as the respect and rapport that they enjoyed with players and coaches alike, gave me a great deal of comfort and a major boost of confidence. I had no doubt that they would always have my back—or so I thought!

We gathered for an early dinner that night in Hacks Restaurant off the lobby of the Chase Park Plaza and tucked in early. While the excitement of the playoffs produces adrenaline in surplus quantities, by this stage the action can wear down players and officials alike. The Blues, piloted by coach Jacques Demers, had won the Norris Division by taking their first two rounds to the maximum number of games. They eliminated the Minnesota North Stars three games to two, then beat the Leafs in seven. Bob Johnson's Calgary Flames, on the other hand, swept the Winnipeg Jets in three straight games before grinding out a seven-game victory over Wayne Gretzky and the Edmonton Oilers to earn the Smythe Division crown.

Fatigue can become a player's toughest opponent. The punishing schedule of games, the often-lengthy travel (especially in the West), and the enhanced physical and mental demands associated with a long playoff run all conspire against him. Costly mistakes can be made, and desperation may lead him to look for an easier path— one that results in infractions. Those penalties may result in power-play goals, adding frustration to the equation, leading to even more penalties. Once that snowball starts to roll down the hill, the result of a game or series becomes a foregone conclusion—it's over.

As a referee, I always hope that a team doesn't get so frustrated they give up. When that happens, all I can do is call everything

I see, eliminate as many of the troublemakers as possible, and to try and keep things as safe as possible. If this happens, I become the focus of the game—not a position I crave. I prefer to find a way to keep them playing. My first act is to solicit the co-operation from a team leader, whether it's the coach or any cooler head who might be willing to intercede with his teammates and restore their focus. At a time like this, they need to know I mean business and won't back off if their play continues to cross the line, but in putting the onus back on them I am quick to remind them of their mission and objective—neither of which can be achieved from the penalty box.

The atmosphere in the St. Louis Arena that night could best be described as energetic. These fans loved their Blues and never gave up on them. They could be a wild bunch, and the old arena was not an overly friendly place for opposing teams—especially not their fans. Whenever the Chicago Blackhawks came to town, a large contingent of supporters would make the five-hour drive or arrive by the busload. Extra police were always added for these clashes—and I'm not talking about on the ice. Whenever fights broke out in the stands, the police were right in the thick of things, punching and whaling away with their billy clubs.

I had a really tough Hawks–Blues game there one night. Several fights had taken place on the ice, and then in the third period the fans started fighting on the other side of the glass. A pier six brawl erupted in a corner of the arena that got so intense that, when play stopped, all of us—players from both teams as well as officials—stood by the glass and watched. The role reversal was the strangest thing I've ever witnessed. I finally suggested to the players that we get the game going and maybe they would stop. Brian Sutter, the Blues' captain at the time, commented that his team could use some of those guys.

This night would be more civilized, I hoped, even though the decibel level in the arena rivalled that in the old Chicago Stadium when Wayne Messmer sang the national anthem. After an opening flurry by a Flames team that looked determined to end the series without further delay, the Blues managed to hold on, and the first period ended scoreless. The second period belonged to Calgary. St. Louis goalie Rick Wamsley was beaten on three shots he later said he should have stopped, and the Blues clearly lost their focus. They took undisciplined penalties, and the energy required to kill them depleted an already low supply. Their frustration mounted, and the steady stream to the penalty box had both the players and their faithful fans singing the Blues.

Just before the second period ended, with the score 4–1 in Calgary's favour, Blues captain Rob "Rammer" Ramage took an aggressive penalty that gave me the sense he had crossed over to the mindset of "I don't care anymore—I'm just going to make them pay the price." It's not uncommon at all for frustrated players to start to play against the third team on the ice—the officials—and defy the referee, daring him to call another penalty. I knew I had to restore order and get them back to playing. While brokering a truce was not an option, reading Rammer the riot act and appealing to his leadership role as captain, in the hopes that he'd help refocus his team's negative energy during the intermission, clearly was.

I met Ramage at the penalty box as the horn sounded. I was very deliberate and direct in the message I wanted him to deliver to coach Jacques Demers and his teammates. I told him I was *not* going to change my standards and that his team was clearly out of control. I would not stand by and watch anyone get hurt by the kind of foul he had just committed. If the Blues continued to play in this fashion, I would bury them in the penalty box. I finished by saying, "Now, you go tell Jacques everything I said and that he had better get control of you guys or this game and the series are over!"

I felt I had hit the target. I didn't get any lip from Ramage. On the contrary, a determined calm seemed to take hold of him. He nodded and said he would deliver the message. At this point, two huge St. Louis police officers, in uniform, stepped out of the penalty box as one of them said, in a very official tone, "Kerry, get off the ice and to your dressing room quickly." They escorted me along the sideboards instead of taking the more direct route across open ice to the Zamboni entrance where officials and visiting players exited the ice. This was the first time I had ever been escorted off the ice, but given the seriousness and urgency with which these two giants issued their order, I complied fully.

Once in the dressing room, I sat down and asked the officers what was up. One of them said, "Kerry, it is our duty to inform you that a death threat has been issued against you."

This really didn't faze me. "That's okay, Officer," I said, "I have had them a couple of times before. Some nut is probably sitting at home with a six-pack and decided he was going to call in and take out his frustration on me."

Looking sterner, if that were even possible, the officer replied, "*No*, Kerry: We traced the call and it came from one of the phones within the arena. His message to us was that he had a gun with him, and that if you came out for the third period he would shoot you!" He then asked me what I would like to do.

I took in a big gulp of air and slowly exhaled in hopes that it would not be one of my last. I looked over at the linesmen, Finn and Scapinello, for some direction. Their eyes were the size of saucers and their mouths hung open.

With very little deliberation—only the time it took to let out that breath—I looked directly at the two officers and replied, "I have no option here. I'm going out to start the third period. The game must continue." To inject some levity into the room, I made a joke about being a small target, so the guy would have to be an excellent shot to nail me. I think Scampy, who was very similar in stature to me, might have been afraid of a possible case of mistaken identity.

We waited until the last possible moment to return to the ice. The long walk from the dressing room had the ominous feeling of what a condemned man must feel as he waits to find out what's on the other side. Just before we reached the end of the protective canopy, I paused, then turned to gain some inspiration from my two colleagues. As I looked back, I found I was alone at the end of the walkway! The two guys who, at dinner the night before, had made me feel certain they would always watch my back, were standing way back, at the top of the runway, with their arms crossed. I beckoned them to join me, but the only thing that moved were their arms, with which they motioned for me to go on ahead, they'd be along shortly. Their feet seemed stuck in cement, while I was up to my knees in quicksand. Even though both of them displayed good-natured smiles, I couldn't blame them for sitting this one out until the coast was clear.

There was no place to take cover if the kook's threat was for real. My plan was to blast out of the tunnel and skate as fast as I could in a zigzag fashion. I figured if I was fortunate to make it to the other end of the rink and back, I'd be home free. My greatest fear in that mad dash was that I'd hear a sound resembling a motorcycle backfiring. After a solo lap of the pond, no gunshot was audible, so my two trusty linesmen finally stepped onto the ice just ahead of the visiting Calgary Flames.

The Blues were a different team in the third period. They killed the balance of Ramage's penalty and showed determination and discipline as they clawed their way back into the game. Calgary started to take some penalties, and with 15 seconds remaining in a five-on-three advantage, Doug Wickenheiser retrieved an errant puck up the right side half-wall, curled toward the top of the right faceoff circle, and fired a wicked slapshot that beat goalie Mike Vernon cleanly to make it 4–2. Their comeback was temporarily stalled as Joey Mullen quickly answered with Calgary's fifth goal. Jim Peplinski had won a battle in the corner and set up

Mullen perfectly. Although Mullen's goal temporarily deflated the crowd, it did not have the desired effect on the Blues' work ethic.

The rally intensified when Brian Sutter scored off a big rebound that Vernon had given up after making a kick save. I have to confess: at this point I didn't think there was any way that the Blues had enough left in the tank to close the two-goal gap. Oh, *me* of little faith!

It wasn't until Greg Paslawski jammed a one-timer past Vernon to make it 5–4 that I became a semi-believer. The Blues were a blue-collar team that relied on the dump-and-chase style that typified Norris Division teams. This goal was just another example of how they outworked their opponents. Brian Sutter, one of the hardest workers I ever saw, beat a Flame defender to the puck deep in the right corner and threw a backhand Hail Mary–style pass toward the front of the Flames' goal. Paslawski was attacking the goal with speed on a direct, unimpeded route through the slot. The no-look pass from Sutter landed perfectly on the tape of Paslawski's stick, and he banged it home. The place erupted.

Privately, I marvelled at how completely the momentum had shifted, and sensed that something special was about to happen. I also saw the dejection in the Flames' faces as they looked at the clock and contemplated the time remaining. Time could either be their best ally or worst nightmare as they tried desperately to hold on to their slim lead. Blues play-by-play announcer Ken Wilson, perhaps accurately sensing the Flames' panic, offered this on-air observation after Paslawski's goal: "If the Blues come up with a miracle finish, these Calgary Flames would have to crawl back to Alberta." While Ken detected that from the distance of his broadcast perch high above the ice, I was in the thick of it.

With 1:17 remaining in regulation time, the Blues once again dumped the puck into the Calgary zone, prompting Vernon to leave his crease and stop the puck behind his cage for oncoming defenceman Jamie Macoun. Vernon stepped aside as the ever-steady

Macoun retrieved the puck, skated behind the goal, and started out the other way. Vernon tried to get back to his crease while the speedy forechecker Paslawski chased Macoun. Just as Macoun rounded the goal and started up ice, Paslawski lifted the Calgary defenceman's stick from behind and stripped him of the puck. Then, all in one motion, he wheeled and fired a desperate shot from a bad angle at the Calgary net. Vernon had not yet been able to set himself in his crease and was caught totally off guard as the shot blew past him on the short side. We were heading to overtime.

Back in the relative quiet and safety of our dressing room, the death threat reported no more than 20 minutes ago had been all but forgotten. Out in the hallway, however, it was a different scene. My oversized bodyguards stood stiffly, like a matched set of Buddhas, outside our door.

The linesmen and I refuelled and rehydrated, not knowing whether overtime would end quickly or if another full 20 minutes—or more—would be required to decide this game. Depending on how it ended, I knew one thing for sure: I was getting off the ice quickly—and I might even use Scampy as a decoy! We all shared the hope that, whichever team scored, it would be a clean goal free of controversy. I suggested it was vital that someone be on the goal line in the event of a fast break. Should I be caught behind the play for any reason, I asked Finn and Scampy to make sure they went in from their blueline position to cover for me. In the remaining minutes of calm, each of us relaxed with our own thoughts about what we had just been part of. The three periods had been like three games rolled into one.

Both teams had glorious opportunities to end the game early in overtime. Vernon made a huge save on a Doug Wickenheiser slapshot. At the other end, Wamsley was equal to the task against Al MacInnis, and got a little help from his best friend, the goalpost, when a Joey Mullen slapper blasted past him, only to clang off the iron.

Jacques Demers credited Bernie Federko as his on-ice leader and a player with a special ability to do something that could change a game. And Bernie got it done for his coach once again by setting up the play that that ended the game.

Ken Wilson called the play this way: "Here's Ramage, for Federko too far . . . Federko steals the puck from Reinhart . . . over to Hunter, who shoots . . . blocked—Wickenheiser scores! Doug Wickenheiser! The Blues pull it off and it's unbelievable!"

Federko had snatched the puck off defenceman Paul Reinhart's skate just outside the Calgary blue line and broke in on goal from the left side. He saw Mark Hunter on the right wing and slid a perfect pass across for a one-time shot. Goalie Mike Vernon moved across with the pass, and Hunter's shot was blocked by a sliding Flames defenceman as Vernon went down as well. The rebound went right to a trailing Wickenheiser, who was moving into the slot. Wick fired a shot into the unattended goal for what many consider the greatest moment in St. Louis Blues history.

As Huck, Scampy, and I followed the disappointed Calgary Flames team off the ice, we entered our dressing room with a sense of accomplishment that we had stood up to the test that had been sent our way. When penalties needed to be called, they were. When courage had been demanded of us, we spit in the face of intimidation and threats. And finally, at the end of the night, we'd simply done our jobs to the very best of our ability. To top it off, we had just witnessed a Monday-Night Miracle. Who could ask for more?

A short time afterward, a baby-faced Doug Gilmour, then just 22, but a player Jacques Demers had already recognized as a tremendous leader, was interviewed. "I just kinda sit there and, you know, think back to myself that, you know . . . *how did we do it?* Somebody must have been looking out for us, you know? Something was going on."

In a city named after a saint, could that something have been a miracle? Most of the 17,801 in the stands that night still think so, and so does one referee!

For nearly a quarter of a century, I wondered if my message for Jacques Demers at the end of the second period was ever delivered by Rob Ramage. As I prepared for this book I spoke with Jacques, for whom I have the utmost respect, not only as a tremendous coach and motivator, but even more so as the good, kind, caring human being that he is. The world would be a better place if there were more Jacques Demerses around.

He told me he did get the message. He knew that his team had some strong leaders, including Sutter, Ramage, and Gilmour. Jacques's team had accomplished a great deal that season even though they were underdogs—and underfinanced under the ownership of Harry Ornest. The work ethic that he promoted and his players displayed had brought the fans back into the building. Jacques did not want to disappoint those fans and end their season the way the second period had finished.

These are some of the points Jacques told me he touched on during that second intermission: the team was trying to do too much and had put themselves in the position they were in; he appealed to them not to take any more stupid penalties; he sensed that everybody was frustrated—even he had lost some control; they needed to get back in the game early; and they needed to score a goal every five minutes.

Jacques also told me that, aside from Game Two of the 1993 Stanley Cup final, which the Montreal Canadiens won in overtime after tying the game while Marty McSorley of Los Angeles sat in the penalty box for using an illegal stick, the Monday-Night

Miracle was the greatest game he'd ever coached. Call it coincidence, call it fate, but it was a tremendous honour for me to have been the referee in both games that the Honourable Jacques Demers, now a Canadian senator, considers his greatest games.

NHL=NO
HOME LIFE

One of the realities of being a member of the "third team" on the ice is that, unless you live in a National Hockey League market, you never have a home game. Over the course of a season, we log between 120,000 and 150,000 miles in the air. Elements of it can be very enjoyable: getting to see some of the greatest cities in North America (and sometimes Europe) is a definite perk, especially when you get to bring your spouse or family along. It's the getting there that is not all it's cracked up to be. Since 9/11, travel has been much more difficult and taxing, both mentally and physically, than ever. NHL officials deal with the long security lines, flight delays, and winter-weather issues on pretty much a daily basis for 10 months of the year. Trust me when I say it's not the life of a jet-setter! The road warriors of the business world know exactly what I'm talking about.

We joke in the officiating business that NHL really stands for *No Home Life*. In a month such as January, I might be home for 10 out of the 31 days. The place setting at the head of the table in an official's home is often unoccupied for birthdays, anniversaries, First Communions, Thanksgivings, and just about every family function except Christmas. (Until 1971, there were even games on

December 25, but the NHL Players' Association gained that concession.)

That degree of absence doesn't always make the heart grow fonder on the home front. I can attest to this first-hand, as my first marriage ended in divorce. I was only 20 years old and too young to understand what love and commitment were all about, especially as I immediately entered the world of professional hockey officiating. I wasn't alone in this regard. More than a couple of guys over the years have come home from a trip to find an empty house. In many cases, not only was the official's wife gone, but all the furniture as well, right down to the curtain rods. The wife of one fellow in the early '80s was at least decent enough to leave his place setting on the floor in the dining room where the table and his chair used to be.

My point is it's not an easy life for a wife or family. It takes someone special at home to provide stability, love, and balance, both for the kids and the husband. I was blessed to have found all that and more in Kathy, my true soulmate. Kathy and her three beautiful young daughters accepted the proposal from me and my three young sons and we were married in June 1988, effectively becoming the "Brady Bunch." In December 1990, Kara Marie Fraser was born and then there were seven!

I couldn't ask for a better head of our household than Kathy. She has taken care of paying all the bills, handling all calamities (which always seemed to happen when I was away), and raising our beautiful children to be good, successful people. She has provided love, warmth, and support to all of our children and grandchildren, seemingly as a single parent. Often, she had to be in two places at once while I was away. It was common for her to run from a high school field-hockey game for Jessica or Jaime to a college field-hockey game that Marcie was in, or Ryan's wrestling meet or Ian's hockey game.

When our daughter Jaime was preparing to receive her First Holy Communion, we set the date—with the co-operation of the pastor, who was very accommodating—to suit my playoff schedule. The day before this very special event, I got a phone call from Bryan Lewis, the director of officiating, telling me that one of my colleagues was injured and I had to travel to Edmonton immediately. To this day, it breaks my heart to see the family album with pictures of Jaime in her beautiful white dress and veil—and big, red, sad eyes.

But such is the reality of the life of a referee. Kathy never complained, she just kept on giving, loving, and caring. She is the true hero in our family.

When you travel as much as I do, you have to be prepared for anything to happen. On January 6, 2010, I faced a six-hour flight to the West Coast to work a game the next night between the St. Louis Blues and the Anaheim Ducks. Another mad rush to get out the door, another goodbye kiss from Kathy and prayer for a safe trip, then off to Philadelphia International Airport. Arriving with enough time to check my bags so they would at least stand a fighting chance of arriving on the same flight I did, I took my place in line, expecting to be placed in first class. However, the boarding pass I was handed revealed that I'd been assigned a seat in coach. I assumed a computer error must have occurred. When you travel 150,000 miles in a year, US Airways makes you a member of the Chairman's Preferred program, and the chairman does not sit in the back of the bus! Except, it seemed, this time. Without a hint of apology or empathy, the counter agent simply said, "Full up front."

I knew it wasn't the end of the world, but in case I needed grounding at any time during the trip, Kathy's response to the news rang in my ears: "Kerry, you are just a referee, you're not Wayne Gretzky!" (Of course, that wasn't what I thought I needed to hear at that moment.) Nightmarish visions of past economy-class seatmates haunted me, from screaming children to the abusive drunk I had to quiet down on a pre-Christmas flight to Chicago.

On that occasion, I had offered to give up my seat in first class and move back, a suggestion the flight attendants gratefully and eagerly accepted. As did the fellow with whom I was trading seats—he practically knocked me over as he raced forward to take my place. As I headed back through the cabin, the faces of the passengers for about 10 rows on either side of this guy made it clear to me just how disruptive and obnoxious my new seatmate had been. All I could glean from the flight attendants was that his name was Bruno.

Two things gave me cause to be relieved when I arrived at my new location: I had the aisle, he had the window, and the middle seat was unoccupied. And, while he had broad shoulders and thick, sausage-like fingers, he was two inches shorter than me. His eyes were glossed over thicker than the ice on the Rideau Canal in February, and his first, heavily slurred, words to me were, "Shooo, yooou're the guy that'sss gonna keep me quiet, are youuu?" Then he hiccupped. I extended my hand, introduced myself, and said, "Bruno, before this plane lands in Chicago, you and I are going to be best friends."

I learned that he was of Polish descent, and told him my wife and I had been to Rome the previous summer and had had an audience with Pope John Paul II, after which we'd had our picture taken shaking his hand. Our mutual affection for the pope established some common ground right off the bat. Next, I asked Bruno if he liked hockey. It turned out he had grown up watching the Broad Street Bullies, and his dad had even taken him to their first Stanley Cup parade in 1974. Since he was a Flyers fan, I asked about Eric Lindros. He loved the Big E. He loved Gretzky. Heck, it seemed he loved everybody! How could it possibly be that the other passengers wanted to throw him off the plane—at 35,000 feet?

"Bruno," I said, "this is your lucky day, because in my bag I have a picture of the opening faceoff of the first game Lindros and Gretzky played against each other. Both players have signed it, and if you're good for the rest of this flight, I will give you that picture as a Christmas gift for your dad." To prove I wasn't bluffing, that the reward was as promised, I produced the picture from my bag. From that moment, Bruno would've done anything for me—even built me a house with his bare, stubby hands. Only twice did I have to remind him about our bargain, and both times it was when he wanted another cocktail because he was tiring of the coffee I was pouring into him.

When we landed at O'Hare, we were all instructed to remain seated. The flashing lights visible outside the aircraft were a dead giveaway that Bruno's next stop wouldn't be the airport lounge. A female Chicago police officer, followed by a much more physically imposing colleague, boarded the plane and walked directly to our row. With a big smile and friendly demeanour, she invited Bruno to a "Christmas party" they were having. For a moment, I actually felt sorry for Bruno; the thought of him being led past his parents in handcuffs saddened me, and I considered advocating for him. Bruno collected his carry-on, which now included the coveted Gretzky-Lindros photo, and as he was led off the plane, he turned and waved to the other passengers, who cheered his fate. I was thankful my negotiation and crisis-management skills were all I had to call upon. Even so, it was the longest two-hour flight I've ever taken.

Surely, my fate on this California flight couldn't possibly be that bad . . . or could it? When I boarded the plane, I found the middle seat occupied by a large woman with a serious chest infection. She was hacking and coughing—the really thick, phlegmy coughs that sounded like they were coming from her toes—and never once did she cover her mouth. I found that I was leaning so far out into the aisle from my seat that I was almost decapitated by the beverage cart. I'm not a big fan of wearing a helmet, as you might expect, but I would have gladly put mine on if it hadn't been packed in the belly of the plane. Still, a full shield couldn't have deflected the germs that were flying around the cabin, and I only had to hold my breath for six more hours! I knew it wasn't a matter of *if* I was going to get sick, but when.

Sure enough, three nights later in San Jose, it happened. A goal was scored against Sharks goalie Evgeni Nabokov, who thought the puck had been batted past him with a high stick. The goal was reviewed by the war room in Toronto, and Mike Murphy confirmed my call—the goal was "good." I got off the headset and switched on my microphone to make the announcement in my very best broadcast voice when, to my dismay, I began to croak like a frog. By the end of the evening, I too was barking like a dog, just like my former seatmate!

I learned early in my career that the best way to avoid jet lag was to adjust my body clock to local time as quickly as possible. Whenever I travelled to the West Coast, that meant staying up as late as possible, at least until midnight. While my body might protest that it was really 3 a.m. and it desperately needed sleep, I would look at the clock and remind myself it was only midnight. This enabled me to reset my body clock and awaken between seven and eight local time the next morning. Kathy could never figure out why my theory didn't work so well when I returned home from the West and would fall into bed, exhausted, right after dinner.

Kathy would watch all the games on the NHL Network so that, like me, she would be on Pacific time when I returned. The problem was that she had to function on Eastern Time to attend to the kids and household duties, in addition to keeping tabs on me out West. But she was so good about watching my games that I would call her and ask, "How did I do?" She would usually say I did a great job, but was never afraid to tell me if she didn't agree with a call. Sometimes, her assessment was as good as those from our NHL supervisors!

Once, she accompanied me on a trip to Boston and met Derek Sanderson, who was broadcasting for the Bruins at the time. She told him she had watched the game I'd worked the week before and heard his comments on a penalty call I had made. He turned a little red in the face and admitted that sometimes "we get a little carried away." They both laughed about it. The next time I reffed a Bruins game, Derek must have deduced that my number-one fan would be watching. "Kerry Fraser is the referee tonight," he commented. "I met his wife Kathy a little while ago, and boy, did she give me the devil about a comment I had made about Kerry. You know what? I like that . . . a woman who stands by her man! Kathy, if you're watching tonight, and I'm sure you are, I promise I'll be fair to your husband."

We moved to the U.S. in 1988, and Kath's greatest sadness, next to leaving her widowed mom and brother Danny, who has Down's syndrome, was not being able to watch *Hockey Night in Canada*. She will tell you to this day that *HNIC* produces the best hockey broadcasts in the world. So, for our first Christmas in our new home in Voorhees, New Jersey, I surprised her with one of those huge, black satellite dishes. Now she could watch Don Cherry (her favourite at the time) to her heart's content.

One night, I was working a game in Quebec City, and the only telecast she could pick up was in French. So she watched the game, not understanding much of what was being said, but she knew the fans weren't very happy with me because I had called a number of penalties against the Nordiques. All of a sudden, she saw these white bombs descending from all over the rink—being thrown in my direction. The broadcasters were very animated, but she couldn't understand what they were saying. Then she caught the word *toilette*. The game was delayed as I made my way to centre ice and just stood there. Kathy called my mom in Sarnia (my other fan) and asked if she knew what was happening. "Yes," Mom said, "they're throwing rolls of toilet paper at him. I think they're going to have to call the game off!" My mother was right: they were throwing every roll of toilet paper at me that they could get their hands on. At first, they were streaming down, but then fans started soaking them in the toilet to give them extra weight and velocity. Even the players skated for cover! I was told that, after that game, the management of Le Colisée re-equipped all the bathroom stalls with single-sheet dispensers.

After Gary Bettman decided to take the names off the backs of the officials' sweaters, we were allowed to choose our own numbers. I chose number two. Not long after that, I was interviewed for a feature article in the South Jersey *Courier-Post*. The reporter asked why I hadn't chosen number one instead. I answered that it was because Kathy is number one—always has been and always will be.

In retirement, I plan to repay Kathy and the kids for all of the events in their lives that I've missed. I am looking forward to having a *New Home Life*. I have given enough of my blood, sweat, tears, and time to the National Hockey League. It is time to be homeward bound.

Great hair from the very beginning! Following this first vacation to Northern Ontario with my mother (Barb) and father (Hilt), I started skating two months later. 1953. FRASER FAMILY COLLECTION

1967–68 Sarnia Black Hawks OMHA AAA Midget All-Ontario finalists team photo. I am in the first row, second from the right, and my dad, Hilt, who was the coach, is in middle row on the left. Wayne Merrick (four time Stanley Cup winner with NY Islanders) is in the back row, third from right. My best friend growing up, Mike Boyle (Hamilton Red Wings & St. Catharines Black Hawks), is in the back row on the right. May, 1968. BROWN PHOTOGRAPHY—FRASER FAMILY COLLECTION

Opening faceoff of final game played in Calgary Stampede Corral on April 18, 1983, as Flames coach Bob Johnson looks on from behind the bench. COURTESY OF AL COATES, ASST. TO THE PRESIDENT, CALGARY FLAMES, 1983

Joe Louis Arena with my three sons looking over my shoulder: Ryan at left shoulder, blond Ian looking down, Matthew next to him with head down, 1986. PHOTO BY JOHN HARTMAN; COURTESY OF BRUCE BENNETT

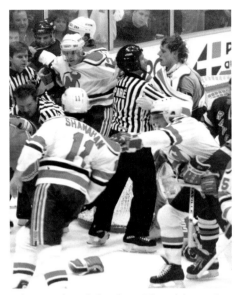

Caught between the Devil and the deep Blue shirts—Brendan Shanahan coming to the aid of Devil's goalie Sean Burke, November 17, 1989.

PHOTO BY CHARLES FOWLER JR.

The Fury of Fleury: Theo Fleury usually directed as much negative energy towards me as he did his opponents even in this confrontation during his rookie season in 1989–90.

PHOTO BY JOHN HARTMAN; COURTESY OF BRUCE BENNETT

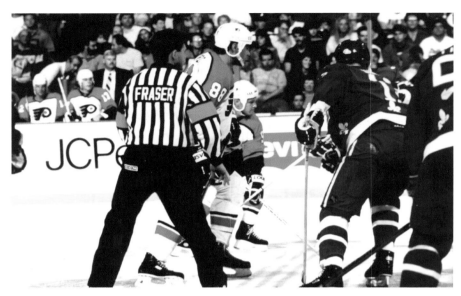

Eric Lindros's first game in the NHL was also the Flyers first pre-season game. The Flyers vs. Quebec Nordiques, the team The Big E refused to play for. September 1992. PHOTO BY BRUCE BENNETT

The Great One vs. The Next One: opening faceoff in first game between Gretzky and Lindros at the Philadelphia Spectrum, 1992.
PHOTO BY BRUCE BENNETT

Relax *paesani*, I never said I didn't like Italian food! With good friends, linesmen Pat Dapuzzo and Ray Scapinello, at Philadelphia Spectrum, November 22, 1992. FRASER FAMILY COLLECTION

One of many cartoon caricatures by the incomparable Dave Elston spoofing my hair. 1994. REPRINTED WITH PERMISSION OF THE ARTIST

Former President of the NHLOA, Assistant Director of Officiating, and friend Dave Newell presents me with my 1,000 game milestone award at Madison Square Garden as Kathy, Mom, Dad and all our children applaud (Kara's going the wrong way!). December 6, 1996.
COURTESY OF BRUCE BENNETT

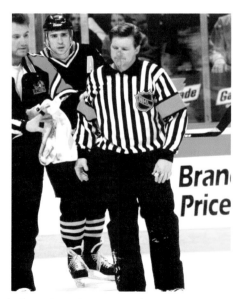

Tony Amonte deflected puck into my face in Chicago Stadium, 1997, resulting in broken nose, fractured tooth, seven stitches to lip *but not a hair out of place!* PHOTO COURTESY OF RAY GRABOWSKI / GRABOWSKIPHOTO.COM

The War Room calling again! December 9, 1997.
PHOTO BY ACTION IMAGE, MARK A. HICKS, COURTESY OF THE DETROIT RED WINGS

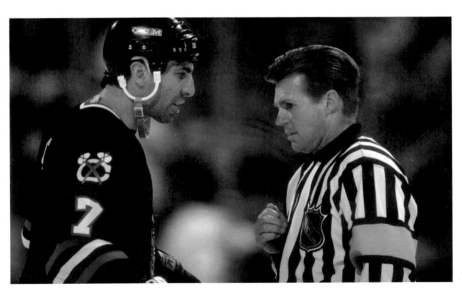

One of many intense debates with Chris Chelios. This one occurred in
a 3–1 Blackhawks playoff loss to the Stars at Reunion Arena in Dallas,
April 18, 1998. Like fine wine, Chris and I both mellowed with age.
STEPHEN DUNN / GETTY IMAGES

Fraser family in summer 2000 in front of Keenan's old house. Back, left to right: Ryan, Matthew, me, Ian. Middle, left to right: Jaime, Kathy, Jessica, Marcie. Front: Kara and Muffin. FRASER FAMILY COLLECTION

Picture commissioned by Kathy for my 1500th game. Artist Phoebe Darlington sketched highlights of my career. Pictured are four of the greatest players I refereed: Mario Lemieux, Wayne Gretzky, Guy Lafleur, and Mark Messier. Inset of my Dad taking me skating and the late John McCauley, friend and mentor. Pucks depict career highlights. Presented by Mark Messier at MSG pregame ceremony November 30, 2004.

ARTIST PHOEBE DARLINGTON—FRASER FAMILY COLLECTION

THE FURY OF FLEURY: CALGARY FLAMES

"I'm gonna fucking kill you! I don't care who you fuckin' think you are. Let's meet outside in the parking lot, you fucking shitbag asshole!" [Fraser] immediately gave me a 10-minute misconduct, throwing me out of the game. It was too much. I took my helmet off and threw it at him.

—Theoren Fleury, *Playing with Fire*

I felt the anger well up in me as Fleury's helmet landed at my feet. For a fleeting moment, I considered kicking it back at him. But I quickly regained my composure and my professional demeanour and ejected him from the game.

It was April 19, 1996, Game Two of a first-round series between the Calgary Flames and Chicago Blackhawks. The Hawks had won the first game, 4–1, and now, in the third period, were up 3–0 and were on the power play. In a corner of the rink, I could see Fleury slashing—in retaliation—at the Hawks' Murray Craven. I assessed a penalty, which would again put the Flames two men down—and which triggered Theo's outburst, in which he threatened me with a passion that only men with nothing left to lose can muster.

It has always been my objective, in a game sometimes characterized by force and brutality, to show respect to all who cross my path, both on and off the ice. I believe that sportsmanship is key and that there is a certain baseline of conduct and comportment that one should never slip below. Unfortunately, there have been a number of times when I, as well as other players, have fallen prey to a crudeness, even a cruelty, that is way out of line.

Theoren Fleury has been on both the giving and receiving side of that equation. He always talked a big game, and wasn't afraid to act on his claims if he thought it could benefit himself or his team. Calgary profited quite a bit from this fiery, controversial character and his great heart, speed, and grit, not to mention the goals he scored prolifically. Theo wouldn't learn, however, until four years later, the venomous potency that words can have when aimed low.

On December 20, 2000, at Madison Square Garden, the buzzer had just sounded to end the first period and Fleury rushed up to me with tears in his eyes, a shocking sight in its own right. This player, known for his Mighty Mouse–like tenacity, now stood beaten down, appealing to a person he'd rather never have contact with. "Kerry, he can't talk to me like that!" he shouted. "He can't talk to me like that! I'm really tryin' to get my life turned around. I've been clean for a month and haven't done any coke or even had a drink since then. I'm really tryin', honest. Don't let him talk to me like that!"

Was this the same Theoren Fleury who had played for three different teams and had never once, while playing for any of them, exhibited any sort of trust in or respect for me? Was this the same guy who'd told me to go eff myself time and time again, who'd thrown his helmet at me, railed against me as an authority figure because he never wanted to play by the rules and, by virtue of my job, I forced him to? Could it be that man who was now pouring out his heart to me?

I had been used to seeing this guy fall far below anything remotely resembling a standard of acceptable behaviour. He was the type to insult your mother, kids, and dog before breaking a stick over your head just to gain an edge on the ice; he wasn't really in a position to judge what other guys were throwing back at him. Yet here he was, almost like a hurt child. He was desperate—I could see that in his eyes, along with a deep sadness and lifelessness. There were lines etched on his face from wounds that not even the best doctors could diagnose or repair; and he wore psychological scars from his troubled existence, despite being a superstar winger in the National Hockey League.

I was confused in this moment by what I was seeing from Theo Fleury, but then again, most things that Theo did were confusing to the average person. In a moment of vulnerability, when I could easily have gotten him back and told him to eff off, I looked into those tormented eyes and felt compassion. I was reminded of my own seven children and how I felt for them when they were in distress, especially my son Ian, who had been to Fleury's hockey school a few years before. Theo Fleury was his favourite player growing up and Ian had a signed poster on his wall. Looking at Theo, I couldn't help but feel a small tug at my heartstrings and a desire to take some of the pain away. Although Theo wasn't looking for a father's shoulder to cry on (he was still too proud for that), he was reaching out to me for the first time in our tumultuous relationship. I saw before me a broken human being with a dangerous combination of vulnerability, volatility, and weakness.

It was in this vulnerability, though, that I saw potential strength and could feel hope for him. He was probably expecting me to disappoint or mock him, as so many with authority had done throughout his life. But that was not my intention; I needed to throw Theo a lifeline. I only hoped he might grasp at it.

I asked Theo which of the visiting St. Louis Blues had said something to upset him so much. Theo told me it was Tyson Nash, with whom he had just been involved in a scrum as the period had ended. Nash allegedly brought up Theo's addiction to drugs and alcohol, which had landed Fleury in the NHL's substance abuse program. I saw the pained look on Fleury's face intensify as he revisited what Tyson had said to him. I looked for Blues coach Joel Quenneville, but he had already vacated the bench and was rounding the corner to his team's dressing room.

I agreed with Theo that Nash's comments were unacceptable, a personal attack that went below the generally accepted level of taunting and trash-talking. Nash's words had cut deeper than any slash from a stick could inflict. I truly felt heartsick for this poor guy. I asked Theo whether, if I could arrange a sincere apology from Nash at the start of the next period, he would accept it and attempt to move forward. He said he would. I told him to meet me right back at the same spot on the ice after the intermission. Before we parted, I said, "Now, if I arrange this, please promise me you won't crack him over the head with your stick, but will accept the apology like a man." Once again, Theo responded that he would.

I immediately went up the hall past the door of my dressing room to the visiting team's room and asked Quenneville if I might have a word with him. Joel, beyond being an excellent coach, is really a class act. He wants to win as badly as anyone I have seen in this business, but in my opinion he places integrity above all else. When I relayed what had just taken place, Joel, without hesitation, rolled his eyes and said, "Do you want me to tell Nash to get undressed?" This is the kind of integrity I'm talking about.

I offered a different solution. I said I thought there could be a lesson in this for his player and would prefer it if we could elicit a sincere apology from Tyson at the start of the period. Joel agreed, perhaps feeling somewhat responsible for the jibes—he had told

Nash, who had played just one full NHL season to that date, that he would remain with the Blues as long as he made himself the most "hated" player in hockey. Joel nodded and sped around the corner into his players' dressing room.

Right before the next period, Theo Fleury and I waited between the two teams' benches as the Blues took the ice from the Zamboni entrance in the end zone. Nash approached us with a look of sheepishness and reluctance. He avoided eye contact and appeared to be on a "drive-by" when I flagged him down and said, "Don't you have something to say to this man?"

Tyson was visibly shaken, and it was my impression that he had also been negatively affected by his comments to Fleury. I detected a quiver in Tyson's upper lip as he delivered a very sincere apology to Theo for what he had said. He then wished Fleury well in all that he faced on the road ahead, and gave him a friendly tap on the shin pad with his stick. I looked at Theo and asked him if he was okay with that, to which he said he was. Both players then shook hands and went out to play the rest of the game, which concluded without any further incident.

I believe that Tyson Nash learned a valuable lesson that night; he continued to fill the role his coach asked of him, but from then on he stayed above the line. The Blues beat the Rangers 6–3. Nash saw more ice time than usual—15 minutes and 42 seconds—and assisted on the second-period goal that put the Blues ahead 3–0. And the score sheet proves he didn't shun his role as the Blues' "agitator." At 18:34 of the third period, with his team defending a 5–3 lead, he provoked New York defenceman Brad Brown into a fight. Brown got a minor for instigating the tussle, as well as five minutes for fighting and a game misconduct. Nash got a roughing minor, a major for fighting, and a 10-minute misconduct.

Looking back over my 30 years in the NHL, I would rank Nash and Matthew Barnaby as the two "hated" players who were most effective at getting opponents to take penalties. There are others who are just plain hated, but who commit as many, if not more, infractions than they draw.

I recently corresponded with Tyson Nash about the incident with Theo. I was most surprised by the lasting impact I'd had by calling him out on his comments and forcing him to apologize. Tyson shared with me that the episode was a low point for him in his career, one that caused him to reflect on what he had done and his need to change. I offer this because there might be some hockey fans who read this who are of the opinion that it isn't the job of a referee to be the morality police, but just to assess the penalties. I disagree, and two of the biggest reasons I can think of are Theo Fleury and Tyson Nash. I hope Theo gained some strength that night from the apology he received. In his own words, here's part of a letter Tyson wrote on April 7, 2010, about the positive impact the experience had on him.

> When I first started playing hockey, I was actually pretty decent and had the ability to put the puck in the back of the net, but as I travelled on in my career I realized, and certain coaches helped me realize, if I was going to make the NHL . . . I needed to play a certain way. I, of course, didn't always agree with them . . . but I listened and am so thankful I did because of the career I ended up having. . . .
>
> Coach Quenneville gave me an opportunity and a role on a great NHL team. When I first got called up to the NHL after four years in the minors, I knew this might be my only chance to show what I can do. . . . I ran around and hit everything that moved and smiled and laughed the whole game through, and in many more after that, for I was living my dream and I was playing in the NHL. . . . Coach Quenneville told me that I needed to be the most hated man in hockey and bring that smile and energy to every game and as long as I did that I would be a St. Louis Blue. The rest was history. From that day I would do

whatever I had to do to stick in the league; I would hit anything and anyone. . . . I would yell and chirp and do whatever I could to get the upper hand or draw penalties. After all, we had the best power play in the league, and in fact we had a stat sheet for penalties drawn—which, of course, I dominated. At least I could say I was good in one stat column.

I am pretty sure I was a ref's nightmare, always in the middle of everything, and it just escalated from there. It was a tough role [to assume] because it wasn't really who I was. I consider myself a pretty nice guy who, off the ice, hates controversy, but on the ice I had to do something totally opposite or I would be gone. I was given a job and I wanted to be great at it, no matter what or who stood in my way—until on a particular night.

Before a game against the Rangers, everyone talked and gossiped, and in the heat of the moment I said some things that I typically never do and [got] personal. I was frustrated with Theo Fleury and in the heat of the moment I . . . attacked him as a person. Obviously, Theo was a very fiery guy and it didn't take much to get him, but instead of fire him up, I apparently struck a chord emotionally and he approached Kerry Fraser about it and, well, that was a huge wake-up call for me that certain things are offsides no matter how bad you want to win the game. . . .

After that, I never went after someone's personal life, and I have Fraser to thank for playing dad in this one.

I believe the insight and honesty of Tyson's candid self-analysis have great value. I am reminded that, while winning at all costs seems to be the accepted aim of our game, from the NHL to youth hockey, the cost might not be a simple two-minute penalty but something so damaging and injurious it cuts to the core of the opponent.

Theoren Fleury wasn't the first player in a Flames jersey who
wanted a piece of me. In the brawling '70s, the Flames were based
in Atlanta. They shared an American Hockey League farm team,
the Nova Scotia Voyageurs, with the Montreal Canadiens. In
1975, the Flames had a player by the name of Rich Lemieux, who
had played three and a half seasons with Vancouver and Kansas
City. But he was traded to Atlanta and they sent him down to
Halifax. As a 23-year-old official, I had the misfortune to have a
run-in with Lemieux one night in the old Halifax Forum. He was
on a one-way contract and was not happy about being farmed
out.

On his first shift, I called a penalty against him; his second
shift also resulted in a trip to the box. Voyageurs coach Al Mac-
Neil quickly cut his ice time, which didn't prevent Lemieux from
getting yet another penalty in the third period for an obvious infraction. That was the last straw for Lemieux, who threw his stick
in the air and kicked it some 30 feet across the ice, where it struck
my skate. With that, I assessed a minor for unsportsmanlike
conduct.

In a little over three shifts, he'd racked up eight minutes in
penalties. I knew this fact left him extremely frustrated, and since
his stick lay at my feet, I realized he would have to come over and
pick it up. And I didn't want to be there when he arrived! I started
to move away from the stick, with my back to the Nova Scotia
bench. As I did, Lemieux threw down his gloves at centre ice and
started to charge toward me. I turned to face him squarely, extending both hands, with open palms facing up, in an appeal for
peace. Not a chance. As soon as he reached me, he threw a punch,
which I ducked. I grabbed that arm as it flew past my head, and
as he threw a right, I caught that arm in the air and pulled his

sweater over his head to prevent him from throwing any more punches. Seeing this, one of his teammates, Ken Houston (a six-foot, three-inch giant I had played junior against), thought I was going to punch Lemieux. He grabbed me from behind and picked me up, my little feet dangling two feet above the ice. Fortunately for me, as Lemieux began to untangle himself from his sweater, a linesman arrived on the scene and escorted him off the ice.

I recognize that players get frustrated and that, as the referee, I'm an easy target for them to vent their frustrations on. I've been punched, spat upon, cursed at, and threatened, but somehow an inner voice has always allowed me to maintain a steely calm.

Fortunately, players who demonstrate this sort of hostility are more the exception than the rule. The current captain of the Flames, Jarome Iginla, is a fine example of the other side of the coin. Jarome is the complete player who leads by example whether his team needs a goal, a big hit, or even a fight to ignite their competitive fires. While Iginla takes losses as hard as anyone who has played the game, there were many occasions when I was on the receiving end of the class that he exemplifies.

In a game on Easter Sunday in Chicago, one the Flames desperately needed to win to keep their slim playoff hopes alive, they were about to fall to defeat. This was the last time that I was to work a Flames game. Iginla approached me during his last shift and extended his sincerest congratulations on my retirement. He said that he had watched me work games in the NHL as a kid growing up, and that it had been his honour to share the ice with me. This ultimate compliment, coming from such a great competitor and superstar, will always be a cherished memory.

WHEN THE GOING GETS RUFF: VANCOUVER CANUCKS

The ringing of the alarm at 5:45 a.m. sent shockwaves through me. Whenever I worked back-to-back games in different cities, the alarm always seemed to go off just as I had fallen into the first deep sleep of the night. In 34 years, my fear of missing a wake-up call—and then my flight—never eased.

After a few moments of disorientation, the fog lifted enough to process which city I had called "home" the night before, and where I was heading for the next game.

My restless night had nothing to do with the minor controversy surrounding my ruling that disallowed a Buffalo goal late in the second period of their 3–2 loss to the Canucks. While the call might have disturbed Sabres coach Lindy Ruff's sleep, it seemed fairly academic to me. Every official likes to have some confirmation that his decision was the correct one, and there is no better vehicle than to review the game DVD provided to each referee by the home club. Viewed in the privacy and quiet of my hotel room, a second, third, or fourth look at a play can be both educational and affirming. In some cases, the video evidence can be cause for a future apology. None of these were forthcoming the previous night since, unfortunately, my NHL-issued laptop would not open the DVD. That left me with the old-fashioned form of post-game analysis: replaying it in my mind and hoping that *SportsCenter* would provide me with a good look at the play before I turned out the lights.

In fairness to Lindy, he developed an acute sensitivity to video replay and controversial goals back in 1999, when he was behind the Sabres bench as Brett Hull snatched a championship from him and his team. In the third overtime period of Game Six of the Stanley Cup final, the Golden Brett, a pure goal scorer with a big gun of a shot, this time stood in front of the Buffalo goal with his back to Dominik Hasek and deflected an incoming shot that Hasek stopped with his stick. Hull's tree-trunk-like legs were clearly planted in the goal crease long enough to take root as he dragged his own rebound out of the crease to his forehand and put it in the net. The ensuing mayhem created by the jubilant celebration and the on-ice presentation of the Cup by Commissioner Gary Bettman made it virtually impossible to give, at the very least, the impression that a thorough video replay had taken place. So many goals had been disallowed in that year's playoffs for players having a mere "toe in the crease" that this play was a bitter pill for the Sabres to swallow. I can't ever recall a more absurd rule or standard of enforcement than the toe in the crease. It wasn't the prettiest goal of the 844 Brett scored in regular-season and playoff action during his Hall of Fame career, but it just may be his most famous.

Lindy is a darn good coach (as well as a good guy), and I found myself hoping he slept well the night before in spite of the outcome. When I disallowed the goal, I thought for sure he was going to blow a gasket. On the play, with Buffalo a man short by virtue of Henrik Tallinder's hooking penalty just 15 seconds earlier, Vancouver turned the puck over, allowing an odd-man rush.

Paul Gaustad, driving hard to the net without the puck, delivered a cross-check on the shoulder of Vancouver defender Christian Ehrhoff with enough force to knock him clean into the net. The net came off its moorings just as the puck entered from the opposite side to where I was positioned. It was a bang-bang play and I wasn't able to even raise my hand to signal the infraction. Traffic obscured my view just as the puck entered the net, and the only thing I could do was wave off the goal to assess an interference penalty—but on which Buffalo player? I'd failed to catch the number of the Sabre who had committed the foul.

I quickly asked my colleagues on the ice which Buffalo player had knocked Ehrhoff into the net, but came up empty. I then asked our video replay guy to give me the name of the player, but he was already on the phone with Mike Murphy, the league's VP of hockey operations, in Toronto. I told him to get the hell off the phone with Toronto, that we had no goal but we did have a penalty to call, and I needed the number of the Buffalo player immediately. During this delay, Lindy thought we were reviewing whether the puck crossed the line before the net was dislodged. That wasn't the case: the puck clearly entered the net just before the net came off the moorings, but instead of a goal, Lindy's team would be getting a penalty that would put them two men short for almost two minutes. The gasket had already blown, so there was no sense in trying to communicate that to him. It wasn't pretty, but in the end I got the right player in the box.

And Lindy and the Sabres escaped the period unscathed. In our dressing room between periods, I said to my colleagues (Mike Leggo, Lonnie Cameron, and Scott Cherrey) that one of two things would happen when we went back out for the third period. Lindy's initial demeanour would tell us what he thought of the replay. Either he would be in quiet agreement that his player had committed the infraction and deserved the penalty, or he'd still think I'd robbed him. If the latter scenario occurred and the Canucks scored on the power play, I envisioned a bench penalty and perhaps an ejection from the game for Mr. Ruff.

When we returned to the ice, Lindy was very calm and did not display even a glimpse of repressed anger. As much as he can blow his top like a Mount St. Helens eruption, I also know Lindy to be fair.

Thirty-five seconds into the period, Vancouver's Ryan Kesler was called for elbowing, which left Buffalo short just one man. They killed off both penalties, and converted the brief man advantage they enjoyed, tying the score 2–2. Unfortunately for the Sabres, journeyman defenceman Brad Lukowich scored his first goal in 111 games a couple of minutes later, and it turned out to be the game winner.

Around the time of this game, the media—broadcasters, writers, and bloggers alike—were abuzz with the allegations made by Vancouver forward Alexandre Burrows that referee Stéphane Auger had a vendetta against him. In Nashville on December 8, 2009, Jerred Smithson of the Predators levelled Burrows, and Auger gave Smithson a five-minute major for charging and a game misconduct. The NHL reviewed the play and concluded that the game misconduct was unwarranted because Burrows had embellished the hit.

A month later, on January 11, the teams met in Vancouver, and Auger was again assigned to the game. Burrows, who scored both of the Canucks' goals in a 3–2 loss, received minors for diving, interference, and—with four seconds on the clock—unsportsmanlike conduct. The last one, incurred when he verbally unloaded on Auger, also earned him a 10-minute misconduct. Afterward, Burrows alleged that Auger had approached him prior to the game, told him he had made him look bad, and that he'd be looking for retribution. It is true that Auger had words with Burrows before the game—videotape clearly shows that—but I don't put any stock at all in Alex's version of what was said.

Stéphane Auger is a professional. Can he get his back up like the rest of us? Sure. Whenever someone crossed the line and pissed me off, there could be no way of misunderstanding my body language, demeanour, and response. I think that's called being human! But that sort of reaction comes in the heat of battle and does not lead to some premeditated plan for revenge. That would be unethical and just isn't in the equation for us officials. Ask any player, past or present, and they will give you a list of those of us they felt picked on them and carried a grudge against them. Being the victim is a heavy cross to bear. I hope all parties move beyond it because it's just not healthy. I also wish the media would take the time to send a pool reporter in to get their facts straight after they interview a player or coach. That, of course, would require that the league grant them access to the officials' room.

One thing that is missing in this "New NHL" is the opportunity for players and officials to develop a professional relationship much beyond an adversarial one. When Gary Bettman took the officials' names off our jerseys and replaced them with numbers, part of the identity and personality that each official brought to the game was lost. I can't tell you how many times players would approach me on the ice and ask the name of one of the other officials so he could at least communicate with him by name. This state of affairs creates an impersonal environment.

Officials need to feel empowered to make decisions without being second-guessed by the "war room" in Toronto. Officials need to be able to develop a feel for the game, and to rely on their judgment rather than falling back on the safety net of saying, "Let's go upstairs." When game misconducts are assessed and the league rescinds them, or plays are deemed "a good hockey hit" by the keepers of the game, it causes confusion amongst the rank and file. Decisions on the ice sometimes become a silent debate with oneself as to how a call will be perceived at "mission control." In other words, as a result of feeling like the league is second-guessing him, the referee begins doing it to himself and does not react instinctively. Those who have never worn the stripes wouldn't understand that. If the league had an objective of creating a more robotic, less personal style of officiating, then I guess it's mission accomplished. If the thinking was that criticism against officials would be reduced, the league has failed.

Over my 30-plus years in this business, I've come to realize that refereeing is an art form. You are dealing with many personalities on the ice, from players to coaches to your fellow officials. You have to take in as much of the game as possible, at breakneck speed, staying in position while skating backwards ahead of the play, staying out of the way of players, and making decisions in a fraction of a second. You read the play and know instinctively where the players are going to go or who they are going to pass the puck to before it even happens. You truly develop a sixth sense, a feel for the game, all the while watching 10 players for any infractions they might commit when they think you're not looking.

On several occasions, I've had to question whether these dedicated men who sit in the war room late into the night have any idea what it really takes to referee in the National Hockey League. Playing the game and refereeing it, although both are worthy of respect, quite honestly require distinctly different skill sets.

I was at home watching a Vancouver game on television one night when there was a disputed goal during a shootout. The referee went to the Toronto war room for a decision. It took *nine minutes* to decide it was a good goal! Watching the replay, I knew right away that it was a goal, but like the announcers, the fans at GM Place, and the viewers on television, I had to wait for the league to dissect the goal ad nauseam for nine excruciating minutes.

There has to be a better way. And there is: give those decisions back to the referee, who is in the arena at ice level. That's where the responsibility belongs. These men have made a career out of making these kinds of decisions.

It is my contention that the very best person to review a goal is the referee on the ice who had to make a decision on the play in the first place. It works very well in the National Football League. The officials on the field know exactly what to look for when they review plays. This is what they do for a living. Give us the same respect by putting a monitor at ice level and trust us to make the decision on a goal that we actively saw develop. It would speed up our game and take away the decisions by committee.

Video replay has brought hockey into the modern age of technology. Back in the late '70s, Leafs coach Roger Neilson was given the nickname "Captain Video" because of his extensive study of videotape and use of it as a teaching tool. And it wasn't always a compliment! It was a novelty in those days. It is hard to believe today, but there was even a time when every game was not televised, which made it difficult for the league to determine suspensions on match penalties. I saw Tiger Williams, while playing for the Vancouver Canucks, use a non-televised game on March 23, 1983, to his advantage and mount the best defence I've ever heard in a disciplinary hearing to avoid a suspension. It was classic Tiger.

The game, a 1–1 tie, was played at the old Capital Center in Landover, Maryland. As there was no videotape of the incident, my report would constitute the only evidence presented at the hearing. Here is my account of what transpired.

Early in the game, Tony Tanti of the Canucks bumped into Capitals defenceman Randy Holt. Holt was neck and neck with Tiger for the league lead in penalty minutes, so you can be sure it didn't take much to upset him. The hit got his back up. Not long after, Patrik Sundström, a skilled rookie who got 30 minutes in penalties by accident that year, bumped into Holt in the corner, and the sticks came up. Holt threw his gloves down and started pounding away on the Swede. I thought, What the hell are you doing, Holt? This guy doesn't fight and the game isn't even five minutes old. I hoped the linesmen would get in quick, and as I turned to look out toward the blue line, I saw that they still had some distance to travel before they arrived. Williams, on the other hand, had less distance to cover.

I saw Tiger charging like the wild jungle cat he was nicknamed after; his stick was out in front of him in a cross-checking position, aimed perfectly at the back of Holt's helmetless head. Tiger was still 20 feet away but closing fast when it occurred to me that if a zebra were to step into his path, he would discontinue his charge. I held my line in this game of chicken for as long as possible, but Williams was looking right through the stripes and wasn't stopping for anything, least of all a referee. At the last second, I stepped aside and watched as Tiger shattered his wooden hockey stick on the back of Holt's head. The impact drove Holt's face into the glass, cutting his lip, but to both Tiger's and my amazement, Randy remained on his feet.

The attack hardly fazed Holt, but it did get his attention. The two started trading punches, but Mike Gartner of the Capitals quickly jumped on Williams. Everyone else then followed suit and ended up in a heap on the ice. Rod Langway emerged from the pile with a nasty gash over his eye and needed repairs. I ejected Holt with a major and game misconduct, while Williams got a 10-minute match penalty for deliberate injury, plus a game misconduct for being the third man in an altercation. It was his third game misconduct of the year, so he would get a one-game suspension for that alone. The match penalty would require a hearing, and I expected Tiger would sit out the remaining games of the regular season, especially since he had already been suspended for using his stick on Islander goalie Billy Smith.

I figured Tiger would throw himself on the mercy of Brian O'Neill after I read his post-game admission of guilt in the *Washington Post*. Tiger confessed that he was coming to the aid of Sundström. "I had no choice but to help my teammate," he said. "In the same situation, I'd do it again. The kid has never dropped his gloves to fight in his life and here all three refs are standing there allowing the second-most penalized guy in the league to hit him five or six times."

An emergency hearing was held in the NHL's Toronto office the next afternoon. Tiger was, and remains, a very popular player from his days as a Leaf, and the media were hovering outside the office. Tiger and Jim Gregory, the former Leaf GM, had a bit of a reunion, and Tiger and I greeted each other cordially as we went into the boardroom for the hearing with O'Neill.

Brian read my report, which laid out the facts without any embellishment of details other than to say that Tiger's stick broke on the back of Holt's head from the force of the blow. O'Neill then asked Tiger for his version and whether he had anything to say in his defence.

For the next 15 minutes, Tiger talked about hunting grizzly bears with a bow and arrow. He was very detailed in describing the size and weight of these huge wild animals he had bagged and turned into rugs. Tiger made it clear that, when one of those beasts charges, you need to make sure you have the equipment to knock it down and stop it dead in its tracks. He said the only way to kill one of those monsters when they charge is with an aluminum arrow. I was fascinated to see where Tiger was going with all this, and then he set the hook.

Leaning forward in his chair a little, toward Mr. O'Neill, he looked the vice-president right in the eye and said, "Brian, that's why I use a wooden hockey stick and not aluminum, because if I hit Holt with an aluminum stick, even with the slightest amount of force, he wouldn't have gotten up—Randy Holt would have been dead just like the grizz."

I couldn't believe this shit, but Tiger kept on going, driving it home. He spoke with such confidence and deliberation, even though it didn't make any sense to me. "Brian, my wooden stick just splintered like a twig. They break easy—that's why I use them. Randy Holt never even fell down when I ran into him, and my wooden stick broke. Ask Fraser."

Now Tiger was using me as an expert witness! Brian asked me to respond, and I said, "Tiger is correct, Mr. O'Neill. Randy Holt did not fall and he turned to exchange punches with Mr. Williams." Tiger finished up by saying he would never try to intentionally hurt a guy from behind and that he had always taken on players straight up and just wanted to get Holt off his Swedish teammate who couldn't defend himself. That was it. Brian said he would advise Harry Neale, the Canucks' coach, later that day of his ruling.

Tiger and I walked out of the hearing room together, and I said, "Tiger, that is the biggest load of horseshit I have ever seen shovelled at one time." With a big grin on his face, he replied, "You know something? I think he went for it. I couldn't believe Holt didn't go down, because I really hammered him." The only punishment Tiger Williams drew was the automatic two-game suspension that came with accumulating game misconducts. What a salesman, what a character, and what a big-game hunter!

Speaking of big game, one of the biggest guys ever to wear a Canucks uniform was Todd Bertuzzi. In 2002–03, Big Bert was an immovable object once he stationed himself in front of the opposing team's goal. When teamed up with Markus Näslund and

Brendan Morrison, the big fella enjoyed his best offensive output to that point in his career. Bert had the habit of standing in front of the crease, and when a shot was coming from the point he would push the defenceman from behind, clearing a wide space for himself as well as gaining unimpeded access to a rebound if the puck didn't enter the net. I told him that was clearly interference, since the guy he blasted from behind wasn't engaged with him. He did it in Calgary one night after I warned him not to. Seeing me raise my hand for a delayed penalty, Bert then slashed the closest Flame. Still with my one arm up, I pointed with the other to signal I was acknowledging a second infraction. When Vancouver touched the puck and I halted play, Todd then tried to take someone with him by punching a defenceman in the face—penalty number three, for six minutes, on the same stoppage. Vancouver was scored on just once during the triple minor. When Bert returned, there were just over 10 minutes left in the period and coach Marc Crawford chose not to play him for the rest of the period. He also benched him for most of the third.

The very next night, I had the Canucks in Edmonton, and as I entered Northlands Coliseum the players were in a circle, warming up and kicking a soccer ball around. As I walked by, the game stopped and Bertuzzi gave me the icy stare. As I passed him, I nodded and said, "Bert." He nodded back, but didn't say a word until I was about 15 feet up the hall, when he called out, "Hey, Kerry, are we goin' for the quad tonight?"

I turned and replied, "That's totally up to you, Bert!"

Bertuzzi didn't take a penalty that night. As a matter of fact, we got along just great from that point on. Any troubles he might have thought he had with me appeared to be over. All he had to do was the math to figure it out.

The off-ice crew in Vancouver seemed very sad to shake my hand for the last time as the referee of record at GM Place. When I arrived for this game on the night of January 25, between the Canucks and the Buffalo Sabres, they had a rocking chair waiting for me in the dressing room. It was set on a rug, decked out with a pair of slippers and an afghan to keep me warm on a cold Jersey night. They also threw in a box of Depends, some Preparation H, and a month's supply of Polident! We all laughed and exchanged hugs, all of us feeling the melancholy of lifelong friends saying goodbye, uncertain when or if we would ever meet again. This great off-ice crew, headed by Dr. Jim Potts, was gracious enough to send me a framed picture of our last time together. The frame also held a picture of me standing at centre ice, helmetless with hand on my heart for the national anthems, with the great Vancouver fans as a backdrop. A third picture showed me helping an injured Vancouver Canucks player, Jannik Hansen, off the ice. I had these very special gifts shipped 3,000 miles from west coast to east coast, a route I'd travelled often over all these years. The beautiful city of Vancouver and this great group of men would be much missed.

EDMONTON
AND THE GREAT ONE:
EDMONTON OILERS

The Air Canada pilot announced our final descent into "balmy" Edmonton, where he reported the temperature at minus-21 degrees Celsius. Looking out the cabin window, I could clearly see that I was about to drop into another major hockey market, one that had fostered so many great memories. The sight of the frozen tundra below, sparsely populated by naked trees sporting their winter-white coats, gave me a sense of what it would be like to land on the moon. Stepping off the plane into the frigid jet bridge brought me to the realization that the early settlers and trappers must have been a hardy breed. The cloud of frozen vapour emitted with each breath I let out immediately took me back to the winter of 1985, when I had to deal with a much different Oilers team.

I was living in Sarnia, Ontario, back then, so I was better prepared for the harsh Canadian winter with fashionably warm attire. I had a wolf-skin coat made by a Toronto furrier to handle the most severe weather that places like Quebec City, Montreal, Winnipeg, and Edmonton could dish out. Given my vertical deficiency, however, the bulky coat made me look like a cross between

119

an Ewok and Chewbacca's infant son! On this trip, the weather forecast (minus-30 in Edmonton and minus-65 in Winnipeg) made the decision to bring along the wolf an easy one, even though it filled the most generous of airplane overhead bins.

Back in those years, the Oilers, like most teams, flew on commercial flights. Hockey players were not yet being treated to the pampering of today's super athletes. Since I was going to see the "Oil" in back-to-back games on consecutive nights, both home and away, odds were that we would be on the same flight to Winnipeg the next morning. In situations like this, an official could only hope for the first game to go smoothly. No matter how good your luck, there was usually one player or coach who was ticked over something. It was also part of the culture that we were perceived as the enemy; one of two teams they would have to defeat on any given night. Sure enough, the Oiler team boarded first and were comfortably seated when the rest of the passengers were allowed to board. Stepping onto the aircraft, clad in my "pet wolf," I could sense the snickers and sneers that were emanating from the peach-fuzzed faces of the players.

Dave Semenko was a giant of a man at a time when there weren't that many large players. The fate of the franchise rested squarely upon his broad shoulders (or should I say fists?). He was assigned the nightly task of protecting Wayne Gretzky. Not many who got the task of shadowing the Great One dared incur Semenko's wrath. I don't know how Barrie Stafford, the Oiler equipment manager, even found a helmet big enough to fit Dave's oversized head. Scanning the rows to find my seat, I identified his big pumpkin head, his face in a toothy grin, sticking up well above the crowd. To my surprise, he adopted a feminine-sounding voice and said, with a wink, "Nice coat!" I didn't have a comeback, and if I did I would have thought better of it. I just crammed the wolf into the overhead bin and sank into my seat for the ride to Winnipeg. I dared not fall asleep with these pranksters on board.

The Winnipeg weather report, it turned out, was way off—no mention of the wind chill. The captain advised us that the air felt like minus-90. When we arrived at the gate the team was, once again, allowed to go first. It was now my turn to grin as I watched big Semenk put on a light leather jacket as his only protection against the extreme temperature. My chance would come that night to give him a shot for being so unprepared for the elements of nature.

Local radio stations warned that exposed skin would be affected by frostbite in just five seconds. It was no exaggeration. I stepped out of the hotel lobby after lunch to catch a breath of fresh air, and immediately there was an audible cracking sound as the hair in my nose froze solid. Within two seconds I felt the harsh bite of Jack Frost on my face and promptly returned to the safety of the lobby, all the while wondering how Dave Semenko was faring.

On the ice that night, I kept an eye out for Semenko. As he skated out for his first twirl around the rink, I approached him. Feeling the need to project my voice upward so that he would catch all of my sarcasm, I said, "Hey, Semenk, I bet you wish you had a warm coat like mine instead of that leather jacket you were sporting." Looking down his nose at me without so much as a grin, the big man dealt me a real zinger: "Fraser, I'd wear a fuckin' coat that size for a collar!" Once again, I had no comeback. As I looked skyward at him, I believed he just might be right!

The Oiler team I would be seeing on the ice in January 2010 was a far cry from the dynasty of the '80s, or even the one that, just a couple of years ago, excited their fans with a gallop through the playoffs to the final, where they narrowly missed the chance to raise the Stanley Cup once more. After 50 games, this group was dead last with 38 points (and just 16 wins), and perhaps their brightest hope was of winning the lottery for the first-overall draft pick. I couldn't imagine how the coaching staff headed by Pat Quinn was suffering through this. Pat returned to the bench this season after a three-year exile. In the meantime, he had taken a group of talented Canadian kids to a gold-medal victory in the World Junior Championships, and I think it warmed him up to the idea of returning to the NHL.

Pat and I have had our disagreements over the years, and I'm not alone in that category. Brian Burke once told me not to take it personally—that Pat just hates all officials! My hope was that, like a fine wine, the old coot would mellow with age or that his memory was failing and he had forgotten our history.

When Pat was coaching the Leafs, I worked Game One of their playoff series in Pittsburgh. It was 1999, and at that time, the video-replay official in the arena was authorized to review goals and make decisions—a responsibility that later shifted to the league's war room in Toronto. The series supervisor, Charlie Banfield, sat in the video-replay booth. Charlie is a good friend and was an excellent NHL referee before he took early retirement in 1979 to become a firefighter in his hometown of Halifax, Nova Scotia. (Chuck's son David is following in his dad's footsteps and is a fine young NHL referee with whom I had the pleasure to work several games during my last couple of seasons.)

In the second period, the video-review process (in particular, the placement of the overhead camera) failed both Charlie and me. I can still see the play as clearly as though it just happened. I was in perfect position, a half-step ahead of the goal line on the opposite side to where the players' benches were located. At my back was the door where the visiting team exited the ice to get to their dressing room, located right beside ours. From this vantage point, my sightline was never obstructed by the goalpost or the mesh of the netting. The Leafs bench, where Quinn stood, was more than 100 feet away, so it was impossible for Pat to see what

I am about to describe. A Penguin fired a rocket and hit the goal post nearest to me. After striking the post, the puck hit the ice flat and slid along the goal line. Less than halfway across the six-foot span between posts, the puck jumped up on its edge and curled along in an upright position. In a split second, I saw the puck cross the inside edge of the goal line, leaving an inch of white ice between the black of the puck and the red of the goal line. I thrust my arm forward, pointing like an Irish setter, to signal the goal. The puck then fell back to flat, once again *on* the line as it continued to curl and exit the other side of the goal area. No goal light came on—nor should have, as the goal judge's perspective would have prevented him from determining that the puck had completely, if narrowly, crossed the goal line. I had to blow my whistle to halt play, as I was the only one in the entire building who had seen that a goal had been scored. At least, that is, until the next day.

After I described the play to Charlie over the phone at the timekeeper's bench, and after extensive review of the videotape, the verdict came back: inconclusive. Charlie apologized and said the overhead camera was positioned so that all he could see was the crossbar. He couldn't see the goal line. It was my call to make on the ice, and I ruled the goal would stand. The Mighty Quinn roared loudly that I had cheated his team that night. The next day, footage shot by an ESPN handheld camera that had been positioned in the corner—behind me and over my shoulder—was broadcast on *SportsCenter*, and it revealed clearly that the puck had crossed the line exactly as I said it had. Even so, Pat would have none of it. He claimed the footage had been doctored.

Fast-forwarding to the season prior to Pat's last as coach in Toronto, I was excited to work a Leafs–Canadiens game in Montreal on a Saturday night. I was working with two Montreal-based linesmen that evening, so after a lengthy walk I arrived back at the Marriott Château Champlain for lunch a little later than normal.

The restaurant was empty and Benito, the waiter who had been there forever, greeted me as old friends do and sat me at a table close to the buffet. Shortly thereafter, Pat Quinn entered the restaurant. Benito brought him over to the table beside mine. Without sitting, Pat looked at me, then looked at our friendly waiter and growled, "Benito, the whole restaurant is empty and you are going to sit me down beside the goddamned referee?" Benito thought Pat was kidding; I knew he wasn't. Nonetheless, Pat sat and began reading his paper. Following that brief period of discomfort, I thought I would attempt some conversation beyond the subject of the weather. I turned to the lawyer in Pat and asked about U.S. immigration and citizenship applications that I had recently filed for Kathy, the kids, and me. The pro bono legal advice Pat offered advanced our conversation from forced to pleasant. After lunch I said it had been nice talking with him and wished him luck in the game that night.

Pat's Leafs won, 2–1, and as he crossed the ice to his dressing room, I said with a smile, "See? All you had to do was have lunch with the 'GD' referee." Pat immediately quipped back with a grin, "If that's all it takes, I would have done it a long time ago."

Pat was behind the Leafs bench at Madison Square Garden on November 30, 2004, when Bill Daly, deputy commissioner of the NHL, presented me with a Tiffany crystal in a special pre-game ceremony in honour of my becoming the first referee in history to work 1,500 regular-season games. As I was being applauded by the crowd and players on both benches, linesman Ray Scapinello skated over to Pat and said, "Come on, Pat, this is Fraser's 1,500th game and you're the only one in the building that isn't applauding him." Scamp said Pat gave a feeble clap and responded with a grin, "One thousand, four hundred and ninety-nine too many, as far as I'm concerned!"

On this day in Edmonton, I was actually looking forward to seeing Pat behind the bench once again. While some aspects of his demeanour hadn't changed, others obviously had. On the very first play that crossed his team's blue line, Pat's familiar voice boomed across the ice at the linesman who he thought had missed an offside. Play quickly stopped when Oiler goalie Jeff Deslauriers was forced to make a good save. I was the back referee on the play and immediately rushed to the Edmonton bench. There, with the same smile I'd left Pat with a few years earlier in Montreal, said in a very audible and demonstrative voice: "Pat, I'm so happy you returned to the bench, because it's been boring as hell around here with you gone. As a matter of fact, I heard you came back to coaching just in honour of my retirement at the end of this season." Pat's initial smile erupted into laughter, something I had never had the pleasure of witnessing before this moment, and I really liked it. The ice had clearly been broken, and Pat's offside protest was forgotten in the moment of levity.

The Oilers were completely dominated by the superior skill and speed of the youthful Chicago Blackhawks in a way that the 4–2 score didn't reflect.

Pat is really a loyal guy and a good hockey man whom, in spite of any differences we may have had, I respect tremendously. After the game, I visited with Kevin Lowe, as well as Pat and his coaching staff—Tom Renney, Kelly Buchberger, and Wayne Fleming—to thank each of them for their co-operation over the many years of our association. Pat invited me to share a beer with them as we reminisced. In that moment, for the one and only time, it seemed as though we were on the same team—or, at the very least, the same page.

I have come across many different coaches, with varied personalities and coaching styles. None could match the wit Glen "Slats" Sather possessed. Glen knew when and how to use it to his advantage, whether to motivate his players, deflect the pressure from their young egos, or throw opposing players off their game. Often, his ultimate purpose was an attempt to intimidate—or at the very least get under the skin of—the officials. In all of this, he was truly the master. From my perspective, I just enjoyed his banter.

Sather has five Stanley Cups to his credit, though it didn't hurt that he had arguably the greatest player of all time in his lineup, along with a supporting cast of superstars in their own right. What Slats did so effectively was mould that brash group of kids into champions. He took their collective blend of cockiness, confidence, and superior talent to a whole different level through the systems he developed. He allowed them the freedom to be kids, but also was able to rein them in like a father who has to take away the keys to the family car on occasion. And I'm not so sure that some of their personalities didn't rub off on him; some nights it was difficult to tell the difference between the kids and the dad. The dead giveaway was Glen's unmistakably high-pitched voice.

In the early '80s, I had an Oilers game in Northlands Coliseum and had just assessed a penalty to an Edmonton player. I lined up inside the blue line, with my back to the Oilers' bench and my hands on my knees, when I heard Glen's voice shout, "Fraser, wake the eff up." Without making a big deal of it, I simply took one hand off my knee, turned my head, and placed a finger to my lips in a "hush" signal to the coach. In the best display of total innocence his body language and facial features could muster, he placed both hands upon his chest and shouted, "It wasn't me, Kerry, it was *him!*" He pointed at the dumbfounded photographer who was shooting from between the two benches. I laughed as Glen and his players joined in on the light moment.

The very next night, the Oilers and I had another engagement, this time in Vancouver. I thought I would set the tone for verbal tolerance right after the national anthem and before I dropped the puck for the opening faceoff. Glen never stood behind the bench during the anthem; he would wait until it was over before making his entrance behind the bench. When I saw him appear, I skated over to the bench and said, "Glen, are we going to have any trouble with that photographer tonight?"

"No," Slats immediately shot back, "we left the son of a bitch at home—he couldn't keep his mouth shut!"

In 1984–85, Glen's team finished first in the Smythe Division with 109 points and went on to win the Stanley Cup for the second consecutive year. One night toward the end of that season, the Oilers took an odd night off in Chicago when the Hawks' scoring hit double digits. Since it was just before the playoffs, Glen didn't want his boys to feel any tightness over such a spanking. With a couple of minutes remaining, Lowe broke his stick over a Hawks player, demonstrating the frustration that Glen might have feared. After assessing the penalty, I looked over at the Oilers' bench, where all the players were standing up with their sticks poised to club a fan on the other side of the glass behind their bench. Glen was the ringleader. I rushed over and got Glen's attention. He immediately directed his choirboys to sit. As they all took their places, I asked Glen if he would like me to get some additional security or remove the obnoxious fan. (The truth was, I just wanted to get the game over without having to write a long report if something broke out between players and fans.) Slats turned down my offering of security by saying, "No, Kerry, everything's all right now. That asshole said the penalty you just gave Kevin Lowe was horseshit, but we stuck up for you!" I laughed, Slats laughed, but most importantly for Glen, his players couldn't

contain their laughter. The coach had deflected the embarrassment of a humiliating loss at the end of the season. His boys were
loose once again.

While the Oilers had a star-studded cast of leaders on the ice,
including Wayne Gretzky, Mark Messier, Kevin Lowe, and other
future Hall of Famers, Glen Sather was the guy at the top who put
it all together and kept it together for as long as he could. The financial woes of Peter Pocklington triggered the exodus of stars,
and over time the nucleus of the Oilers was playing elsewhere.
Sather himself moved on to work for the New York Rangers.
You'd be hard pressed to find a more astute businessman anywhere. It was an absolute honour and delight for me to deal with
Glen Sather during my 30 seasons in the NHL.

From the time that I arrived in the NHL in 1980, it was plain to
see that the Edmonton Oilers were Wayne Gretzky's team. In his
rookie season, 1979–80, Wayne tied Marcel Dionne for the scoring lead with 137 points. Dionne was given the Art Ross Trophy,
awarded to the league's highest scorer, because he had scored one
more goal than Wayne. The next year, it was Gretzky's turn, as his
164 points outpaced Dionne by 29. Wayne was a 19-year-old
sophomore in 1980–81, while I was a 28-year-old rookie!

Wayne eclipsed the 200-point barrier in his third season in the
National Hockey League, with 212, and repeated that feat in
three of the next four seasons (in 1982–83, he had an "off year"
with 196 points). He's the only player to break that barrier, and
upon his retirement he held 40 regular-season records, 15 playoff
records, and six All-Star records. Gretzky was called "the greatest
player of all time" in *Total Hockey: The Official Encyclopedia of
the NHL.* I missed being on the ice with Bobby Orr, Gordie Howe,
and others who came before, but I can tell you without hesitation

or reservation that Gretzky was the very best player I ever skated on NHL ice with over my 30 seasons in the league. What may come as a shock is that, in the early going, we clashed on more than one occasion.

Wayne Gretzky did not enter the NHL and become a phenom; he arrived fully formed. In many ways he was mature well beyond his years, but at times he was still just a kid, not unlike those who followed him—Super Mario, "Sid the Kid," and others. All needed to scale a learning curve and endure some growing pains; some completed the process more quickly than others.

The same is true of officials. Even though I was a man with a family, I was a long way from possessing the maturity I now know is required to handle the pressure and abuse that often came my way. Unfortunately, when I was challenged on the ice, I did not always respond appropriately. I too had a lot to learn.

Each official has inherent strengths and weaknesses that we bring to our game. The obvious physical attributes and mechanical skills—size, skating ability, positioning—are easily detected. The less obvious—but, in my opinion, most important—qualities the job demands are strength of character, integrity, judgment, and the ability to communicate effectively and cultivate and develop professional relationships with players, coaches, and other officials. That was where I had some early flaws.

As a player, my physical stature could be best described as "vertically challenged." In an effort to compete, I often fought the biggest opponents in an attempt to gain a measure of respect. I gained courage through these sorts of encounters, an important attribute that I would call upon countless times throughout the course of every game as players, coaches, and fans tried to sway my decisions in their favour through some form of intimidation.

But while I brought an abundance of courage and confidence to the ice each night, when I came under fire these positive qualities would morph into the less attractive and effective indicators of

"Little Man Syndrome." When that negative side of my personality kicked in, observers were left with the perception that I was cocky and arrogant. Unfortunately, quite often their perception was correct. The more I was challenged, the more this character flaw would surface. I felt the need to let "them"—whoever "they" were—know that I was in charge and would not be intimidated. In a one-on-one confrontation with players or coaches, I usually won the battle to establish myself—or so I thought—by imposing a misconduct or bench penalty. In fact, however, I was losing the war.

What infuriated me most was when a player, especially in his home rink, would take a dive in an attempt not only to draw a penalty but to unleash the wrath of the crowd against me. Any time a player persisted in these attempts, I became extremely stubborn. The more they tried, the less likely it was I'd give them the benefit of a call, warranted or otherwise. I adopted the attitude "You made your bed, now lie in it." I kept a mental list of players who belonged to my "springboard club" and tried to make sure they didn't fool me whenever they were on the ice. One night in Edmonton in 1981–82, Wayne Gretzky joined this undesirable club!

Wayne's young Oilers were playing host to Bobby Clarke and the Philadelphia Flyers in Northlands Coliseum. It had been a close-checking, hard-fought game from the very beginning and Gretz had, in my judgment, fallen down a couple of times in an attempt to trick me into calling a penalty and give Edmonton the man advantage. Generally, if Wayne and his supporting cast were given the extra space a power play afforded, the end result was pretty much a foregone conclusion. The dead giveaway when a player is trying to draw a penalty is that they look at the referee before they hit the ice. On two occasions in the first period, Wayne was looking for me long before the perfect entry of his landing. The partisan crowd already believed that Wayne could walk on water, and with what he gave them each and every night, who could blame them? They didn't subscribe to my "frozen pond" theory that, just because there wasn't a splash didn't mean it wasn't a dive. There was no penalty on the books for embellishment back then. The best recourse was to heighten my awareness and make sure I wasn't fooled in the future. Since that approach didn't seem like much of a deterrent to me, my preferred response was to adjust the standard relative to penalty selection on that particular player. There was no grey area at that point; only high-definition black and white. Wayne and I became locked in a duel where there could be no winners, only losers. With each failed attempt to draw a penalty, Wayne complained more vehemently, making me even less tolerant.

With under a minute to play, the Oilers were down by one goal. They were attacking hard in the Flyers zone, and at that stage of the game their very best option was to get on the power play and try to tie it up. Wayne was positioned in "his office" behind the goal line and to the side of the Flyers net as Pelle Lindbergh caught the puck and I whistled the play dead. With no one around him, Wayne leaped into the air, threw his hands forward, his feet stretched out behind him, and executed a belly flop worthy of a perfect score. Bobby Clarke skated up to Wayne and said, "Get up, you effin' baby."

I was on the scene and said, "Wayne, what are you doing? There was nobody within 10 feet of you." Wayne hit the boiling point as he responded, "You wouldn't have called it anyway; you haven't called an effin' thing all night!"

I said, "You're right, and I'm going to start right now: you've got two minutes for unsportsmanlike conduct." As Wayne stormed past me on the way to his dressing room, he shouted, "Good! It's about effin' time you called something!" He didn't even bother to go to the penalty box. I had to go over to Glen Sather and tell him to put someone in the box in Wayne's place.

That was the first, but not last, time a player would thank me for giving him a penalty.

I was deeply troubled by my attitude on the ice that night. I've always believed that two wrongs don't make a right, and the message I sent to Gretzky was not in the best interest of the game. For my part, I was clearly wrong. I felt I had compromised my integrity and that of the game. On both counts, this was totally unacceptable to me. I needed to change, and it didn't stop with players who tried to draw penalties. I made a much deeper examination of my conscience as I tried to recognize and correct the flaws that became evident.

At the end of that season, I met with Scotty Morrison for my year-end review. Scotty opened the book of supervision reports and went through them rather quickly. He mentioned a lot of good comments that appeared in those reports, and said, as he closed his book, I was on target and that he was looking for great things from me in the future.

I asked if he would mind reopening the book, since it was my desire to be the best I could possibly be and whether he could advise me on some of the areas I needed to work on. More specifically, I asked if there was a common thread that ran throughout the reports. Scotty perused them once again. Some examples of the phrases that held the key to failure were: "While Kerry displays confidence, he sometimes gives the impression of being cocky;" "Occasionally appears arrogant with his body language and gestures"; "On occasion can challenge and incite players through his actions." As strange as this might sound, it was exactly what I wanted to hear.

I looked across the desk at Scotty, only five-foot-six himself, but a giant of a man in my eyes. Scotty was extremely respected, both in his days as an on-ice official as well as in his role as referee-in-chief. Given our similar size, I thought he might have ideas as to how to solve my real and perceived problems. Scotty was amazingly kind and helpful in guiding me. He suggested that I slow down my thought process and articulate what I wanted to say in my head before I spoke aloud—to think about how it would be taken at the other end. Scotty also suggested I relax my body language, especially at the shoulders, when I skated and not appear so rigid and stiff. This was really about changing 31 years of learned behaviour and a Type-A personality. I immediately went to work on applying Scotty's suggestions, and my career skyrocketed. There were times in the beginning of my transformation that I would stop in mid-sentence during a conversation with a player or coach and apologize for what I had just said and rephrase it the way I had intended it originally. When I asked a player to put his stick down for a faceoff, I always used the word "please"—it became a request as opposed to an order. Don't get me wrong: I wasn't handing out roses, but I was definitely handing out fewer misconducts. That season, 1982–83, I was selected to work in the opening round of the Stanley Cup playoffs for the first time. Two years later, I was selected to work my first Stanley Cup final, between the Flyers and Oilers.

I had weathered the storm while Wayne Gretzky was making hockey history. Some nights, I even had the pleasure of being on the ice when he shattered records. One that I got to see from 20 feet away was on December 30, 1981, when Wayne scored five goals against the Philadelphia Flyers (four against goalie Pete Peeters, the fifth into an open net) to reach 50 goals in just 39 games. (He went on to score an incredible 92 goals before the season ended.)

While Wayne Gretzky's exploits on the ice are legendary, what he contributed off the ice can never be accurately measured or, as we have come to realize, truly appreciated. "The Trade" from

Edmonton to Los Angeles on August 9, 1988, rocked Canada. The New Democratic Party even put forward a motion in Parliament to block the trade, declaring Gretzky a national treasure. The popularity that the NHL enjoys in the United States today would not have been possible had it not been for Wayne's move south.

I want to share just one story of the kindness that this man displayed to a child in need at a time when some might not have bothered. In '87–88, Mario Lemieux won the scoring title by 19 points over Gretzky. It was the first time since 1979–80 that Wayne had not won the Art Ross Trophy. The following year, Super Mario was on a real tear and picked up where he had left off, finishing with 199 points to Gretzky's 168. About the middle of that year, I caught up with Gretzky and his Los Angeles Kings in Calgary, at the end of a lengthy road trip. L.A. had lost every game on the trip. The media in each city asked the same question 99 different ways: Had Mario grabbed Wayne's throne? Gretzky answered their questions with class as well as respect and reverence for the talent Mario possessed.

Prior to leaving from my home in New Jersey for Calgary, my wife learned of a young boy who was suffering from a serious illness. The youngster had asked if it would be possible to get an autograph from Wayne Gretzky. This is not something I make a habit of doing, or even like to do, but for a sick child I would do practically anything if it brought some cheer. On that night in Calgary, the Kings were being beaten badly once again. Wayne looked physically drained. His eyes were sunk back in his head and he had beard stubble that gave him an unkempt appearance I had never seen on him before. This trip had obviously beaten him up pretty good. During the final commercial timeout, I approached Wayne as he came out to take the faceoff. I apologized for bothering him at a time like this, but quickly explained about the little boy and asked him, if he thought of it after the game, to just sign a piece of paper and I would make sure he got it.

Wayne nodded and dragged himself over for the faceoff. The game ended, and the linesmen and I had just gotten off the ice and into our dressing room. I hadn't even untied my skates, when there was a knock at the door. It was David Courtney, the Kings' travelling secretary, who said, "Wayne asked me to give you this and to wish the little boy well for him." The very first thing Wayne Gretzky did when he left the ice was not to think about how miserable he must have felt before facing another media onslaught, but simply to demonstrate an incredible act of kindness for a sick child back in New Jersey.

There are many stories like this about Wayne Gretzky, and about many other players around the league. What makes Wayne exceptional off the ice is that he never puts himself above anyone. He is a compassionate, quiet gentleman who often said, "Nobody is above the game." Not only did he often say it, he always lived it. He obviously had been raised this way. Kathy and I have had the pleasure of meeting Wayne's dad, Walter Gretzky, on a few special occasions. He is an amazingly kind man who is very proud of all his children. Let me give you an example.

During the 1996 World Cup of Hockey, the final series between the U.S. and Canada finished up in Montreal. On the day of the final game, Kathy, my mom and dad, and I entered the lobby of the Marriott Château Champlain from the elevator to find Team Canada and their families enjoying a reunion. My dad was in his glory, rubbing elbows with all these great players, many of whom he had met at the 1990 All-Star Game in Pittsburgh with Kathy and me. As I stood and enjoyed watching my father mingle with these gracious stars, Walter Gretzky approached me. He is such a sweet man, and my recollection of him on that day actually brings tears to my eyes as I write this. Walter extended a hand and said, "Kerry, it's so good to see you. I have this little friend that lives across the street from me in Brantford and his name is Daniel Eickmeier. He's a big hockey fan and listens to all the games. He

loves when he can hear Wayne play, but you know, he is a real fan
of the officials. I think it's maybe because the sound of the whistle
intrigues him, because he is blind. He would be thrilled if I told
him I talked to you, and if you could sign an autograph, I'll take
it back and he'll be so excited." I was so touched by this request,
and with seven children of our own, I envisioned this youngster
sitting by the television or radio, listening to the games. I offered
to get one of my referee jerseys made up with my name bar and
number two on the back so he could feel the name, number, and
NHL crest on the front. Walter was humbled by this offering, and
said, "Kerry, you'd do that for me?"

"Oh, please, Mr. Gretzky, anything for you. Your son is one
of the most giving guys I've ever seen."

Walter and I exchanged addresses, and I had CCM make up
the jersey and sent it off to Walter's home in Brantford, Ontario,
along with one of my new referee whistles. A couple of weeks later, I got a beautiful letter from the young man's mother, along
with a picture of him sitting at the breakfast table, wearing his
new referee jersey and spooning cereal into his mouth with the
whistle in his hand. "Dear Mr. Fraser," the letter began. "We
thank you for the kindness that you extended to our son Daniel.
He is absolutely thrilled to have both of your gifts, as you can see
by the photo. I must tell you, however, that your sweater would
have been more than sufficient, as we could have done without
the whistle. Daniel hasn't stopped blowing it since Walter brought
it over."

It was Walter's kindness that made it happen. The apple sure
doesn't fall far from the tree!

Wayne Gretzky's graciousness extended over his entire career
and even after retirement. As I'm about to walk through that same
door, eleven years after the Great One hung up his skates, I understand the tears that he shed as he stepped away.

STUDIES IN DISCIPLINE: THE ISLANDER DYNASTY

In 1979–80, the year before I arrived in the National Hockey League, the New York Islanders had just won the Stanley Cup. At that time, the closest I had been to the Islanders franchise, admitted into the NHL in 1972 to keep the rival World Hockey Association out of the Nassau County Coliseum, was by working games involving their minor-league affiliates, first in New Haven, Connecticut, and then Indianapolis.

The master builder of the franchise, general manager Bill Torrey, started with—and made the correct decision to stick to—a plan to build his team through the amateur draft. Teams that had stockpiled talent by acquiring draft picks preyed on expansion teams in those days. The brilliant GM of the Montreal Canadiens, Sam Pollock, was famously the most hawkish in this regard. But Torrey resisted the pressure to trade for marquee players near the end of their careers, which would deliver short-term benefits on the ice and at the box office at the expense of the team's future.

In their inaugural season, the Islanders were far and away the worst team in the NHL, with just 12 wins and 6 ties to go with their 60 losses. The only plus was that they had the first-overall pick in the 1973 amateur draft. Despite several overtures from Pollock, Torrey held on to the pick and used it to select superstar defenceman Denis Potvin from the Ottawa 67's. Potvin had been a man playing among boys in his last couple of years in junior; NHL rules were all that kept him from turning pro until after his 18th birthday. Potvin arrived with the credentials—and expectations—to be the next Bobby Orr. He did not disappoint, winning the Calder Memorial Trophy as rookie of the year.

Torrey continued to build his team through the draft, selecting the likes of Bryan Trottier, Clark Gillies, Mike Bossy, Bob Bourne, John Tonelli, and Bob Nystrom. He also acquired key players such as Butch Goring and my old childhood friend and teammate Wayne Merrick through trades. Goring won the Conn Smythe Trophy in the Islanders' 1980–81 Stanley Cup victory, while Wayne Merrick centred the best third line in hockey, lining up between wingers John Tonelli and Bob Nystrom.

Torrey made an acquisition off the ice that turned out to be as important as any he ever made in the draft when he hired Al Arbour to coach his team. Arbour made his NHL debut in 1953–54, the year after I was born, and played his last games in 1970–71. He was a big, steady, stay-at-home defenceman who had earned the nickname "Radar" because his eyesight was so poor that he was forced to play while wearing glasses as thick as the bottoms of Coke bottles. The discipline that Al instilled in his players was something I very quickly became aware of upon my arrival in the NHL. And his patience with the mistakes his young players made was evident to a young referee like me.

In 1982–83, the Islanders had won three consecutive Stanley Cups. But the Edmonton Oilers were coming of age and challenging the dynasty that Torrey and Arbour had assembled. Near the end of that season, I had a game in which the visiting Oilers were down by a goal late in the third period. There was a faceoff in the neutral zone, and I was positioned in front of the Islanders bench. Very clearly, I could hear the players reminding one another to be careful not to take a penalty. Looking back, I am sure that whoever initiated the pep rally had done it in no small part to plant a seed in the head of the relatively inexperienced referee.

With less than two minutes left in the game, the Oilers were pressing hard but were still down by a goal. A power play was always their best weapon, given the offensive firepower—and collection of future Hall of Famers—Glen Sather had assembled. Jari Kurri was carrying the puck deep into the Islanders' zone along the boards and was being defended by Potvin. Denis put his stick on Kurri as he had angled the Oiler forward toward the side boards, just past the faceoff circle. Kurri immediately started to "chug" in his motion. Fearing that Kurri might fall in an attempt to draw a penalty, Potvin had the presence of mind to immediately remove his stick from the Oiler player and shadow him to the perimeter. Kurri was forced to carry the puck behind the Islanders' goal while Potvin moved in front of his own net and called for his defence partner to pick up Kurri when he came out on the other side of the Islanders' goal. The game of chess that I witnessed all happened in a flash. Potvin showed me such incredible intelligence about the game in that moment, but the words I had heard while standing in front of the team's bench were still ringing in my ears: "Don't take a penalty, boys." Arbour had coached them well.

Very seldom did I ever hear Al Arbour raise his voice behind the Islanders' bench. If and when he did, I knew it was for good reason and that I probably had screwed up. One night in Chicago Stadium in 1983, I heard his voice just 10 minutes into the game. It gave me a wake-up call I desperately needed, because my head had clearly been up my ass.

It started out as just one of those nights when, for whatever reason, my head just wasn't in the game from the opening puck drop. I was in a fog that I just couldn't seem to pull myself out of.

The Islanders took four penalties in the first 10 minutes; not because they were any less disciplined than usual, but because I was that horrible! After the fourth penalty, which now put the Islanders two men short, Arbour stood in the open door of the visitors' bench with his hands on his hips and a scowl on his face. A hundred feet away, I stood waiting in the end zone for him to put three players on the ice so that we could drop the puck. None were forthcoming. We were in a standoff.

Al waved his arm at me and yelled, "Kerry, get over here!" I had such respect for him that I skated over with my head down, ashamed of my performance to this point. When I arrived at the bench, I felt like a little kid standing in front of the school principal. In obvious frustration, Al said, "Kerry, what the *hell* are you doing out here tonight?"

I responded, still with my head down, eyes focused on the cold ice under my skates, "I don't know, Al. I'm really struggling tonight and don't know what's wrong with me." Finally, I raised my eyes to see this coaching icon scratching his head, uncertain what to say. He stared back at me, silent for just a moment, then pressed his lips together and said, "Well, get the hell out there and try harder," as if admonishing one of his players. Like a child who had just been scolded by his father, I responded, contritely and meekly, "Okay, Al, I'll do my best." We weren't all that far from Notre Dame University, and I felt like I had just been told by Knute Rockne to go win one for the Gipper.

The fatherly treatment I received from a frustrated Al Arbour stood in total contrast to what I would encounter 10 years later, in a similar visit to the bench with Quebec Nordiques coach Marc Crawford (more on that later). I would, however, remember this lesson of respect and self-control that the veteran coach had demonstrated to me as a young referee. Al Arbour and Scotty Bowman were, without a doubt, the two best coaches I have ever known in the NHL.

Arbour retired from coaching after the 1994 season, after the Islanders were swept in the first round by the New York Rangers, who went on to win the Stanley Cup that spring. Al had won 739 regular-season games as the Islanders' coach, and a banner bearing that number was later raised to the rafters of Nassau Coliseum. And on November 3, 2007, at the age of 75, Al Arbour was signed to a one-game contract and, at the behest of then coach Ted Nolan, took his place behind the New York bench to coach his 1,500th game. Al is the coach on record in a 3–2 win over the Pittsburgh Penguins, giving him 740 victories as an Islander. It was my good fortune to be the referee of that game, and I remained on the ice immediately afterward as the old banner was replaced with one bearing the number 1,500. Al was joined for the ceremony by the current players, his family, and Islanders alumni including Bryan Trottier, Mike Bossy, and Pat LaFontaine. On this particular night, the coaching legend didn't have to call me over and tell me to "Get the hell out there and try harder." He got the best I had to give; he deserved nothing less.

MEADOWLANDS MEMORIES: NEW JERSEY DEVILS

An hour up the New Jersey Turnpike from my home, there's a sports complex that rises out of a swamp. Legend has it that a Devil once resided there.

When Dr. John McMullen purchased the Colorado Rockies and moved them to their new home at Brendan Byrne Arena in the Meadowlands in June of 1982, the only things that changed were the team's name and geographical location. The Devils were still the same hapless group that posted a league-worst record of 18–49–13 in their final season in Denver. The New Jersey Devils made their debut with an almost identical 17–49–14 season—though the Pittsburgh Penguins and Hartford Whalers were even worse in 1982–83.

After a 13–4 shellacking at the hands of the Edmonton Oilers in their second season, Wayne Gretzky labelled the organization "a Mickey Mouse operation" that was "ruining hockey." I worked an Oilers–Devils game in the Meadowlands a little later, and those Devils fans who showed up wore Mickey Mouse ears and shirts. I'm not quite sure whether they were in agreement with Wayne's statement or mocking him. Somebody was listening, however, and a coaching change was made. Billy MacMillan, who came over from Colorado, was replaced by a fire plug, Tom McVie. I first ran into Tommy in 1973 in Dayton, Ohio, when he was the playing coach of the Gems of the International Hockey League. Tommy's voice always reminded me of the big cartoon rooster Foghorn Leghorn. McVie is a great guy and always seemed to keep things loose. I could hear that booming voice from anywhere on the ice when he would yell, "BATTLE STATIONS, MEN—BATTEN DOWN THE HATCHES!" When Tom took over the Devils that year, he had to keep his sense of humour, because his battleship was a leaking rowboat.

McVie's replacement at the end of the season, Doug Carpenter, would benefit from some reinforcements added in the 1983 entry draft. Defenceman Joe Cirella and forwards John MacLean, Kirk Muller, and Pat "Beeker" Verbeek would form a good nucleus to build on. Beeker was born in my hometown of Sarnia, and played with a lot of grit and determination. His family farmed in the neighbouring town of Petrolia, and in 1985 Pat put his hand into the fertilizer machine to pull out a piece of a bag that had gotten stuck in the cutter. He didn't pull his hand out in time and had his thumb cut off. Pat's dad, Jerry, rushed him to hospital in London, 45 miles away, while Pat's brother found the thumb, packed it in ice, and brought it to the hospital. Pat's thumb was reconnected, and he was back on the ice that year. It was truly amazing. When I saw Pat in a game in New Jersey, I asked him if it was true that, because the thumb was so well fertilized, it grew back twice as long. He laughed, thank God. He was a very intense player and made an instant difference on that team.

As the Devils' young players improved, so did their record, but the Patrick Division—with the New York Islanders and Rangers, Philadelphia, Washington, and Pittsburgh—was a tough one to move up in, and the Devils missed the playoffs in six of their first seven years. That was all about to change when McMullen went outside the old boys' club of coaches and general managers and plucked the saviour of the franchise from Providence College. Lou Lamoriello was the long-time hockey coach and athletic director at that school, and was a relative unknown outside the college scene. Lou became the Devils' president and general manager just before the 1987–88 season, when New Jersey posted a winning record of 38–36–6 and made the playoffs for the first time, reaching the Wales Conference final against Boston. That series lives in infamy for the phrase "Have another doughnut!"

I was the referee at Chicago Stadium on April 3, 1988, the final day of the regular season, when the Devils clinched their playoff berth. Both New Jersey and the Rangers had 80 points heading into that last game, and during the game, the out-of-town scoreboard reported that the Rangers had shut out the Quebec Nordiques, 3–0. The Devils now knew they had to win in order to reach the post-season; a tie would not be enough. If both teams ended up with 82 points, New Jersey would make the playoffs because they had won more games over the course of the season.

It was an extremely hard-fought game, and the Devils were behind 3–2 until John MacLean tied it up halfway through the third period, off a rebound given up by Chicago goalie Darren Pang. At the other end, rookie goalie Sean Burke stopped a Rick Vaive breakaway late in the game that would have ended the Devils' season. The third period ended with the score tied 3–3, and we were headed to overtime. John MacLean was the hero again, as he scored from the high slot on another big rebound, and the Devils bench erupted as the players jumped over the boards and mobbed MacLean and Burke. It was the biggest goal in franchise history to that point. The celebration was reminiscent of a Stanley Cup final. Coach Jim Schoenfeld went wild and hugged every player on the ice before they headed off to celebrate their victory in the bowels of Chicago Stadium. It wouldn't be the last time that season that

Schoenfeld would let his emotions run wild. The next time, however, there would be a price to pay for his lack of control.

The Devils were a team possessed as they disposed of the first-place Islanders in six games and Washington in seven, putting them in the conference final. During that series, I found out the hard way that John MacLean used his hands for more than scoring goals.

Director of officiating John McCauley assigned me to Game Two in Boston on May 4. The Devils won the rough-and-tumble affair 3–2 in overtime, but before we reached that point a line brawl broke out when Bruins player Moe Lemay went hard to the Devils goal, bumping Sean Burke. The cavalry came to the defence of their goalkeeper, and linesman Gerry Gauthier was tied up with Willi Plett of the Bruins and Perry Anderson of the Devils against the boards in the end zone. Linesman Ron "Huck" Finn was trying to separate Lemay and MacLean, but they had dropped their gloves and were ready to rumble. Poor Huck Finn was on his own, so I came in from behind to grab Lemay and pull him out of the altercation just as the punches started. I moved around Lemay to tie up his right hand and skate him out of the exchange when, unfortunately for me, Finn didn't realize that MacLean's left hand was free. MacLean unloaded with his best shot from over the top. The closest head to the punch was mine—he drove me right in the freakin' head. It staggered me momentarily, but thank heavens he was a better goal scorer than a puncher. I was still on my skates. More than anything, the punch just made me mad. I aggressively tied up Lemay and moved him out of there so that I wouldn't have to take any more shots. When the dust settled, MacLean got 14 minutes in penalties and Lemay ended up with 17. Coach Jim Schoenfeld was sending a message to the Bruins and their coach, Terry O'Reilly, who had prevailed by a score of 5–3 in Game One. The Devils' subsequent overtime win sent the series back to "The Swamp" tied at one game each.

The next dust-up of the series didn't occur on the ice. McCauley assigned Don Koharski to referee Game Three, and the Bruins really put it to them by a score of 6–1. I don't care what anyone says: if a referee misses one or maybe two calls in a game, it sure as heck doesn't result in a 6–1 rout. The responsibility for that kind of shit-kickin', especially in your home arena, needs to be readily accepted by the losing coach and his team. But the pressure of playoff competition makes people react in ways they normally might not. Schoenfeld let his emotions get the better of him and confronted Koho after the game in the hallway as he and linesmen Ray Scapinello and Gord Broseker were heading to their dressing room. Aside from the fact that it never should have happened, the confrontation became highly personal and very public as the television cameras rolled. Schoenfeld cut Koho off a bit, causing him to stumble into the wall. A shouting match ensued, and Koharski told Schoenfeld he was "Gone!" (The game was over—Koharski's reference to "gone" meant a report to the president of the NHL, John Ziegler, would be written and suspension might result.) Schoenfeld fired the last salvo with the infamous line "Good, because you fell, you fat pig. Have another doughnut! Have another doughnut!"

NHL vice-president Brian O'Neill suspended Schoenfeld for Game Four. But, 40 minutes before the game, Judge James F. Madden of the New Jersey Superior Court granted Jim Schoenfeld a stay. Dave Newell was the referee assigned to work that game, with the linesmen from the third game, Scapinello and Broseker. Newell was the president of the NHL Officials' Association and brought the association's lawyer, Jim Beatty, with him to the game in the event that a legal opinion was required. Beatty's presence certainly was needed, because Newell flatly refused to work the game if Jim Schoenfeld was behind the bench.

John Ziegler was out of the country on family business and unavailable for consultation about the incident. Instead, Bill

Wirtz, chairman of the NHL's board of governors and owner of the Chicago Blackhawks, instructed McCauley to advise the officials that they would be fired if they did not take to the ice immediately. McCauley pleaded with Newell to work the game and let the matter be settled in court. Newell remained firm and would not allow the linesmen or standby official to work the game either. It was a show of solidarity for Koharski, who was back at his home in the Hamilton, Ontario, area by this point.

The game was delayed for over an hour. John McCauley's efforts to broker a truce failed, and three amateur officials from the off-ice crew were pressed into service as replacement officials. Goal judges Paul McInnis and Vin Godleski served as referee and linesman, respectively, while official scorer Jim Sullivan worked as the second linesman. They officiated while wearing bright yellow practice jerseys. I don't know what they got paid, but those poor guys earned every cent of it. The game turned into a free-for-all. It was a mess.

McCauley tried to referee the game from the penalty box, instructing the replacement crew. John's two sons, 16-year-old Wes (now an NHL referee himself) and 12-year-old Blaine, were at the game with John and saw the stress their dad underwent as this bizarre situation unfolded. Gang warfare broke out; it was so bad at one point that Bruins coach Terry O'Reilly, one tough hombre when he played, challenged Devils players on the ice—as well as their coaches behind the adjacent bench.

While all this was going on, I was sitting in the comfort of my hotel room at the Detroit Marriott Renaissance Hotel, watching the game on ESPN. I was scheduled to work Game Three of the Western Conference final between the Red Wings and Edmonton Oilers the next night. I had already gotten a call from Newell, who said he, Scapinello, and Broseker had been fired and that Jim Beatty was trying to arrange a meeting in Toronto the next morning to restore peace. My crew would be advised as to our status before game time the next day. I also got a phone call from Bill Clement, who was covering the game on air as a colour analyst and asked me what we were going to do. I informed Bill that we would not take to the ice in Detroit until our colleagues were reinstated. The stage was set to see who would blink first.

Back in New Jersey, the Devils may have won the game 3–1, but the sport received a bigger black eye than any player involved in the multiple brawls that took place. It all could have been avoided. Jim Schoenfeld's behaviour in Game Three was an embarrassment to the game. Schoenfeld had been a tough competitor when he played, and nothing changed when he got behind the bench as a coach. That's commendable, but he should have taken his medicine and sat out the one-game suspension. (He ended up missing Game Five, when John Ziegler returned from abroad and convened a hearing on May 10. Ziegler also fined Schoenfeld $1,000 and the Devils $10,000.)

Back in Detroit, the day after the "yellow jerseys" worked the game in New Jersey, I got a call around 4:30 in the afternoon from Jim Beatty, who said that the matter had been successfully resolved and we were able to work the game that night. As we entered Joe Louis Arena, I encountered an amateur official from my hometown who asked if I was working the game. Much to his disappointment, I told him, "Yes. You can keep your referee bag in your car."

For the next couple of seasons, Devils fans and management felt they were being paid back by the referees for the doughnut incident. While I would admit to having less tolerance for any abusive conduct Schoenfeld might direct toward us, the issue was dead as far as I was concerned. I told Don he should open a franchise of shops called Koho's Donuts and retire a millionaire.

I turned in one of the poorest performances of my career in a game at the Meadowlands in October of 1989, a game the Devils won over the visiting Chicago Blackhawks. In the early evening the night before the game, Kathy suffered a miscarriage. We were devastated. I called Bryan Lewis, who had succeeded John Mc-Cauley as director of officiating. John had tragically died at the age of 44 from pancreatitis shortly after the '89 Stanley Cup final. I explained to Bryan the situation at home, and asked if he could send a substitute to New Jersey. He was sympathetic and said he would do his best. Unfortunately, the NHL referee corps had been hit by a rash of injuries and there was absolutely no one to fill in. I had to go up the turnpike and work the game.

I remained with Kathy for as long as I could and rolled into Brendan Byrne Arena an emotional wreck. I couldn't tell you a thing that happened in that game, other than that, when the final horn sounded, Duane Sutter—who's really a great guy—approached me and said, "Kerry, this was the worst effin' game I've ever seen you work. You were horrible." With tears in my eyes, I softly replied, "I know, Suds. I'm really sorry about my poor performance. My wife had a miscarriage last night and they couldn't get anyone else here to work the game. Please apologize to your team for me." For a brief moment, our eyes connected in mutual sadness, then I broke away and skated off the ice before the tears began to flow. I quickly showered, dressed, and hurried home to Kathy.

A week passed, and I travelled to Chicago for a game. As soon as I got to Chicago Stadium I found Duane Sutter by my dressing-room door, awaiting my arrival. Duane was heartsick, and he apologized for being so insensitive that night in New Jersey. He had no way of knowing, and I told him not to be so hard on himself. Duane said he had been hardly able to sleep for the past week thinking about it, and when he told his wife what had happened, she was furious with him. He and his wife both understood how difficult this loss was for Kathy and me. As we shared a moment more, both of us recognized that, while the game was important, it needed to be kept in the proper perspective. I appreciated the kindness and caring that Duane Sutter demonstrated, and for that moment we were on the same team.

The craftsman of the Devils franchise, Lou Lamoriello, continued to change coaches and acquire the right player personnel to legitimately challenge for the Stanley Cup. It finally happened in 1995, with Jacques Lemaire behind the bench and a remarkable group of players Lou had assembled, led by captain Scott Stevens, Scott Niedermayer, Ken Daneyko on defence, and snipers Claude Lemieux, Stéphane Richer, and John MacLean up front. Goaltender Martin Brodeur became the number-one goaltender in 1993 and would be a cornerstone of the franchise for many years to come.

Working that Cup series in '95, I got to see what an outstanding performer Claude Lemieux truly was. Claude and I became friends in a most unusual fashion. During a playoff series, Matthew Barnaby, the king of agitation and trash talk, was all over Lemieux, trying to get him off his game. During a game at the Meadowlands, Lemieux came to me, emotionally distraught over something Barnaby had said to him on the ice. Not unlike Theo Fleury's appeal to me, Claude asked me to tell Barnaby not to speak to him about his personal life. He told me he was going through a terrible divorce and that Barnaby made some extremely derogatory and obscene comments about his estranged wife. As I've said before, certain things are off limits, and a guy's family is one of them.

Matthew Barnaby always had that choirboy look to him—minus the halo. He would flash a big smile, complete with the removable silver tooth he used to pull out of his mouth if a stick came up near his face. Barney would then show the referee a broken tooth that was now visible in his mouth, and tell the referee the opponent had broken his tooth with a high stick. He got me once, but when he tried it again in another game a little later, I caught on.

Anyway, I called Barnaby over to us as soon as Claude told me what had been said. When I asked Matthew if he had said those things about Claude's wife, he flashed his silver-toothed smile and said proudly, "Yeah, I said those things." I told him to apologize immediately or I would throw him out of the game by assessing a gross misconduct. Barney said, "You wouldn't do that," to which I responded, "Try me!" Matthew gave Claude a half-assed apology, and I told him it wasn't good enough—it needed to be very sincere. Barney then made what I thought was a pretty good second attempt, and I asked Claude if he was okay with it. Claude thanked both Barnaby and me and then skated away, his face still reflecting the emotional stress of his off-ice difficulties. I gave Barnaby a stern lecture and told him I never wanted to hear that stuff out of him again.

On December 31, 2006, I had an early game in Phoenix, and Kathy and our daughters Jaime and Kara joined us to ring in the new year. After the game, we went to the Sanctuary resort on Camelback Mountain, where we bumped into a now-retired Claude Lemieux and his family and shared a drink and reminisced about old times. Claude took my two daughters aside and told them they should be very proud of their father because he is a "great man." All he would tell them was that I helped him out during a very difficult time in his life. It's not just about the game or winning that counts.

Lou Lamoriello had a knack for including all the necessary ingredients on his teams so that the chemistry was right. This was true right down to the fourth-liners. One such player was six-foot, four-inch, 221-pound Jim McKenzie, who played for nine teams over a 15-year NHL career. Aside from being a heavyweight champion, he was the nicest, most unassuming guy you could ever meet. Aside from Wayne Gretzky, McKenzie is the only other player ever to thank me for giving him a penalty.

It was in his first or second year in the NHL as a member of the Hartford Whalers, a nothing game on the last day of the season in Washington. Both teams just wanted to get the game over with before the playoffs. As I waited for the visiting team to exit the ice ahead of me, one player straggled along behind. It was big Jim McKenzie. His quiet and gentlemanly demeanour did not befit his giant stature or his role as an enforcer. Very quietly and politely, Jim asked whether, if he told me to eff off, I would give him a penalty. He had a grin on his face, and I thought he was kidding. He wasn't, and went on to explain that he had a bonus in his contract for penalty minutes and he was four minutes short. I looked at Jim and shouted, "What did you say?" Jim quietly responded, "Fuck off." I then shouted back, "SAY IT LIKE YOU MEAN IT." Practically at the top of his lungs, he thundered, "FUCK OFF!" I hollered, "YOU'VE GOT 10!" Jim smiled and quietly thanked me before walking up the rubber mat to the dressing room.

One of the things I remember most vividly about my experiences with the Devils involves Game Seven of the 2000 Eastern Conference final, when Captain Crunch, Scott Stevens, laid out Eric Lindros with a legal bodycheck. The bone-shaking, brain-jarring hit resulted in the most frightening outcome from a check that I have ever witnessed. I was following the play and saw the Big E, as was usual for him, carrying the puck up the left side of the ice with his head down. Eric pulled the puck back just as he made the tragic miscalculation to cut along the blue line into Scott Stevens's path. The play was offside, and the whistle was approaching the linesman's lips. Stevens saw the deer in the headlights, lowered his shoulder, and rocked Lindros. A millisecond later, the whistle blew to signal offside. Eric was knocked out from the impact of the hit and crumpled to the ice. I saw him lying there, motionless in the fetal position, and I thought, *Oh my God, he's dead.* I saw him move and try to raise his head. My initial fear was calmed.

I drew a bead on the remaining Flyers players on the ice, expecting some form of retaliation. Stevens backed away and readied himself in anticipation of the same, but the moment of retribution never materialized. Linesmen Jay Sharrers and Kevin Collins rerouted the Flyers away from Stevens, just to make sure nothing further developed. John Worley, the Flyers' athletic therapist, flew over the boards to attend to the felled redwood.

I looked at Scott Stevens standing by his team's bench, and for the very first time in his career I saw fear in his eyes. The blood had drained from his face and I detected a nervous twitch. It appeared to me that this ultimate power hitter might have been thinking he'd gone a little too far this time.

Eric was taken off the ice on wobbly legs. His eyes looked shallow and lost. He was the second Lindros I had seen in this condition; I worked a game with Eric's younger brother, Brett, before he was forced to retire. I saw in him the effect of one too many hits to the head. Brett, who played for the New York Islanders, brought his elbow dangerously high on an opponent one night. I advised him that he was getting close to penalty territory. There was no response, just a glazed, catatonic look. I spoke louder, almost hollering, as I tried to elicit some response: "*Hello?* Is anybody home?" There was none forthcoming. He skated to the bench, took a seat, and never played another shift. A short time later, I read that Brett Lindros was retiring.

Scott Stevens's hit was legal by everyone's account. That play-off season, so many players were hit in the very same fashion. Flyers forward Daymond Langkow was planted by Stevens earlier in the series and was forced to miss a game. At the very least, opponents should have been vigilant every time Stevens was on the ice, especially when they were crossing the Devils blue line. In his case, Eric Lindros should have given way to the defenceman, but the Big E never gave way to anyone throughout his playing career. I am, unfortunately, reminded of the answer to a question my wife asked me after Eric's very first game in the NHL; a game I refereed. Kathy asked me what I thought of the young Mr. Lindros. I recall saying, "He'll be great if he lasts. He plays with reckless abandon and is used to playing against boys. Now he's playing against men." When the ultimate power forward met the sheer brute force of the ultimate power defenceman, it was Stevens, the defenceman, who was left standing. Lindros was never the same player again.

Scott Stevens led the Devils to a Stanley Cup championship over the Dallas Stars and earned a Conn Smythe Trophy as playoff MVP. He won the Smythe trophy on the basis of the crushing bodychecks he delivered throughout the playoffs. He had certainly mastered the art better than anyone who'd ever played the game in his position.

The Devils no longer reside in the swamp, where they were forced to celebrate Cup championships in the parking lot of their arena, because there wasn't a main street to parade down. They now play in the beautiful new Prudential Arena, a.k.a. the Rock, in Newark.

The trap that they became famous for changed the team's reputation as well as the face of the game. Instead of Mickey Mouse, they became Mighty Mouse through the efforts of Lou Lamoriello. This team, his team, boasts three Stanley Cups and is a force to be reckoned with every year. The league and its owners have changed rules to try to neutralize the style the Devils were so famous for. Great players are now allowed to move more freely around the ice, making for a much faster, more exciting game. The New Jersey Devils, under Lamoriello's shrewd guidance, have made adjustments of their own to the "New NHL." I worked my last game at the Rock just before the Olympic break where the Nashville Predators would be defeated by the Devils 5–2. The story this night was newly acquired superstar, Ilya Kovalchuk, who scored his 32nd goal of the season and added an assist as he delighted the fans with his explosive offensive talents. Zach Parise, who also had a goal (his 27th) and an assist now had a player to complement his extensive skills.

The Devils have certainly come a long way from their original home in Colorado, where I, as a 28-year-old rookie, began my NHL career.

COLORADO:
ROCKIES TO AVALANCHE

My very first game as a referee in the National Hockey League, on Friday, October 17, 1980, was in the mile-high city of Denver. It was more of a Western cowboy town back then, as opposed to the cosmopolitan city of today. The team was called the Rockies, and I only had to look out the window of my hotel room to understand where they got the name. The snow-capped mountains seemed close enough to reach out and touch. The air was clean to the taste and the crowd at McNichols Sports Arena, as befitted their rugged mountain lifestyle, was a raucous group that enjoyed the rougher side of the game.

I arrived as a cocky, baby-faced, 28-year-old rookie referee with a whistle in one hand and the rule book in my back pocket. I was paired with seasoned linesmen Jim Christison and Ryan Bozak, both great guys and well-respected officials.

The Minnesota North Stars were the visiting team that night, and their roster was loaded with such young stars as Dino Ciccarelli, Bobby Smith, and Craig Hartsburg. Their coach, Glen Sonmor, was very tough on me during my early years in the NHL until fellow referee Ron Fournier and I met up with Glen and Los Angeles Kings star Charlie Simmer while on vacation in Hawaii.

We bumped into them around the pool during happy hour one afternoon. (I told Sonmor I heard the hotel thought of cancelling it when he arrived.) After a few drinks, we arranged a game of golf for the next day. I rode with Glen in the golf cart. Aside from seeing what a great guy he really was I also learned that he had only one eye. I had to look for his ball constantly during the round. I busted his chops about always yelling at me from the bench and asked how the hell he could see what was going on with only one good eye. Without breaking the rhythm of his back-swing, Glen said, "Between the two of us we've got a pair!"

The Rockies, a team that Billy MacMillan had inherited as coach from Don Cherry the year before, were not very successful. Now a hockey icon in Canada, Cherry was as much a player and fan favourite then as he is now. Under Grapes, the team had adopted the slogan "Come to the fights and watch a Rockies game break out," and it boosted ticket sales. It didn't matter who was coaching, however; aside from a few great players in Lanny McDonald (35 goals) and 21-year-old defencemen Rob Ramage and Joel Quenneville, they just didn't have the horses. Two future general managers also played on that team as 21-year-olds: Steve Tambellini (now with the Edmonton Oilers) and Mike Gillis (Vancouver Canucks).

In the rule book I was carrying in my back pocket was an addition that had just been implemented that season, one that none of the players, coaches, or fans had read yet. The league was concerned about the impact of all the brawling throughout the mid- to late '70s on the image of the game; during that period, the NHL had lost its network-TV contract in the U.S. Historically, whenever a fight broke out between two players, the remaining players on the ice would drop their gloves and hang on to one another to keep someone from jumping in. With their dance partner in hand, they were often content to watch the main event from a distance. In 1980, the NHL decided that any player who dropped his gloves after the original altercation was to receive a 10-minute misconduct. Early in the first period of my very first game, the Rockies' second home game of the season, a fight broke out. All the players instinctively dropped their gloves—and ended up in the penalty box as per the new rule. Not long afterward, a second fight broke out, with the same result. I had both penalty boxes filled beyond capacity; short of sitting on each other's knee, their only option was to stand. The players and the crowd turned hostile against this rookie referee who they thought was making up the rules as he went. Debris littered the ice at various intervals, and the boo birds sang in unison.

The penalty-filled game ended in a 5–5 tie. On the way out of McNichols Arena, Bozak, Christison, and I walked through the tunnel to where the North Stars' bus was being loaded up. Along the way, we marched past players Glen Sharpley and Al MacAdam. The area was exposed to the fans, who stood above the ramp behind a chain-link fence—usually, hoping to catch a glimpse of the players. This night, they wanted a piece of the referee they thought had screwed up the game. They started shouting obscenities and firing things over the fence as soon as they saw me. As we walked past the North Stars' bus, Sharpley said to Christison, "Hey, Chris, if you guys need any help, we're right here for you." Without skipping a beat, the witty Jim Christison replied, "No thanks, Sharp. I've seen you fight!"

We jumped into a cab and, after unpacking our gear back at the hotel, I bought the beer all night at Zangs Brewing Company, as was the first-game tradition. While I had survived my first NHL game, I only hoped that it would get easier from that point on. I, like all rookies, would experience growing pains, but I worked hard to minimize my mistakes and learn from the ones I was bound to make. I had realized a dream that night, but also recognized I had an awful lot to learn.

There was a small nucleus of fans who mourned the loss of their Rockies when they were sold and moved to New Jersey to become the Devils in 1982. These loyalists would be rewarded in 1995, however, when they got a team that was poised to win the Stanley Cup.

The Quebec Nordiques had concluded they could not survive in their small Canadian market, given the economic climate of the NHL at the time. A lockout interrupted the 1994–95 season, resulting in a shortened schedule of 48 games. The Nordiques finished second in the 26-team league that season, and I could tell that wherever the team landed, one of the first orders of business in the new location would be to apply at city hall for a Stanley Cup parade permit and start building floats.

In 1989–90, the Nordiques had hit rock bottom, losing 61 of 80 games. Some talented players, including Joe Sakic and Mats Sundin, were already in the pipeline, but the turnaround really shifted gears when they got the first-overall pick in the 1991 entry draft. Ironically, the player they chose never played a single game for Quebec. Eric Lindros was already a controversial figure; in 1989, he refused to join the junior team that drafted him, the Soo Greyhounds. He had warned the Nordiques that he would not sign a contract with them, but they chose him anyway. True to his word, he spent the season in junior and playing for the Canadian Olympic team. A year passed, and Lindros's resolve showed no sign of weakening. On the day of the 1992 draft, the Nordiques traded him—twice, to the Philadelphia Flyers and New York Rangers. An arbitrator ruled that the Philadelphia trade stood. In return for Lindros, Quebec received what seemed like half the Flyer franchise: future MVP Peter Forsberg, whom they'd chosen in the first round in 1991; goalie Ron Hextall, who had won the

Conn Smythe and Vezina trophies in his rookie season of 1986–87; high-scoring defenceman Steve Duchesne; role players Mike Ricci, Kerry Huffman, and Chris Simon; a couple of first-round draft picks; and $15 million in cash. Overnight, Quebec went from a 21st-place team to fourth place overall in 1992–93, and Forsberg hadn't even joined the team yet. He would become the league's rookie of the year in 1995.

Another rookie, Marc Crawford, was hired as the Nordiques' coach in 1994–95. His team won 12 of their first 13 games, and he went on to win the Jack Adams Award as coach of the year. He also received a "career warning" from me for the vilest verbal assault to be levied against me from behind the bench in my entire career.

Just before the playoffs, Crawford's team hit a patch where they couldn't seem to win on the road and the coach was at a loss as to what to do. I caught up with them during a trip to Florida for back-to-back games. They lost 5–2 to Tampa Bay, a team that finished 28 points behind them in the 48-game schedule, and two nights later were upset 4–2 by a Florida team that was struggling to make the playoffs. Ten minutes in, the Panthers were up 3–0, despite having taken only seven shots at goalie Jocelyn Thibault. Florida had scored on their first two power plays—quite a feat, as they were one of the weakest clubs in the league with the man advantage. Despite a first-period goal, the Nordiques couldn't seem to get anything going, and they were obviously frustrated. With about a minute and a half remaining, Peter Forsberg broke his stick on a Panthers player. I called him for interference. It was a tactical error on Forsberg's part, because Quebec might have wanted to pull their goalie for an extra attacker in a bid to tie the score. Now, they'd have no such advantage.

The ensuing faceoff was to be held in the neutral zone, and Crawford refused to put his penalty killers on the ice for the faceoff. I had been in the league 15 years by now, so I knew what he was trying to do. He wanted me to skate over to the bench so he could vent his frustration on me. I could have chosen to wait him out, I could have assessed a delay-of-game penalty that would serve no purpose, or I could approach the bench and let him get it off his chest so we could finish the game. Never in my wildest nightmare could I have imagined the garbage that would spew out of Crawford's mouth. It's funny: I'd seen him as a rookie player in 1981–82 and throughout his six-year NHL playing career, and I didn't even know he could talk. I had never heard him say anything. He had obviously found his voice.

I stood directly in front of him and politely said, "Marc, I need four guys on the ice now, please." He paused, then said, "Kerry, you really fucked us tonight. As a matter of fact, you fucked us right up the ass without a condom." Blood drained from my face and my mouth ran dry. Marc wasn't finished. "You were fucking horrible tonight and you really put it to us. That was the worst fucking game I've ever seen refereed in my entire fucking career." Which, I thought to myself, amounted to 42 games as an NHL coach, but I let him continue. He went on for another 20 seconds or so as I remained outwardly stoic, even though I was ready to explode. Finally, I asked, "Are you just about done?"

He said, "Yeah, I'm done."

I guess he thought I was going to throw him out of the game. Not tonight, Bucko. Forcing words through the sawdust in my mouth, I replied, "Marc, that is the most disgusting, unprofessional dialogue I have ever heard from a coach in this league or any other, and it's totally unwarranted. There isn't one guy sitting on this bench who believes what you just said. Your team didn't show up tonight and they deserved every penalty they got, and could have probably gotten more, but you and I will save that for another day because *right now,* I need you to put your players on the ice and I need them NOW, please!"

As I skated across the ice, the muscles in my arms were twitching from an overabundance of adrenaline flowing and no place to discharge it. Four players followed me to the faceoff location, and when the game ended I was still burning up inside. I entered our dressing room and felt physically sick.

I had just taken my skates and sweater off when there was a knock at our dressing room door. I always sit closest to the door, just for moments like this. I opened it, and there stood Crawford with his head down. He asked my permission to talk, so I invited him in. The last thing I wanted was for the French-language media to see or hear anything they might blow out of proportion in the papers. I offered him a seat and a beer, both of which he accepted. Marc then offered an apology and confirmed that everything I had said on the ice was correct. He explained that his team, heavily favoured to win the Stanley Cup, was heading south (figuratively, of course, as we were already in Florida!) at the worst possible time, and he just didn't know what to do.

He asked if his team was the worst culprit when it came to whining and complaining. I referred that question to my two linesmen, Ray Scapinello and Greg Devorski; both of them agreed without reservation or hesitation that the Nords led the league in that category. I then provided Marc with my perspective, gained over 15 years in the league. I talked about the great New York Islanders dynasty and the discipline they demonstrated to achieve their success. I told him it came straight from the man behind the bench, Al Arbour. Scotty Bowman, the other coach I would rank among the two greatest I've ever seen, also instilled the same quality in his teams. I told Crawford that when those two men spoke, I listened because they so seldom had anything to say. When they did, I knew I must have screwed up. He got the message, but before he left, I had one last statement to make: "Marc, I accept your apology and want you to know that I don't hold a grudge, but I need you to understand and agree to what I am about to tell you. Right here in this very room, in front of these two fine colleagues of mine as witnesses, I am issuing you a career warning—which means that, from this moment forward, if you ever curse or yell at me inappropriately from behind the bench you will receive a bench minor penalty! Do you understand and consent to what I am telling you?" Marc's handshake sealed the agreement between the two of us.

In late January of the following season, I refereed a game between the Ducks and Avalanche in Anaheim. Midway through the third period, I had assessed minors to Sylvain Lefebvre (for holding) and Craig Wolanin (cross-checking), which put Colorado two men short. Thirteen seconds later, Paul Kariya scored to put the Ducks ahead 2–1. From the Colorado bench, I could hear Crow's distinctive, high-pitched voice: "Kerry, what the fuh—" That's as far as he got before I wheeled and gave him a bench penalty. Crawford hung his head the same way he had done that night in Miami and clammed right up. Claude Lemieux, a fantastic guy and one my all-time favourites, came up to me and appealed to me not to extend Anaheim's two-man advantage. I looked Pepe in the eye and said, "Go say the word 'Florida' to Crow." Claude looked at me as if I had two heads and said, "Flo-*ree*-da? What da 'ell you mean? We are in Ana-'eim, not Flo-ree-da." I asked Pepe to please just humour me and deliver the message. I assured him Marc would get it. He got it. A few months later, the Colorado Avalanche won the Stanley Cup by sweeping the "Flo-*ree*-da" Panthers in four straight games. And I never heard another caw out of the Crow.

One of the most memorable Stanley Cup final series of the dozen I worked was Colorado's seven-game victory over the New Jersey Devils in 2001. The primary reason for that is because it was Raymond Bourque's first and only time he would hoist the Stanley Cup. In his 20 full seasons with Boston, the Bruins had come up short against Edmonton in both 1988 and 1990. This guy was a champion in my mind, even if he had never ended up with a Cup. I give Harry Sinden full marks for arranging a trade at Ray's request, one that gave him a chance to close out his career with his name engraved on the Cup. At the age of 40, the five-time Norris Trophy winner as the league's top defenceman led all Avs blueliners in scoring, with 59 points, was named to the first All-Star team, and was a runner-up to Nicklas Lidström of the Detroit Red Wings in the Norris Trophy voting. He also scored the winning goal in Game Three of the final.

I worked Game Seven of that series, and I must tell you the city of Denver was electrified from the moment the sun came up that morning. The only minute of calm I found that day was at 8 a.m., when I went down to the Pepsi Center for a skate before the teams arrived. I skated alone in the empty, dimly lit arena for 30 minutes, while outside the building, television trucks and equipment filled the nearest parking lot. I had never seen so much media coverage for a final, and the big story was Raymond Bourque.

The Avalanche won Game Seven that night, and in a remarkable display of class and respect, team captain Joe Sakic, after posing with the Cup, handed it directly to Ray Bourque so that he could be the first to skate a victory lap. Three days after the Cup victory, Bourque arranged to take the Cup back to Boston for an emotional rally in City Hall Plaza. The event was attended by 20,000 cheering Bostonians. I don't think there is a hockey fan anywhere, no matter which team they cheered for, that wouldn't have been happy for Bourque's Stanley Cup victory.

Over the years, an intense rivalry developed between the Avalanche and the Detroit Red Wings. It began in 1996, during the Western Conference final, when Claude Lemieux checked Kris

Draper into the boards from behind. Draper suffered a broken jaw, shattered cheek and orbital bones, and a concussion. On March 26, 1997, the teams met for the fourth time that season, but it was Lemieux's first appearance in a game against Detroit. As a result, brawls broke out repeatedly, including one between the goalies, Patrick Roy of the Avs and Mike Vernon of the Wings, at centre ice. Detroit and Colorado would meet again in the 1997 conference final—a series won by the Red Wings—and tempers flared up in Game Four. This time, coaches Scotty Bowman and Marc Crawford went at each other verbally, earning Crow a $10,000 fine.

My final game in Colorado, March 1, 2010, was between these same two teams. While the rivalry isn't dead in the minds of the fans in either city, many of the players who participated so aggressively in the feud have moved on. But Kris Draper was still playing his usual tenacious checking game for the Wings, while Adam Foote was crashing, as always, from his position on the Avs defence.

This was the first scheduled game played after the Olympics, and I felt refreshed and ready to go again after a much-needed break. The NHL schedule had been compressed to accommodate the shutdown for the Winter Games, so Kathy and I had spent 10 glorious days in Aruba.

I was also especially excited about this last game in Colorado because my youngest daughter, Kara, was with me on this trip. Although Kara is now a college freshman at Mount St. Mary's University in Emmitsburg, Maryland, she will always be Daddy's little girl. We flew together from Philadelphia to Denver the night before the game. It was her first trip to this beautiful city. We spent part of the day touring the foothills and had a pre-game lunch in an old mining town outside of Golden, Colorado. Our eight-year-old grandson, Harrison, had given Aunt Kara the task of getting an autograph from his new favourite player, Avs forward Paul

Stastny, who was fresh from winning a silver medal at the Vancouver Games. Behind the Red Wings bench tonight was the gold medal–winning coach of Team Canada, Mike Babcock.

The game featured lots of energy and speed right from the get-go. It appeared that the players recognized that if a playoff spot was to be gained, the push must start now. Tomas "Homer" Holmström, the nightmare of every goalie *and* referee, hadn't lost a beat, as he jammed the crease and made contact with Avs netminder Craig Anderson, resulting in a Red Wings goal being disallowed and two minutes for goalie interference for Homer. At the end of the night, however, the pesky forward was chosen as the game's third star after scoring a goal and assisting on both of Detroit's others in a 3–2 Red Wings victory.

Nicklas Lidström, the first star, scored the winner on a power play after I called a tripping penalty on Kyle Quincey when he hauled down a Red Wing behind the Avs' goal. With Anderson pulled for an extra attacker, the Avalanche peppered Detroit goalie Jimmy Howard, who made several big saves. For me, it was a pleasure to see young Paul Stastny one last time. His father, Peter, was not only a tremendous player but a wonderful person. Kathy and I spent some time with Paul's mom and dad in Bratislava at the start of the '08-09 pre-season when the Tampa Bay Lightning played the locals before moving to Prague to open the NHL season against the NY Rangers. It is certainly easy to see why young Paul is such a respectful and talented kid. After the game, my daughter Kara and I caught up with Paul, who was on his way out of the building, and he insisted that she put his silver medal around her neck as they posed for a picture together. I told Paul that the game I remember most from the Quebec Nordiques era was Game Seven of the Adams Division final in 1985, when his father scored the winner in overtime against the Montreal Canadiens, propelling the team to the Wales Conference final. Paul commented that it was ironic I should bring that up, since he and his teammates had talked about that very game during their morning skate. The game certainly has no generation gaps. Peter's goal will be remembered forever, and I am sure that Paul will also be remembered for many contributions he will make. I find it remarkable that I am four years older than Peter, and that I have had the honour to be on NHL ice with two generations of Stastny superstars.

As Kara and I left the Pepsi Center, in sharp contrast to my first NHL game in Denver, there were no fans waiting to assault me, verbally or otherwise. The assistance of Glen Sharpley wouldn't be needed this night, either. Just as well, because I'd seen Sharp fight, too!

CENTRE OF THE HOCKEY UNIVERSE: TORONTO MAPLE LEAFS

On March 27, 2010, I was scheduled to work my fifth game of the season at the Air Canada Centre, the centre of the hockey universe. This would also be the last appearance of my career on Toronto ice—try not to all cheer at once, Leafs Nation! For me it is an honour and a privilege every time I step onto the ice in that large cash register they call the ACC.

The Leafs could play on a slushy Toronto Harbour and draw a record crowd, but the only other hockey home that most of us can recall was Maple Leaf Gardens. The sound of that hallowed building still resonates in my head. On my final visit to Toronto for the game, I felt I must walk over to pay my respects to that historic building. It was a walk I would take by myself before teaming up with my associate referee for the game, Wes McCauley.

Unlike its cousins in Boston, Chicago, and Detroit, Maple Leaf Gardens is still standing, having been spared implosion or demolition. I circled the building and walked past the back door that NHL security representative and dear friend Al Wiseman, long since deceased, snuck me and my family out of on April 9, 1988, after the Leafs lost 6–3 to Detroit in Game Four of the Norris Division semifinals. This exit had been engineered so that I could avoid Leafs general manager Gerry McNamara, who had gone on a tirade. John McCauley, with his two young sons Wes and Blaine by his side, tried to calm the out-of-control McNamara. The Leafs survived two more games in the series, but Gerry was replaced by Gord Stellick after their season ended.

There were many years in the '80s, when Harold Ballard owned the team, that the Leafs were not very good. Even so, business was always good and the fans were very forgiving—at least in ways I have yet to experience. It would be a safe bet to assume that "Mike the Scalper" on Carlton Street made as much as some of the players in those days. If on-ice officials wanted to take a family member or friend to a game at the Gardens, we were given the privilege of purchasing a ticket through the "special ticket office" at Maple Leaf Gardens. What that meant is that we paid an extra five bucks over the ticket's face value just to buy it and for the "special handling" that was involved by one of Mr. Ballard's staff.

I approached the façade of Maple Leaf Gardens on my nostalgic stroll and tried to dream my way into the boarded-up building. I wanted to recall what it was like in those days on a game night, especially a Saturday night. It all came back to me in a flash. Transported back in time, I was suddenly approaching the brightly lit blue-on-white marquee from across the street: SATURDAY NIGHT—MONTREAL CANADIENS 8:00 PM. I was going to be the referee this night in Toronto. On Saturday nights, the game wasn't just played on this corner; it was *Hockey Night in Canada* and the entire nation showed up. In English-speaking Canada in the days before NHL expansion into western Canada, the Toronto Maple Leafs were (and to some extent are still) regarded as Canada's team, with a profile akin to those of the Dallas Cowboys and New York Yankees in the United States. Hockey is the heart and soul of Canadian culture.

I had my father with me and my little three-year-old son Matthew in tow. While it was only a pre-season game, for me, at the infancy of my NHL officiating career, it was what I imagined a seventh game of the Stanley Cup final might be like. I held Matthew's hand as we waited for a streetcar to pass by. That in itself was a new experience for both of us, since we don't have any of those in Sarnia. The trolley was swollen with people as it approached the Gardens stop. With a clang of the bell it departed empty as all of its cargo swarmed the main entrance and Doug Laurie Sports to check out this season's souvenirs. As we crossed the street, the scalper didn't bother to ask if I needed tickets. While he didn't know me from Adam, he recognized the bag I was carrying and simply said, "Have a good game." I picked up the tickets for my dad and Matt, then we went around to the press gate to enter a building that was now completely foreign to me after having seen it thousands of times on TV from childhood. We passed Guy Lafleur and some other Montreal players lounging in the hall outside their dressing room. They also recognized me from the bag I was carrying and took little Matthew on a dressing room tour to meet some of the players. I wasn't sure he would re-member any of it, but I was thrilled to see these players up close for the first time. Dad and Matthew were seated while I went to prepare for my first game at Maple Leaf Gardens.

Our dressing room was small and located next door to the Leaf directors' lounge. We sat on wooden benches that ran along either wall, and we could reach across and shake hands with the guy opposite. To access the ice, we turned left after passing through the dressing room door, then up a step, a quick right through the crowd a short distance, and finally through the penalty box. On this night, I didn't know whether to step on the ice or get down and kiss it. I wisely chose the former. I wanted to show everyone that I belonged.

On my first turn around the rink, I looked up at the gondola I had seen so many times on television, from which Foster Hewitt and his son Bill broadcast the games. Everything looked so much more immense and bright. Making the turn, I looked directly into Harold Ballard's "bunker." There he sat, with King Clancy beside him. It was then that I heard the familiar voice of an old friend: the distinctive monotone of Leafs PA announcer Paul Morris, who held that job for 38 years and worked 1,585 consecutive games before retiring, at age 61, in 1999. I froze in midstride and tried unsuccessfully to find the face that went with the voice.

The teams came onto the ice and paid little or no attention to me, but I studied each one of them. As I stood at centre ice to drop the puck between Darryl Sittler and Doug Jarvis, I wasn't sure which was shaking more, my knees or my hands. I immediately thought, *Get your shit together, if you hope to be in charge of this game.* Once I got into the flow, everything went great. By the third period I felt like I really belonged, and nobody had even yelled at me yet—until I missed a penalty against the Leafs, or at least that's what future Hall of Fame defenceman Guy Lapointe thought. The Leafs were winning by a goal with a couple of minutes to play, and Lapointe was quite animated in his protest of the non-call. Wanting to appear like a veteran, I thought it wise to call him by his first name, which I hoped would make him feel comfortable with me. I put my hands up with palms open and said, "Relax, Serge!" Well, Lapointe shot me a look of disgust and said, "My name is *Guy*, you fucking rookie!"

Other than that case of mistaken identity, my first experience in Maple Leaf Gardens was fairly successful. The three of us travelled back to Sarnia the next day. It didn't take long to find out whether little Matthew had retained anything from his visit to the

Canadiens' dressing room. The next day, I heard him out on the front porch, telling his little buddy from next door about the players he had met. In Matthew's words, Guy Lafleur became "Gooie Laflew," while the goalie, Bunny Larocque, became "The Rabbit." I couldn't help but laugh and think that my three-year-old had the same difficulty with names as I did!

As a postscript, a few nights later, I was in Montreal for a game and I sent my skates in to Eddie Palchak of the Canadiens to be sharpened. I was all dressed and ready to go and was looking forward to hearing Roger Doucet sing the national anthem, but my skates had not yet been returned. I asked Raymond, our room attendant, to please hurry and get my skates. He hadn't returned before the two-minute warning, so I told the linesmen to go on without me and I would join them as soon as I had my skates. Shortly thereafter, Raymond came running in with a smirk on his face and said, in broken English, "I am so sorry, Monsieur Fraser, they were very busy up the hall." In a rush, I jammed my feet into the skates . . . and shaving cream came flying out of both of them. I had no choice but to quickly tie them up and rush to the ice, just as Roger was about to sing. As I stepped on the ice, my left skate went in one direction and the right in another. *Guy* Lapointe was standing beside *Serge* Savard on the Canadiens' blue line with a big grin on his face. After the anthem, he skated over and asked, "How are your skates tonight, *rookie*?" I replied, "Perfect, *Guy*— just the way I like them." We both laughed and the ice was broken. I think that was when I realized that acceptance would come if I didn't force it. Though I did have to get my skates resharpened, since I think Guy had done the honours the first time.

My tour of the old Gardens was complete. While I couldn't physically get inside, I most definitely *journeyed* there through the inner recesses of my mind. I visited with ghosts of old acquaintances, such as great players Börje Salming, Darryl Sittler, and Ian Turnbull; my old teammate Bob Neely; captains Rick Vaive—I pointed to the net when he scored his 50th goal for the first time in '82—Wendel Clark, and Doug Gilmour; coaches Pat Burns and Pat Quinn; general manager Cliff Fletcher; and so many more. We were all friends on this imaginary reunion, even though I could clearly see I was younger, cockier, and much less travelled in those days, when this Temple of Hockey allowed me to pass through her turnstiles. Looking at the old building, I would have to say that Maple Leaf Gardens is more weather-beaten than me, at least on the outside.

I hustled back to the Renaissance Hotel at the Rogers Centre (formerly SkyDome), just up the street from the ACC, to pick up Wes. Later, I would try to mesh my memories of the old with the reality of the new at the morning skate. The New York Rangers would be the guests; while the Leafs were once again out of the playoffs, the Rangers were in a dogfight with Philadelphia and Boston for the final spot. They needed every point they could get.

I found Wes waiting for me in the lobby at 10:30 a.m. sharp, and it took us only five minutes to walk to the Air Canada Centre. There was a large crowd assembled in the lower bowl seats, watching coach Ron Wilson put the locals through their drills. Many school-age children were on hand to watch their heroes perform. It spoke to the depth of the hockey culture in this city and country, where the national game is revered. I can't blame them. I love going to the rink to watch the morning skate. You get a chance to explore the vastness of the building when it's less full, and the sounds of the pucks hitting the boards or the glass resonate throughout the upper level like the echo your voice makes while standing in a canyon.

Down in the hallway by the dressing rooms, Wes and I encountered the large contingent of newspaper scribes and radio and television broadcasters who cover both teams. The atmosphere was like that of a family reunion. The press corps of both towns are extremely professional, and for the most part were very fair with me. I accommodated their questions as a scrum gathered, and of course one of the questions they asked—the subject of which would likely form the lead paragraph of their stories— pertained to the missed call in 1993. It probably didn't help that Doug Gilmour was in town with the Kingston Frontenacs junior hockey team he was coaching. They had a game in Brampton, just 30 miles up the road.

Before reaching the room, I bumped into Leafs coach Ron Wilson as he exited the ice, as well as Glen Sather, president and GM of the Rangers. I had a brief but pleasant visit with each of them. Later, just as we were about to leave the building, Börje Salming walked out of the Leafs' dressing room. They called him the King when he excited the fans for 16 years with his end-to-end rushes as a Leaf defenceman. It was wonderful to visit briefly with Börje before Wes and I headed out for our pre-game lunch. I left it to Wes to decide where he would like to eat. Of course, he chose Wayne Gretzky's restaurant.

With all the walking I had done since early that morning, I was happy to shut it down for three solid hours of sleep during my standard pre-game nap. I woke up ready to go to work. Unfortunately for the New York Rangers, they appeared to be taking their naps during the third period, and they blew a two-goal lead and a glorious opportunity to pick up two points on Philadelphia and Boston. They ended up losing in overtime on a stinker of a wraparound goal by Nikolai Kulemin that would surely haunt goalie Henrik Lundqvist. The single point for the OT loss would ultimately haunt the Rangers.

Late in the second period, New York lost Sean Avery when he injured his knee in a race for the puck on an icing play. While the Rangers bad boy can be a major pain in the butt, he can also be a very effective player. After establishing acceptable limits, I developed a good working relationship with Sean. I hope he turns the corner and finds some peace in his life, on and off the ice.

After the final TV timeout in the third period, defenceman Dion Phaneuf—a great late-season acquisition by Leafs GM Brian Burke—approached me quietly to offer his congratulations on my retirement. "You always do such a great job, and it has truly been my honour to have played in games that you refereed," he said. "The game is really going to miss you." I was humbled by his kind remarks. My sincere objective over these past 30 years had been to make a positive difference to this great game of hockey. To have been appreciated by those who matter most within the game makes any abuse that came my way secondary and insignificant.

That being said, as I left this great Canadian city, I could still hear the chant "Fraser sucks!" ringing in my ears. I have to smile as I wonder how the fans will carry on this tradition in the absence of one Kerry Fraser.

GHOSTS OF THE FORUM: MONTREAL CANADIENS

Another morning after a game, and another departure at the crack of dawn as I boarded the shuttle outside the Minneapolis Marriott at 5:30 a.m. to catch a flight to Philadelphia at 6:45. This wouldn't be unusual if I had to work back-to-back games, but my next game wasn't until the next night—in Montreal. So why the early start and the roundabout route to *la belle province*? Because Kathy would be waiting there for me, to accompany me on this last "official" visit to a city that holds so many memories for both of us.

Growing up in Ontario, both Kathy and I were Leafs fans (she much more devout than I). The Canadiens were the hated arch-enemy. The Flying Frenchmen combined the speed and skill of Rocket Richard and his brother Henri (the Pocket Rocket), Jean Béliveau, Bernie Geoffrion, Yvan Cournoyer, and Guy Lafleur with the toughness of John Ferguson and Ted Harris. Their defence corps boasted a seemingly endless supply of future Hall of Famers, from Doug Harvey and Butch Bouchard to Jacques Laperrière, Serge Savard, and Guy Lapointe. For decades, the stability and leadership that had been provided by general manager Frank Selke and coaches Dick Irvin and Toe Blake continued under Sam Pollock, Ronald Corey, Scotty Bowman, Jacques Lemaire, and Jacques Demers. Throughout their storied past, the Canadiens didn't just do business in a unique way, they espoused a philosophy of pride in the organization that every member was expected to live by. I could feel it in the air each time I entered the old Montreal Forum.

The Habs' fans were very demanding, expecting nothing less than a Stanley Cup every year. These high expectations were a by-product of the deep sense of pride that flowed both ways between the team and the community. A player walking into the Canadiens' dressing room for the first time would get an instant history lesson, as the walls were adorned with photographs and names of past players. If anyone brought disgrace to the CH crest, it wasn't long before they found themselves playing elsewhere. Even the walls of the officials' dressing room are decorated with photos of past Canadiens legends. If I were asked to describe the Montreal Canadiens organization, the two words I would use would be class and tradition—qualities that the organization possesses in abundance above all others in the NHL.

Upon our arrival in Montreal, Kathy and I had a dinner reservation at Guy Lafleur's restaurant, aptly named the Bleu, Blanc, Rouge (Blue, White, Red). We wanted to drink deep from the cup of nostalgia that both of us felt. However, this was not the first time that I had arrived early the day before a game involving this famous team in the hockey-crazed city of Montreal.

On May 1, 1985, I packed my bag early in the morning and headed off to the Sarnia Airport to catch a flight to Montreal. Even though my playoff curfew wasn't until 10 p.m., I wanted to arrive at the Sheraton Centre on René Lévesque Boulevard around noon. This was only the third time I had been assigned to the Stanley Cup playoffs, and the first time I had been chosen to work Game Seven of a divisional final series. The magnitude of a seventh game is important in any series; after all, once it's over, one team advances and the other goes golfing. This particular game had taken on a whole life of its own and was unlike any that could have been played in the NHL before or since. This was the Battle of Quebec!

While there have been other provincial or local rivalries— Edmonton vs. Calgary, Toronto vs. Ottawa, Rangers vs. Islanders—the Battle of Quebec transcended the game of hockey and crossed over to the political and corporate arenas. Clashes between the Nordiques and Canadiens pitted the smaller provincial capital against the metropolis. The tradition of the Canadiens against the upstart Nordiques organization, born as part of the "rebel league," the World Hockey Association. Some even present it as a battle between Quebec separatists and Montreal federalists. The rivalry between the teams was as bitter as the battle for market share between its owners: the Montreal-based Molson brewery owned the Habs, while Carling-O'Keefe, which marketed its products heavily throughout the province, owned the Nordiques. Both sides knew that consumers preferred to drink a winner. When the Canadiens initially opposed a merger between the NHL and WHA, it is said that a boycott of Molson beer by fans in Edmonton, Winnipeg, and Quebec City cost the brewery so much it changed its mind.

Throughout the province, the media—particularly the competitive French-language newspapers in Quebec City and Montreal—were relentless in their coverage and would pull no punches in their pursuit of sensational headlines. On more than one occasion, I was advised by John McCauley to be very careful about what I did or said in public in either city. Even the officials were fair game! Denis Morel found that out after working a Nordiques–Canadiens game.

We weren't paid a lot then (some might say we still aren't) and often worked a summer job. Using his hockey connections, Denis got a job in sales and marketing for Molson one summer. The day after this particular game, which Montreal won, a picture of Denis in a Molson bottle cap appeared on the front sports page of a French-language paper. The radio talk shows percolated to the boiling point every day and night. There was no escape from the "controversy."

As soon as I landed in Montreal and collected my luggage, I noticed how intently I was being stared at by arriving passengers and airport workers. As I passed a skycap, I was greeted with a nod of the head along with *"Bonne chance."* Once I hit the line for the taxis, it seemed that everyone I met, from the man who loaded my bags in the taxi, to the cab driver, to the doorman at the hotel, to the people at the front desk, greeted me with, "Oh, M'sieur Fraser, it is good to see you here for da big game".... "We are so happy you are doing the game".... "I heard you were doing the game on the radio this morning and I tell my wife, Chantal, I be so pleased it's you...." My personal favourite: "Who do you think will win?" It was wild. I went for a walk to clear my head and look for a place to eat dinner, but I was stopped so many times on the street that after 10 minutes I returned to the Sheraton, locked myself in my room, and ordered room service. I even avoided television because you couldn't turn a channel without something about the game popping up. When my linesmen for the game, Ray Scapinello and John D'Amico, arrived that evening, I was already in bed. Scampy called, and I told him I'd see him in the morning for breakfast—I was in for the night.

I woke early with the sensation that something was crawling all over my body. Upon inspection, I discovered I was covered head to toe in big, red, itchy welts. At least they weren't on my face. I thought, *What the hell is this*? I was too embarrassed to mention it to anybody—I certainly didn't want McCauley to think he had made the wrong choice in choosing me for Game Seven. Scampy would have busted my "stones," while J.D. would have given me a pill from his supply of medicines and told me to wash it down with a Dr Pepper. Actually, John was a hypochondriac, so I was afraid he'd immediately "catch" whatever was ailing me. All I could do was put on a long-sleeved shirt, buttoned at the neck, and go out for the pre-game meal with the guys.

I'm sure that my subconscious was not letting me forget the now-legendary Good Friday brawl that these same two teams engaged in Game Six of their series the year before. That one broke out at the end of the second period, and everyone, including the backup goalies, ended up on the ice. When the teams took to the ice for the third period, the hostilities resumed, even as the penalties were being announced. Some of the players involved at this point had already been ejected, but did not know it yet! It was an impossible situation for referee Bruce Hood and linesmen Bob Hodges and John D'Amico to control. The first five games of the 1985 series had similarly been penalty-filled affairs. The bottom line was that these two teams hated each other. I had no idea what I could expect once I dropped the puck. For now, all I could see when I looked down was red—all over my body.

After lunch, I walked into a pharmacy and discreetly showed the pharmacist my blotches and asked him what I had. We discounted food allergies, and then he asked if I was nervous about anything. After my emphatic "YES!" he recommended an antihistamine that he said wouldn't make me drowsy. I told the other guys I would meet them at the Forum; my alibi was I had to go ahead and get some equipment repairs. The truth is, I didn't want to have to change in front of them. By the time Scamp and D'Amico arrived in the room, I was totally concealed by my long underwear.

As soon as I stepped on the ice, all was forgotten, other than the energy inside the Forum. It was an unbelievable, end-to-end game. Both teams came to play, and there was none of the rough stuff that we might have anticipated. At the end of regulation time, it was all tied up at two.

I can't tell you what a sense of relief I had with D'Amico and Scapinello working the lines. There were others who would have made me feel the same way, but as a young referee being put into this position for the very first time, I fed off their quiet confidence.

Once I dropped the puck to start the overtime, it didn't take long for the game and series to end. After a faceoff in the Montreal zone, Peter Stastny drew the puck back cleanly to Pat Price on the left point and headed toward the Montreal net. Price drove a slapshot right at Steve Penney in the Montreal goal. Stastny pounced on the rebound, and Penney made another stop but still couldn't control the rebound. Stastny would make no mistake the second time, putting the game and series in his pocket at 2:22 of overtime.

I remember driving to the net from my position on the goal line as the scramble for the loose puck took place, and as I signaled the goal I felt an overwhelming sense of relief that it could not be disputed. All three of us were jubilant as we returned to the officials' room, not because we had scored a tangible victory, but because we knew we had performed our duties well and the game was better for it.

Cautiously removing my long underwear, this time in front of my colleagues, to my pleasant surprise, the only thing I saw was my lily-white skin. Either the antihistamine had kicked in or, more likely, I had avoided controversy with the help of my two colleagues.

As Bruce Hood can probably attest, a year or two can make a big difference. I got caught in the crossfire between these two bitter rivals in Game Five of the Adams Division final on April 28,

1987. The Nordiques had stunned the Canadiens by taking the first two games in Montreal, while the Habs won the next two at Le Colisée. Late in the third period of the fifth game, with the score tied at two, I disallowed a goal by Alain Côté, and Nordiques coach Michel Bergeron was transformed from "*Le Petit Tigre*" into a roaring lion—or, depending on your perspective, a raving maniac. To this day, the thought or mention of that call causes Bergeron's already high blood pressure to boil out of control.

We had a rule, even back then, that a goalie should be allowed to stand in his crease and do what his job description entails— namely, to defend his net by stopping the puck without being interfered with. This was the premise that later led us to the ridiculous interpretation that a goal could not be counted if a player had his foot—even a toe—in the goal crease, or even on the goal line.

Players went hard to the net, and goalies such as Billy Smith and Ron Hextall had a technique for keeping their goal crease clear—and not the same one used by the "ice girls" on Long Island or in Philadelphia, who scrape away the debris during commercial timeouts. I made it clear to goalies that I would not allow them to be bumped, jostled, interfered with, or bodychecked when they were within the confines of their crease. On the other hand, if they decided to do their own housekeeping with their stick or any other appendage, I would penalize them accordingly. The arrangement worked extremely well.

It looked as though this game might continue for a while, since the game in Quebec two nights earlier had been sent to overtime with the exact same score. Montreal scored five and a half minutes into the extra period. When I saw Quebec's Paul Gillis attacking the net hard, with Mats Näslund of the Canadiens chasing him on the backcheck, I immediately recognized all the makings of trouble in the crease. Sure enough, Näslund gave Gillis a little bump from behind that Gillis took advantage of to speed right into the goal crease, where he made solid contact with the left side of Montreal goalkeeper Brian Hayward. Gillis was not content with that contact, however: he hooked his skate around the left skate and pad of Hayward while he applied pressure with his stick to the goalie's upper torso. Gillis then used his momentum and force to drag Hayward to the side of the goal crease and beyond.

Seeing this take place, it would most likely not have drawn a penalty or a reaction from anyone in those days, especially given the score and the time remaining. Unless, that is, there was a consequence to Paul Gillis's actions. Therein lies the problem. In the same instant that I saw Hayward being dragged out of the net, I also saw Côté ready to fire a shot from the high slot into the now-empty Montreal cage. Before the puck left Côté's stick, the whistle was in my mouth and I was blowing as hard as I could. The Nordiques' celebration was short-lived as I waved off the goal and penalized Gillis for goaltender interference. I also gave Näslund a token interference penalty for his nudge on Gillis that triggered the events. The penalties were a wash, and I felt justice had been served.

With a faceoff in the Montreal end, the Nordiques seemed to be in shock. The Canadiens won the draw and marched down the ice. Guy Carbonneau set up Ryan Walter for the winning goal with 2:53 remaining. With his team down one goal, and certainly with enough time to score an equalizer, the very last thing I wanted to do was to give Bergie a bench penalty—or, worse yet, throw him out of the game. As *Le Petit Tigre* began to growl and bare his fangs, he was providing me with all the ammunition I would need to make such a call, but none would be forthcoming at this particular time. After the horn sounded, though, the fireworks started up in the hall outside our dressing room. Michel was out of his mind, his face so red I thought he was going to blow up. There was no sense pouring gasoline on an inferno, so Bob Hodges,

Leon Stickle, and I made our way into our dressing room as Michel and his people were moved elsewhere.

I had worked the Stanley Cup final the previous two seasons, and to this point in these playoffs, I had worked in seven games in the first round and now five games in the second. I returned home to Sarnia the next day to await the call for a sixth or seventh game if needed. That night, the Leafs played Game Six of their series in Detroit. The next games were played in Quebec and on Long Island. I was not assigned to any. I was listening to radio station CHOK in Sarnia when it was reported that a lawsuit had been filed against Sarnia native and NHL referee Kerry Fraser by a group in Quebec claiming prejudice. I couldn't believe my ears. Wait a minute, I thought. I had just worked a game involving two teams from the province of Quebec, and I was being sued for prejudice? Against whom and on what grounds? I called the NHL office in Toronto, got Jim Gregory on the line, and told him what I had just heard. I asked if there was anything to it. Jim's response was, "Have you been served with a summons yet?" I thought, *Holy shit, this is bizarre.* Jim said they'd had a report that a group of fans in Quebec City were behind the suit and that he had notified the NHL's legal department in New York. He told me that, if served, I should just send the paperwork to New York and that the league would stand 100 per cent behind me. That was reassuring—for the time being.

When all three playoff series went to Game Seven, and I wasn't called on for any of them, I knew I was done for the year, even before John McCauley completed the unfortunate task of telling me. I know it was not something John relished doing. Not only had he relied heavily on me to that point in the playoffs, John knew I was going through a very difficult divorce at the time. He had been extremely supportive as I maintained a balance between my work and caring for my three boys. If all this weren't enough, I contracted hepatitis in late June after a terrible allergic reaction to medication I had been prescribed for a sinus infection, and missed the first five months of the 1987–88 season. As I recuperated, John told me that he got calls from all over the league on the Quebec ordeal and that I had many friends in very high places. He promised that someday he and I would sit down and he would let me in on all that had transpired. We never did have that conversation as John passed away after the 1989 Stanley Cup final in which Calgary beat the Canadiens in six games. I cherish the many moments that we got to spend together during his final series of life.

In the summer of 1987, I received a personal letter from Serge Savard, general manager of the Canadiens, along with a videotape with enhanced footage of the play. It clearly showed Paul Gillis hooking Hayward's skate and using his stick to drag him out of the crease, as I suggested had been the case. With the class that Serge Savard always demonstrates, he said it had taken courage to make that call and he thanked me for being able to put the game ahead of my own self-interest. That, in a nutshell, is why I think of the word "class" when I think of the Montreal Canadiens organization. Serge's letter came at a time when I felt alone and abandoned and his kindness will always be very much appreciated.

Savard's sentiments were repeated by E.M. Swift of *Sports Illustrated*, who wrote, "Kerry Fraser's only fault with the Montreal–Quebec call was that he had the courage to make it."

After Michel Bergeron had retired from coaching and moved on to become a very popular television and radio personality in Montreal, I got word that he had been hospitalized. In his first return to radio, I arranged to call in and surprised him on the air. I had written a message, which my friend and colleague, linesman Pierre Champoux, had translated into French. Bergie was a good sport, and we both had a laugh over my poor French dialect.

A couple of years later, while I was in Montreal for the play-offs, Denis Morel's wife, Debbie, arranged a round of golf for us at Le Mirage Golf Club, where she is director of golf. The course is owned by Céline Dion and her husband, René Angélil. Ray Scapinello, Dave Newell, and I were playing the last couple of holes, while Bergeron and René were on the opposite fairway. We yelled and joked with one another, then played on. Later, we were sitting in the clubhouse, about to order a beer and a sandwich, when Michel came by and said that René wanted us to join them for lunch in the private dining room. I was on my cellphone with Kathy, so I said I would join them shortly.

As I entered the private dining room, there was a long table with one vacant seat at the opposite end to where René sat. To my immediate right—not by accident, but by René's design—sat *mon bon ami* Michel Bergeron. Behind me, there was a giant flat-screen television. René proudly announced that, before we started lunch, he wanted to give us a preview of a commercial Céline had just shot for Callaway, in which the old-fashioned microphone she is singing into is transformed into a Callaway driver, with which she makes a perfect swing. It was a great commercial, and we applauded. "Not so fast," René said. "I have one more thing to show you." Immediately, the disallowed goal was shown, complete with Michel standing up on the bench and looking more like Don Cherry than Grapes himself. Sitting beside me, Bergie went crazy again.

When the laughter had subsided, I called Kathy back on my phone and told her to please speak to Michel Bergeron. I said he still didn't agree with the call, and suggested maybe she could convince him otherwise. I handed the phone to Michel, who sat patiently through Kathy's attempt to convince him her dear husband is never wrong! When Michel's turn came to respond, he said, "Kat'y, I knew you love dat man, but it was an awful fucking call!" We roared with laughter and then enjoyed a wonderful lunch as Céline joined us after a practice session with Debbie.

At the Bell Centre, on the occasion of my final visit as a referee, I stood alone outside our dressing room and waited for the media scrum to arrive. Like a swarm of locusts, 20 or 30 members of the media rounded the corner, led by Michel Bergeron! We embraced as friends do, and Michel offered his most sincere congratulations on what he described as a Hall of Fame career. It was very touching for me to be received by him at this time and in this special way. Michel was an outstanding coach, and the passion he brought to the game was like no other I have ever witnessed. Michel and I then bid each other adieu in a much more peaceful and civilized fashion than we had the night of April 28, 1987. This was a new building, and a new foundation of friendship had been laid with it.

After answering all of the media's questions, I had one last request for a private meeting. It was from Canadiens coach Jacques Martin. In a very sincere and meaningful way, Jacques wanted to congratulate me on my (as he put it) tremendous career and thanked me for the way I had always shown respect for players and coaches and communicated with them. He appreciated that particularly after the lockout season, when I attempted to explain and "coach" the players on the new rules, to help keep them out of the penalty box. Nothing goes unnoticed by astute coaches like Jacques Martin, and I thanked him for all his co-operation over the years. Everything that Jacques said, I could tell, came from his heart.

It was now time to go to work for the last time with this great franchise. Tonight was not only my final game in Montreal, it was also the last for linesman Mark Paré. Mark joined the league in 1979 and has been a steady performer for all those years. He certainly goes about his business much more quietly than I have, but his integrity and character are what quiet heroes are made of. Mark is not only a trusted friend, he is the most outstanding employee the National Hockey League could ever hope for. His young protégé this evening was linesman Steve Barton. It has been my honour to observe this fine young man and his outstanding work. So much of what it takes to do this job well and in the best interest of the game comes from a depth of unshakable character. These two fine men, now at the opposite ends of their respective careers, have this quality in common.

The Carolina Hurricanes were the visitors. They suffered through an early-season drought and just ran out of time after Christmas to catch the rest of the pack. After the Olympic break, they beat teams on a consistent basis and were not to be taken lightly by anyone. Tonight, the Canadiens and their coach, Jacques Martin, with a trip to the playoffs riding on the outcome, showed a great deal of discipline, but Carolina hung on to win 2–1.

When the game concluded, Mark Paré and I were met by the majority of the Hurricane players, coaches, and trainers, as we received their expressions of appreciation for our many years of service to the NHL. It was an extremely classy thing for them to do, and I know that Mark appreciated it as much as I did. No different from Montreal, where class starts at the top, Hurricanes boss Jimmy Rutherford is one class act as well.

I have far too many memories of the Montreal Canadiens to chronicle in just one chapter. I could write a whole book about them. I worked the very first game at the Bell Centre, the site of our game tonight. Then there are the many playoff battles with Boston; the night Chris Chelios knocked poor Brian Propp of the Flyers out with an elbow; the penalty I called on Mark Hunter, then with the Calgary Flames, in the 1989 Cup final when, at the end of double overtime, he drove Shayne Corson's head into the boards from behind, and on and on . . .

There are a couple of stories, however, that I *must* share with you. The first incident worthy of mention was a call I made that turned a playoff series around. This one happened on June 3, 1993, in Game Two of the Stanley Cup final between the Los Angeles Kings and these Montreal Canadiens. The Kings had won the first game of the series, 4–1, and with 1:45 left in Game Two, they were up 2–1 and set to take a commanding lead back to the Great Western Forum. Habs coach Jacques Demers sent captain Guy Carbonneau and alternate captain Kirk Muller over to me, and they requested that I measure the curve of Marty McSorley's stick blade. I approached Marty and asked him for his stick, informing him that a request had been made to measure it. I eyeballed the blade and said, "Marty, what are you thinking? I don't even have to measure this thing; it is clearly illegal." Over at the penalty box, I meticulously measured the blade not once, but twice. I did not want there to be any question as to the accuracy of this crucial call.

Wayne Gretzky was standing at the edge of the referee's crease, and I showed him the result of one of the measurements. Thirty-two seconds later, with Marty sitting helplessly in the penalty box and Patrick Roy pulled for an extra attacker (a very gutsy move by Demers), Éric Desjardins scored the tying goal from the point to force overtime. Desjardins became the first defenceman in NHL history to record a hat trick in a Stanley Cup final game, when he scored his third of the night just 51 seconds into overtime to end the game. Montreal won the next three games, and their 24th Stanley Cup. Wayne Gretzky later admitted that it was the most bitter defeat he ever suffered.

While it was speculated that someone from the Montreal organization or coaching staff had snuck into the Kings' locker room to measure McSorley's stick, I firmly believe that was not the case. I spoke with Jacques Demers personally about this very allegation as I wrote this chapter. Jacques responded this way: "Kerry, you and I have talked at length on previous occasions.... From those conversations, I know that both of us are religious people. I can tell you and swear to God that I would never lie and I would never cheat to win, and I never measured or had Marty's stick measured.

"After the first game, some of my players told me that Marty McSorley was playing with an illegal stick. I filed it away in my mind. Had we gone back to L.A. down two games, I doubted that we could win. On the strength of what my players told me, and the desperation of our situation, I called for the measurement. Our power play wasn't going very well, so I decided to pull Patrick (goalie Patrick Roy) for an extra attacker."

Jacques said that he felt bad about having to resort to this call, but that his general manager, Serge Savard, told him after the game that if he and his players believed that McSorley's stick was illegal and Jacques had not called for a measurement, he (Serge) would have been very upset with Jacques. Jacques Demers is a very good and honorable man. If he said it, you can bank your life on it—it is the absolute truth!

Kathy sat at the game this evening with my dear old friend, Brian O'Neill, who was a VP at the National Hockey League on the day I signed my first contract in September of 1973. Working under President Clarence Campbell, one of Brian's many duties was to conduct hearings as chief disciplinarian and hand out suspensions to players when he deemed them warranted. Colin Campbell has that thankless task today. Whenever a player was assessed a match penalty, Mr. O'Neill invited him to visit his office in Montreal. No RSVP was required, as attendance was mandatory.

Often, it was a repeat offender, or, at the very least, an aggressive player who had earned his respect and reputation the old-fashioned way: with his fists or stick. On occasion, the accused felt aggrieved, as though he was the victim, and would go to some unusual lengths in stating his defence. Let me give you a classic example in which I was involved.

Chris "Knuckles" Nilan was a member of the Montreal Canadiens in the early '80s, when Hall of Fame defenceman Serge Savard was the general manager. Chris was a tough, hard-nosed guy who always played on the edge. I would want him on my team because he was a leader on the ice and in the dressing room—he held people accountable. He was fearless and earned his nickname honestly. That's often where the honesty ended. Chris would take advantage and get away with whatever he could. I don't fault him for trying, or as Dale Hunter once told me, "Frase, if you ain't cheatin', you ain't tryin'!" Simply put, Knuckles always gave much more than he got, and in the process took his share of penalties—in his mind, more than his share.

Like many enforcers, he believed the referees (and me in particular) were always gunning for him. John D'Amico told me very early in my career to always know which players are on the ice every second of the game. It was great advice, and a lesson I took to heart from the moment I received it. One night, the Canadiens were in Boston and the Bruins' skilled winger, Rick "Nifty" Middleton, somehow ended up on the ice during a shift with Knuckles. This mismatch set off alarm bells for me. With the play moving out of the Boston end, I looked across the ice and saw Nilan skating close to Middleton. Under normal circumstances, this would be done to establish a backcheck. More important than me seeing Knuckles, he saw that I was looking at him. In that moment of eye contact, the trap was set! I turned my eyes up ice for a split second, then snapped my head back toward Nilan and Middleton to catch Knuckles jamming the butt end of his stick into his

Doing my best impersonation of "Jack the Giant Killer" as I attempt to save Vinny Lecavalier from imminent peril at the hands of the giant, Zdeno Chara, in Game 3, Eastern Conference quarterfinal, April 25, 2006. THE TAMPA TRIBUNE

Wayne Gretzky presents me with #1 of 99 special edition signed prints by Gordie Howe and himself in honour of my 1700th game, November 15, 2007, in Phoenix. WAYNE GRETZKY & GORDIE HOWE—FRASER FAMILY COLLECTION

Take me out to the ball game! Fraser family members skate at Fenway Park the day before the Winter Classic. Back, left to right: son-in-law Harry Dumas with Brady on shoulders, Ryan Gano. Middle, left to right: Jessica, Jaime. Front, left to right: Kara, me, and Harrison. January 1, 2010. FRASER FAMILY COLLECTION

I am greeted by the face of the Philadelphia Flyers franchise, Bobby Clarke, a co-captain at the Winter Classic, as I step onto the ice in Fenway Park, January 1, 2010. ZACK HILL—PHILADELPHIA FLYERS

A loving wave to Fraser family, my angels in the outfield, before dropping the puck for the opening faceoff at Fenway Park, January 1, 2010.
KARA FRASER

The heartbeat of the game. The National Anthem is always a time of intense prayerful reflection and thanksgiving for me as demonstrated in Vancouver on January 25, 2010. JEFF VINNICK—VANCOUVER CANUCKS

FRASER

OMHA ALL-TIME GREAT

SARNIA

www.OMHA.net

Banner that hangs in Sarnia Sports and Entertainment Centre after selection to OMHA 75th Anniversary season All-Time Great team. Team selection includes Wayne Gretzky, Doug Gilmour, Syl Apps, Bobby Orr, Rob Blake, Curtis Joseph, Roger Neilson, Jim Rutherford, Ray Scapinello, Bill McCreary. COURTESY OF ONTARIO MINOR HOCKEY ASSOCIATION

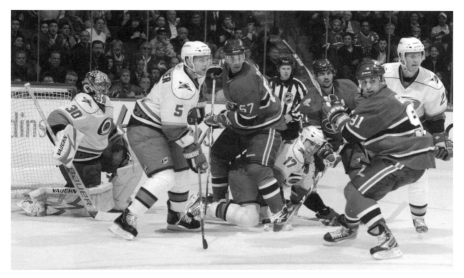

After 20 seasons in the NHL, soon-to-retire warrior Rod Brind'Amour was never afraid to put himself in harm's way by blocking shots, as seen here in his (and my) final game in the Bell Centre on March 31, 2010. COURTESY OF BOB FISHER / CHC

Kerry Fraser and Michel Bergeron: *bon amis* at last! March 31, 2010.
FRANCOIS ROY / LA PRESSE

While the teams were on the Wachovia Center ice during their pre-game warm-up, linesman Darren Gibbs and I stretched and warmed up together in preparation for my final game on April 11, 2010.

RON CORTES, COURTESY OF THE PHILADELPHIA INQUIRER

A pre-game moment of reflection at zamboni entrance of the Wachovia Center, home of the Philadelphia Flyers. Scanning the crowd, I realize it will be for the last time. April 11, 2010.

RON CORTES, COURTESY OF THE PHILADELPHIA INQUIRER

Prior to dropping the puck in my final game, I say to Flyer Jeff Carter and Ranger Artem Anisimov, "Boys, this isn't about me; this game is about you. And this is your time, not mine." April 11, 2010.

RON CORTES, COURTESY OF THE PHILADELPHIA INQUIRER

Leaving the ice for the final time in my career, as I raise my helmet high above my head in a farewell gesture to the crowd as well as to the game. It is my last stride before stepping off the ice and into retirement! April 11, 2010. JIM McISAAC / GETTY IMAGES

The Hair Evolution 1: 1980s.

The Hair Evolution 2: 1990s.

The Hair Evolution 3: 2000s.

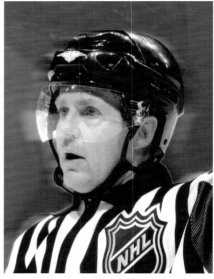

The Hair Evolution 4: League
Imposed Helmet Head! 2007

opponent's mouth, knocking out some of Nifty's front teeth. Up went my arm, and I assessed a 10-minute match penalty for deliberate injury, at the time the most severe penalty that could be assessed.

In those days, we not only had to write a detailed report immediately after the game and send it to Brian O'Neill, we were required to appear at the hearing as well. The player, with his general manager, also attended to plead his case. As we sat on opposite sides of the table in the Montreal boardroom, I received a courteous, but businesslike, greeting from Serge Savard. A nod of the head was the best I could expect from Nilan, who cast a steely gaze my way that sent an icy chill around the room.

Mr. O'Neill, as always, meticulously laid out the parameters of the hearing and made the "accused" know exactly why he was there. Knuckles' fate could largely depend on his testimony, since the primary evidence against him was contained in my game report, along with supporting reports from linesmen Kevin Collins and Gord Broseker, who worked the game with me. The linesmen, however, were not required to attend the hearing. After reading all the officials' reports of the incident, Mr. O'Neill looked at Knuckles and said, "Chris, do you have anything to say in defence of yourself?"

Knuckles immediately sprang to the offence. He said, "Yeah, I got something to say. Fraser has it in for me and he gives me more penalties than any other ref in the league. No matter what I do, he's always watching me. Just to prove my point, if Fraser had've been watching what he should have been [the play up the ice], he never would have seen me butt-end Middleton in the mouth!"

Well, Serge Savard just about upchucked his coffee, placed his hand on Chris Nilan's arm to silence him, and tried to convince Brian that that was not what Chris meant to say. Mr. O'Neill took the floor and, looking directly at Knuckles, said, "Mr. Nilan, there isn't a referee in this league that would be worth a pound of salt if he didn't watch you every second that you are on the ice, given your history. Now, would you like to see a replay of the incident?" Nilan and Savard refused his invitation to look at the incriminating replay. The evidence against him was overwhelming and he was suspended for eight games for the butt-end delivered to Rick Middleton's mouth.

Looking back on the many hearings I've attended, I realize there was great value in having the opportunity to explain a serious call and for the player to explain things as he saw it to a "judge," in this case Brian O'Neill. This open dialogue was a mechanism for communication between all parties and forced accountability on the player, the referee, and the league. It provided a fair, open hearing, face to face, with all parties understanding the final ruling.

As Kathy, Mark Paré, and I left the beautiful Bell Centre, I reflected on a very special visitor I had had years before at the 1990 All-Star Game I worked in Pittsburgh. Legendary Montreal Canadien, 69-year-old Maurice "Rocket" Richard, was the honorary captain of the Wales Conference team. I guess the "Rocket" had been hearing about this young referee Kerry Fraser for some time, since I arrived on the scene in earnest with my first Stanley Cup final appearance in 1985. Brian O'Neill entered our dressing room just before we were ready to go out for the anthems, told me the "Rocket" wanted to meet me, and asked if it would be okay to bring him in. I said, "Oh my God, Brian, I'll postpone the game for as long as it takes to get him here. What an honour—please bring him in." As I sat in my chair, facing the door that had just been flung open, I was pierced by those infamous eyes, black as coal. I got up from the chair and immediately extended my hand to Mr. Richard. It remained there, suspended, while the Rocket sized me up thoroughly. He stood there, grizzly-like, leaning toward me in expectation, as if studying this "upstart" referee, deciding if I deserved my reputation. I thought this was going to be a casual introduction to a legend of the game, but, I quickly realized, with the Rocket standing before me, that this man didn't do anything casually. In spite of his age, I realized that this was indeed the fierce competitor that had struck fear in all his opponents. The first words out of his mouth were, "Fraser, you're not so fuckin' young!"

I burst out laughing, as did the others in the room, and we shook hands. In this moment of reflection I could still recall the firm, powerful grip of his hand that I was so honoured to shake on that memorable occasion in Pittsburgh.

As I crossed the Bell Centre parking lot that I would be exiting for the last time, his statement rang true…you're right, Rocket, my baby-faced youthfulness has given way, and like the old plaque that adorns the great Montreal Canadiens dressing room says, "To you from failing hands, we throw the torch . . ."

HOCKEYTOWN, USA: DETROIT RED WINGS

Growing up in Sarnia, 60 miles upriver from Detroit, I was able to watch the Red Wings frequently on television. As a young hockey player, I often made that short journey to play against the Detroit Little Caesars organization, sponsored by the hockey-crazed pizza mogul and future owner of the Detroit Red Wings, Mike Ilitch. My peewee team would play there in a rink that looked like a converted factory, bearing the name "Gordie Howe Hockeyland."

Before it was known as Hockeytown, USA, Detroit was the home of Mr. Hockey, Gordie Howe. When I was 10 years old, Gordie came to our Sarnia Minor Athletic Association year-end banquet. I was awed to be in his presence. I stood in line to get his autograph, and couldn't help feeling excited but nervous. He took my program and autographed it, and then gently, with a smile, rubbed my short brush cut, not realizing that one day that hair was going to be famous. Through my 10-year-old eyes, I could see what a true gentle giant Howe was—off the ice. On the ice, however, he was a fierce competitor famed not only for his skill but his toughness.

I experienced that Howe toughness years later—not from Gordie, but from his son, Mark. When I was 19 years old, I played against Mark when he was a member of the Detroit Junior Red Wings. Mark was 16, but he was physically developed beyond his years. I was five-foot-seven and 140 pounds, whereas he was several inches taller and 50 pounds heavier. He had just returned from playing at the 1972 Winter Olympics in Sapporo, Japan, against some of the best players in the world. The U.S. team Mark played for pulled off a miraculous upset by beating the Czechs and Finns to capture a silver medal; the Soviet Union won the gold. That cold night in 1972, my team, the Sarnia Bees, played Mark and his Junior Red Wings in the old Detroit Olympia. We were down a goal, and as the captain of my team, I wanted to make something happen. I saw my chance when a Detroit defenceman floated a long, lazy pass to Mark. I was bearing down on him at full speed, and I timed my hit perfectly. As soon as he received the pass, I hit him head-on with all the force I could generate. I thought I had just run into a brick wall! Neither of us went down after the crisp *pop* sound the open ice hit had produced. I don't know whether Mark felt any effect of the impact, but my insides vibrated within my rib cage with the force of the hit.

It was at the end of that season that I decided to trade my hockey stick for a whistle. The hit I tried to deliver on Mark Howe that night in the Detroit Olympia was all I needed to convince me that it was time to look for a safer line of work.

While Gordie Howe is still the traditional face of the Red Wings, I am sure that Mr. Hockey would willingly share that distinction with his more recent counterpart, Steve Yzerman. Jim Devellano, the Wings' general manager at the time, used his first-round pick (fourth overall) in the 1983 draft to land Yzerman, after missing out on Pat LaFontaine, who grew up in the Detroit area and was claimed by the New York Islanders with their number-three pick. While Yzerman may not have been Jimmy D's first choice, he went on to become one of the most important players in franchise history: a team captain, a multiple Stanley Cup champion, and a Red Wing for all of his 22 NHL seasons.

In 1988–89, after his team had made back-to-back trips to the Campbell Conference final against Edmonton, Stevie Y's scoring prowess shifted gears, propelling him to heights normally touched only by Gretzky and Lemieux: 65 goals and 90 assists for 155 points. That spring, he won the Lester B. Pearson Award (the league's most valuable player as chosen by members of the players' association) and was a finalist for the Hart Trophy (the league's MVP award, voted on by NHL writers). Beyond the statistics, the captain brought a level of intensity and leadership to every game that was seldom demonstrated by others. To say that Steve Yzerman is a classy, friendly individual off the ice would be an understatement; he is one of the best. But his demeanour was often much less friendly during a game. He brought such an intense desire to win every night that no one was immune to the wrath he could inflict. Steve demanded as much out of everyone around him as he did of himself. If he felt someone—whether it was a teammate or, as in my case, the guy in stripes—wasn't giving enough or had made an error, they heard about it immediately. People talk about Mark Messier and "The Look"—his patented death stare—but I can tell you that Steve had a look that could blow open the door of a bank vault. There were many times when it was directed at me, particularly in the early to mid-'90s.

In spite of Steve's phenomenal scoring numbers, not to mention the addition of players such as Dino Ciccarelli, Sergei Fedorov, Ray Sheppard, Paul Coffey, Jimmy Carson, and Nicklas Lidström, the team had not yet won a Stanley Cup. Worse yet, a series of early exits from the playoffs fuelled rumours that the captain was going to be traded to Ottawa. Scotty Bowman, who took over as the Wings' coach in 1993, had a rigid coaching style that emphasized two-way play. On occasion, he would clash with offensive stars over this philosophy. Yzerman became Scotty's project—or target, depending on whom you asked. I actually didn't mind it when Stevie Y was feuding with Scotty during the early stages of his transition from a scoring machine to a strong defensive forward. He tended to leave me alone at these times, and instead focused his anger and frustration on the man behind the bench. Being the ultimate leader and team player that he is, Yzerman eventually bought in the defensive responsibilities that Bowman demanded of him. As a result, Stevie Y is generally regarded as one of the best two-way players in the history of the games and Scotty Bowman is considered the greatest coach.

In 1995, Steve led the Red Wings to their first Stanley Cup final series since 1966. As I worked that series, it became obvious that Detroit didn't quite have what it took to win the Cup. It seemed to me that the Wings were content just to have arrived and did not fully understand how to finish the job. Their education was provided by the New Jersey Devils, who swept in four straight games. Two years later, they were back, and it was clear that they had learned their lessons well, as they swept the Philadelphia Flyers to win the Cup for the first time in 42 years. I worked Game Three and stood by as the backup referee for Game Four in Detroit, and I got a first-hand look at how "the Captain" would not be denied the chance to hoist the Cup at home. There was a wonderful mood of celebration on the ice and in the stands, but unfortunately, it spilled out into the streets, as it had in Montreal in 1993. The Detroit police escorted our officiating crew, with wives in tow, over the Ambassador Bridge to Windsor, Ontario. Kathy sat beside me in the van and squeezed my arm tightly in fear as we drove past burning cars and looters and raced through red lights toward the safety of our Canadian hotel.

In spite of the negative aftermath, I will forever remember the boyish joy displayed by Steve Yzerman, as all of his effort, heart, and leadership came to fruition and he finally got to raise the Cup over his head. He went on to do so twice more, in 1998 and 2002. In 2001–02, he not only led the team to victory, but did it through excruciating pain after re-injuring his knee and missing 30 games. During those playoffs, he was effectively playing on one leg. I remember watching Steve win a race to a loose puck through sheer will as he hobbled like a wounded deer looking to the forest for cover. The pain that was etched on his face was overshadowed only by the grit and determination to win the battle, no matter the cost. He would not give in to the pain or to a younger, healthier opponent. You needed to have the vantage point that his teammates, opponents, or I had to truly appreciate just how amazing his accomplishments were. How could a teammate not be inspired by his courage and effort? I know I was. When I was awakened in the middle of the night due to the arthritic pain in my left knee, in which I had long since blown out my ACL and cartilage as a 16-year-old, I only had to recall Yzerman's fortitude.

As intense as Steve Yzerman could be on the ice, he demonstrated the same degree of kindness and caring for others off of it. On a bleak, frigid morning in February 2001, I was waiting for Kathy's niece, Margaret Krumholtz, and her family. Margaret had been battling a very rare form of cancer for four months, but was determined to attend an NHL game between Detroit and Toronto at my invitation. She would meet her favourite Leaf, Tie Domi, after the morning skate at Joe Louis Arena. Margaret was snuggled in a blanket and seated in her wheelchair, while her husband and their two teenage daughters stood by her side as they waited for their Leaf heroes to appear. Scotty Bowman very kindly invited the family on a tour of the Red Wings' dressing room. Yzerman and Darren McCarty were leaving when they noticed Margaret and her family with me in the hallway. They very graciously returned to meet the family and pose for pictures. The life and sparkle returned to Margaret's big, beautiful brown eyes one last time. It was a very memorable day for all of us, myself included. She lost her battle with cancer on May 21, 2001, but told her husband, Gary, before she passed, that that game in Detroit was one of the most special moments of her life. Sometimes we are led to believe the National Hockey League is just a game or a business, that it's not life or death. On this particular day, however, for one courageous hockey fan and her family, the NHL and its players represented life in the face of death.

The sound of a beeping metal detector brought me back to the present day. I rolled my bag past security and entered Joe Louis Arena on the afternoon of my final game at "The Joe."

Forty-seven years after I stood in line to receive Mr. Hockey's autograph, I rounded the corner to enter my dressing room and ran smack into a famous Gordie Howe elbow, one that so many players had the misfortune to experience and so few referees ever caught. I sure didn't see this one, either!

I'm no different than his millions of adoring fans. I am mesmerized by the aura that surrounds Gordie Howe. In this moment, I felt a special connection to the game of hockey and its unrivalled history, similar to the way I feel every time I enter the Hockey Hall of Fame in Toronto. This meeting was even more special, however, because being in the presence of Gordie Howe actually brought the game and its history to life. I felt like a 10-year-old kid again. There was no hero-worship at work here; nearly 30 years had passed since Gordie scored his last goal and hung up his skates in retirement—for the second time. I have worked in more than 2,000 NHL games myself and skated beside many of the greatest players the game has known. But this was something different. There is an ease and comfort that Gordie makes everyone around him feel, even though he is a hockey icon.

He congratulated me on my fine officiating career and we chatted for a few minutes about other legends of the game—Rocket Richard, Sid Abel, even the Great One, Wayne Gretzky—but he also talked about officiating greats: Red Storey, Frank Udvari, and Bill Friday. I could have spent all day with this living encyclopedia of hockey knowledge, but I knew it would have to wait for another time. I had to concentrate on the present, and the game that would begin in just over an hour. Gordie wished me all the best and took note of the time I would now have to enjoy with kids, grandchildren, and Kathy. He advised me not to take anything for granted and to use the time wisely. It was clear to me his good counsel came from the wisdom and life experience one acquires through sadness, as he continues to bear the loss of his dear wife, Colleen, who succumbed to Alzheimer's. Our time together had come to an end; there were others waiting up the hall to be graced by his presence. I vowed to hold this great man's words of wisdom close to my heart for the rest of my life.

Now it was time to refocus. In the dressing room, my fellow referee, Wes McCauley, and I discussed the game and its significance for both teams. The Predators, with three games left to play, had 96 points and sat fifth in the Western Conference. The Wings, with five games left, had 95 point and were sixth. The winner would clinch a playoff berth. Close behind, in seventh, were the Los Angeles Kings. Wes and I had worked a number of games together and meshed well both on and off the ice. We moved and thought a lot alike. He has a very good feel for the game from his experience as a Division I collegiate player at Michigan State University and as a pro player after being drafted by this same Detroit Red Wings organization. Wes is following in the footsteps of his late father, John, a dear friend and mentor of mine. This would be the last time we worked together, and I was savouring the moment.

It would also be my last game alongside linesman Mark Paré, the 31-year NHL veteran who, as noted in the Montreal chapter, was also retiring at the end of the season. Mark lives in Windsor, and this would be his final game at Joe Louis Arena as well. We both found it hard to get a handle on how fast the years had passed. As we prepared to share the ice one last time, I reflected on the mutual respect we had for each other and the friendship that will last long after the whistle and skates are put away. We share a long history in the business together, with lots of memories—good, bad, and ugly!

Very early in both of our careers, it turned real ugly one night. We were working together, along with linesman Leon Stickle, at Joe Louis Arena when I unknowingly made NHL history. It was February 11, 1982, and the Vancouver Canucks, coached by Harry Neale, were in Detroit to play against Wayne Maxner's Red Wings. It was a lean period in Red Wings history; that season, they finished last in the Norris Division (and 20th in the 21-team league) with 54 points, just five ahead of the bottom-dwelling Colorado Rockies. The Red Wings were leading 4–2 midway through the third period when Detroit defenceman Jim Schoenfeld grabbed the puck with his hand in the goal crease during a scramble around the net. I immediately blew my whistle and assessed a penalty shot to Vancouver. The shot could be taken by any Canuck player who had been on the ice at the time of the infraction. Neale selected Thomas Gradin, and he buried it against Detroit goalie Gilles Gilbert. The score was now 4–3 Detroit and remained that way with just over a minute to play, as Neale gave the signal to his goalie, Richard Brodeur, to come to the bench for an extra attacker in an effort to tie it up.

With the Canucks' net empty, Detroit turned the puck over, all their players focusing on trying to score on the open net instead of defending the lead. Stan Smyl picked up a loose puck at the

Vancouver blue line and raced in the other direction on a break-away. Detroit defenceman Reed Larson was the closest Red Wing to Smyl and chased him down from behind. Just as Smyl was about to let a shot go from about 15 feet out to the left of Gilbert, Larson took a two-handed swing and chopped the Stanley Steamer down, causing the Canuck forward to slide into the goalpost and injure his leg. With just 30 seconds left in the game and the Red Wings up by one goal, I blew my whistle and pointed to centre ice to signal another penalty shot for the Canucks. It was the first time in NHL history a team had been awarded two penalty shots in the same period. I was later informed that only once before had two penalty shots even been called in the same game. The referee to do that was former NHL president Clarence Campbell.

The safest thing for me to do (and the easy way out, especially in those years) would have been to call a two-minute slashing penalty. Penalty shots were rarely awarded. A referee in that era might be lucky to call two in his career, and I had just handed out two in the same period—against the home team. It certainly didn't make me a popular figure with Detroit coach Wayne Maxner, any of the Red Wings players, or the entire crowd of about 11,000.

Vancouver trainer Larry Ashley had to come out and assist Stan Smyl off the ice. The injury he had sustained on the play meant he wouldn't be able to take the shot. Once again, Harry Neale had to select one of the players who had been on the ice at the time of the infraction. Czech star Ivan Hlinka was his choice. Neale told me later that his instructions to Hlinka were very clear: "If you don't score on this penalty shot, just keep skating right out the end of the rink, all the way back to Czechoslovakia!" At the time, I wondered why Ivan looked so nervous as he bore down on Gilles Gilbert. Lucky for Ivan Hlinka—and unlucky for Kerry Fraser—he scored. The moment I signalled the goal, beer cups (many of them still full) and everything else that wasn't nailed down in the arena rained down in my direction.

After the debris was cleaned up, we still had another 30 seconds left to play. I dropped the puck and held my breath, hoping nothing else stupid happened. The horn sounded and I made a bee-line for the end of the rink. Then I saw Reed Larson, with a powerful arm worthy of a Detroit Lions quarterback, launch a water bottle 30 yards—and I, or perhaps my head, was the intended receiver. I didn't drop the ball on this one, either; I gave Larson a 10-minute misconduct (instead of a 10-yard penalty), even though the game was over. The fans were still firing any debris that remained as Paré, Stickle, and I headed for cover in the officials' room. Mark was driving back to Windsor, so he left the room on his own. Leon and I left with a police officer by my side. Approaching our exit, we noticed that a fan stood by the iron gate, blocking our path. From 20 feet away, the police officer said, "Oh no, not this guy—he's a real pain in the ass. We've had trouble with him before."

I said, "If you want to get him, just hang back about 10 feet, but be ready to jump in if I need you." I felt pretty brave with big Leon right behind me. As I got closer, this guy removed his glasses and put them in his shirt pocket. I walked right up to him, not taking my eyes off of him, and dropped my bag at his feet. He started on me about the rotten calls I had made. I said, "Listen, I don't know who you are or what you do, but I notice you took your glasses off and I assume you did so for a reason. Either you get out of my way right now, or I'm going to go right through you. The choice is yours to make."

The guy pulled his glasses out of his pocket, stepped aside, and—to the policeman's amazement—we walked right past. Turns out the guy was all mouth.

The veteran hockey columnist with the Montreal *Gazette*, Red Fisher, wrote a column the day after the incident and likened me, this new little referee in the NHL, to Popeye, with forearms of steel and carrying anchors in both hands, just for having the courage to call two penalty shots against the home team, especially in light of the time remaining and the score of the game. John McCauley called me the day after the game, told me about Red's article, and congratulated me on making those calls. Late in the next season, the referees attended a meeting prior to the playoffs. Scotty Morrison, the referee-in-chief, commented that a total of eight penalty shots had been called in the NHL to that point, and one guy (by the name of Fraser) had called six of them. He urged all of us to call penalty shots whenever warranted to restore a scoring opportunity that had been lost.

I know that the league recognized the excitement that penalty shots created for the fans. They certainly were excited that night in Detroit, perhaps for the wrong reason, but nonetheless, there was a dramatic increase in the number of penalty shots after Scotty's appeal. For me, it was just another call. Personal consequences that might result from making any tough call were never part of my decision-making process. If I clearly saw a play, it either was or wasn't a penalty. I didn't alter my judgment according to who might get most upset by it. Courage and integrity are two qualities that officials in any sport must possess. The integrity of the game rests squarely on the shoulders of its game officials.

Tonight, as every other night, that integrity is what would be expected of us. With two minutes showing on the digital clock in our dressing room, it was time for us to take to the ice before the teams arrived for the introductions of the starting lineups and the national anthem. As Wes McCauley, Mark Paré, Mark Shewchyk, and I exited the officials' dressing room, we were escorted to the ice by two Detroit police officers. My hope for this afternoon was that this short walk would be the only time we required their services. I felt the energy in the building as the Red Wings' fans showed their appreciation for the surge their team had been on since the Olympic break. Not that long ago, there was fear that this powerful team might miss the playoffs. With the return of some key performers from injuries, they were now hitting on all cylinders—teams like that are always dangerous in the post-season.

Right from the opening faceoff, both teams showed tremendous speed through the neutral zone and attacked the net. At this crucial point in the schedule, teams do everything they can to manufacture goals, especially when they are playing against a hot goalie. This game had one at each end, in Jimmy Howard of the Red Wings and Pekka Rinne of the Predators. Each team had at least one player we had placed on a "watch list" for goal-crease violations: Patric Hörnqvist of Nashville and the biggest "crease pest" in the entire league, Detroit's Tomas Holmström.

The other guy I kept an eye on and gave a wide berth to was Nashville's Jordin Tootoo. Ever since Jordin separated my rib in a game between Detroit and the Predators in Nashville on November 22, 2007, I've been sure to steer clear. In that game, after I signalled a Detroit goal, I backed away toward the corner and side boards as Tootoo and Detroit tough-guy Aaron Downey circled in front of me. Downey gave Toots a little bump, and Jordin, who has been known to embellish (i.e., dive) on more than one occasion, launched himself into the boards—back first—and threw a fist against the boards, hoping to make a big noise and sell a call that wasn't warranted. The problem was, the sound that was made was from the air that left my lungs, along with a loud groan of pain—*aaaagghh*—I let out when his fist nailed me right in the sternum. I thought I had been shot. My rib popped out and I was flat on my back, unable to breathe.

I was gasping for air and turning blue as big Detroit defenceman Andreas Lilja stood over me with a concerned look on his face and shouted at me, in a thick Swedish accent, "Breathe,

Kerry, breathe!" Just as it seemed as though I was going to pass out, some oxygen returned to my lungs. I finished the period and went to the medical room for an X-ray. My rib had been displaced, but nothing was broken, and for the next couple of months tears came to my eyes every time I coughed, sneezed, or farted! I found it easier to suppress the first two of those bodily functions.

Nashville and Detroit played hard, and as I anticipated, I would have to step up from my position at the blue line and call a penalty on Holmström at 19:04 of the first period. Mickey Redmond, a former 50-goal scorer for Detroit and long-time colour commentator on Wings television broadcasts, didn't agree (imagine that), but it was a phenomenal call. Some things that the untrained eye might take several replays, even in slow motion, to detect, we officials only have a fraction of a millisecond to see and make a judgment on. This was one of those times, and from 65 feet away.

The Wings were cycling the puck low in the Nashville end zone. Holmström came out of the corner from a scramble behind the net and occupied his favourite real estate, right at the top of—if not inside—the blue paint of the goal crease, his back and butt in the face of Pekka Rinne. As one of the non–puck carriers, Tomas was part of my area of coverage, along with the other players who weren't immediately involved in the action around the puck. Wes covered everything to do with action on the puck.

Tomas never seems to want to take up space on his own; he usually attracts a crowd, which he uses to his advantage by jamming up the goal crease even more. With the puck on its way to the front of the net, Tomas grabbed the stick of Nashville defenceman Shea Weber, tap-danced over Rinne's pads, and pulled Weber down to the side of the goal crease, all the while flipping a one-handed shot at the goal with his stick. Before the puck floated overtop of the net, I had my hand in the air to signal a penalty against Holmström. With all the action around him, Pekka Rinne didn't realize there was a delayed penalty being called against Detroit, so he remained in his crease until the whistle blew once Detroit gained possession of the puck. Tomas had that confused look of innocence on his face as he went to the penalty box for the remaining 56 seconds of the period.

Prior to the start of the second period, I was standing near the penalty box when Holmström skated over to occupy the real estate *I* had rented him for the next 64 seconds. Again flashing me that confused look, Tomas asked me what I'd seen—notice, not what he'd done! I explained that I'd seen him engage the Nashville defenceman at the edge of the crease, grab his stick, and pull him down, while trying to make it look as though he was the one being fouled. A wide grin broke out across Holmström's face, as he smiled and said, "That's why you're the *best!*" and then stepped into the penalty box.

Tomas Holmström makes things happen. He creates opportunities for his team and takes a huge beating in front of the net to do so. He is just as valuable to the Detroit Red Wings as any of their other star players, and they have a boatload of them, including Nicklas Lidström, Henrik Zetterberg, Pavel Datsyuk, Johan Franzén, Todd Bertuzzi, and Brian Rafalski.

The Nashville Predators grabbed a 3–2 lead with just 43 seconds remaining in the second period when J.P. Dumont scored. It looked as though that lead would hold up, until Datsyuk tied the score for the Red Wings on a beautiful effort with just 37 seconds remaining in regulation, and Jimmy Howard removed from the Detroit goal for an extra attacker. When the horn sounded, we were heading to overtime.

Fans who had gone to grab one last slice of Little Caesars Pizza didn't even have time to return to their seats as Nashville defenceman Ryan Suter scored just 16 seconds after Wes McCauley dropped the puck for the opening faceoff of overtime. It was a clean goal, and there were no beer cups or debris thrown by the

Joe Louis fans at the end of this game. I would be able to walk out of the building without the police riding shotgun.

Leaving behind the memories of Gordie Howe, Stevie Yzerman, Scotty Bowman, and the fabulous Russian Five (defencemen Vyacheslav Fetisov and Vladimir Konstantinov and forwards Igor Larionov, Sergei Federov, and Slava Kozlov) that Bowman assembled in 1997 to return the Stanley Cup to Detroit, I rushed to the airport to catch a flight to Chicago for an Easter Sunday game the next afternoon—and a date with Scotty Bowman, the Blackhawks' director of player personnel and his son Stan, their general manager. Together, they are busy assembling another potential Stanley Cup champion, this time in the Windy City.

While I was editing this book, it was announced that Steve Yzerman was hired as the general manager of the Tampa Bay Lightning. Having just returned from my niece Lynsey's wedding on Mackinac Island, Michigan, I can tell you first-hand the fans of that state are heartbroken. It was all I heard about from the locals the entire weekend. It comes as no surprise to me, however, that Stevie Y was lured away from the franchise that he played his entire career for and, as I documented extensively in this chapter, took the Red Wings from obscurity to Stanley Cup champions with his stellar play and leadership. The depth that the Wings possess is not just limited to the players on the ice. The same is true of their management team. General manager Ken Holland has done a fantastic job in putting together a collection of talent and is a pillar of the organization. His assistant general manager for 12 seasons, Jim Nill, is a guy that could also be in charge of his own NHL team but has been retained by Holland. While I still believe Steve Yzerman will always be the face of Red Wings hockey, he is a "front-line player" that needs to be challenged and lead.

The Tampa job will do just that. New owner Jeff Vinik has placed his franchise on very solid ground. Acquiring Stevie Y demonstrates Mr. Vinik's commitment to assembling a winning team on and off the ice. They have a great nucleus of players but have been rudderless since the return from the lockout season. "The Captain" will no doubt right the ship just as he did as an 18-year-old rookie in the Motor City. Mark my words, "Lightning" will strike again!

HERE COME THE HAWKS!: CHICAGO BLACKHAWKS

In the summer of 2009, the management of the United Center in Chicago announced that part of the arena's upper level was being renamed the Madhouse on Madison. The name conjured up images of the old Chicago Stadium, which stood across the street from 1929 until 1995 and deserved the nickname. A visitor to the stadium couldn't help but revel in the sights and sounds of the massive Barton pipe organ, the steep, overhanging balconies, and the dignified way in which the old barn had aged. There came a point when you felt the fans couldn't possibly cheer any louder, but then the national anthem, often sung by Wayne Messmer, would reach its crescendo and your eardrums felt like they were going to rupture from the incalculable decibel levels. If your heart didn't get pumping when you stood on that ice, you were probably dead.

Chicago Stadium was my favourite place to work in those days—I loved it. Everything about the arena smelled historic—the musty seats that had seen so many triumphs and defeats, the faint waxy residue of the scuffed wood floors, the hint of the hockey equipment worn by some of the greatest players the game has known. Whenever I stood at centre ice, the monumental horn, taken from the owners' yacht, the *Black Hawk*, hung overhead and never failed to scare the hell out of me whenever Chicago scored. It sounded like a ship was being scuttled upon the waves of avid hockey fans. When you walked down the stairs—yes, stairs!—to get to the dressing rooms, you passed vast numbers of beer kegs waiting to be served to the thirsty patrons above.

It was October 14, 1993, and the Blackhawks were battling it out with the Hartford Whalers in the Hawks' third home game to the start the 1993–94 season. Rookie defenceman Chris Pronger sat on the visitors' bench, wondering what the hell he had gotten himself into. There was 3:19 left in the third period with Chicago trailing 6–2. It had been a rough game from the start for the Blackhawks, and now it seemed like they were bent on making their opponents pay for it. Chicago centre Jeremy Roenick had already earned a reputation for playing full out all the time. He only knew one speed and that was pedal to the metal, never letting the score of a game slow down his legs—or his mouth. That's why he was so much fun for the fans to watch and for me to referee. I always had to be aware, as did his opponents, of when JR was on the ice, especially when he was on the forecheck. If a defenceman didn't hustle back to retrieve a puck, JR was on him in a flash.

On this night, the Whalers were ready to roll out of the Stadium with a nice early-season road win. The problem was that somebody had forgotten to tell veteran defenceman Brad "the Beast" McCrimmon that Jeremy Roenick could neither tell the time nor the score. Brad sauntered into the corner to pick up a loose puck. Before he had even touched the puck, JR had given him a decent tap with his stick, then slammed the Hartford defenceman into the boards. The whistle blew and a pod of Whales swam around Roenick. Brian Propp confronted him, and the two engaged in some verbal sparring. Chicago defenceman Chris Chelios, who had knocked Propp out with an elbow in the 1989 Wales Conference final (at the time, Propp was a Philadelphia Flyer while Chelios was with the Montreal Canadiens), came flying in and challenged him. Before Propp knew what hit him, Chelios was throwing bombs. All Propp could do was cover up as linesman Bernie DeGrace and I attempted to pull Chelios off him. Linesman Randy Mitton blanketed Propp to protect him from taking more of Chelios's punches.

In the meantime, a second fight had started in the middle of the ice, between Adam Burt of the Whalers and Brian Noonan of the Hawks. It was a real dandy; they traded punches until they finally ended up over near the side boards at the blue line. An enraged Chelios charged his way across the ice toward the Burt–Noonan fight, dragging Bernie DeGrace along for the ride. Chelios was able to get a right hand free and smoke Burt with a sucker punch right in the eye that really left a mark. Burt, now receiving punches from both sides, was staggering. Chris Chelios was beyond just being out of control and his best defence in a future hearing should be to plead temporary insanity. Linesman DeGrace had to exert what some might deem excessive force (but in this case necessary) to hog-tie Chelios and get him the heck out of there and off the ice. Mitton had hold of Adam Burt, so I stepped in and bear-hugged Brian Noonan just as he was about to throw a wild right that would have caught me by mistake. Muscle memory kicking in from my scrapping days as a player, I restrained Noonan long enough to talk him down from trying to maul Burt while also staying fully intact myself.

With the fight now over, Chris Chelios had the distinction of setting two Hawks records for penalties that night: 51 minutes for the game and 37 in the one altercation. I gave Chris a total of eight penalties that evening, including a double game misconduct. Brian Propp didn't even get a penalty in the aftermath of the brawl; there was nothing I could give him for being on the receiving end. When it was all over, Chris Pronger, the 18-year-old rookie, looked for some wisdom from the veteran Brad McCrimmon. "What the hell was that?" he asked. "I couldn't believe Chelios was bouncing around, suckering guys. Does this happen often?" The Beast could only reply, "Welcome to the NHL, kid."

After the game, we officials filed our reports with the league and I spoke with Brian Burke by telephone. He had seen the game from his home in Hartford, so he had a pretty accurate sense of what had transpired. Chelios received a suspension for his tirade, and obviously wasn't all that happy about it.

I was back in Chicago for a New York Islanders game not too long afterward—November 4, to be exact. Before the game, I stopped up the hall to see the Blackhawks' equipment trainer, Randy Lacey, about getting my skates sharpened. Randy, a great guy, was from Barrie, Ontario, and did an excellent job sharpening skates. As I was talking to him, Chelios stepped out of his dressing room into the trainers' area and gave me a dirty look. He returned a moment later and said, menacingly, "You will get yours someday, Kerry." I ignored this threat and continued my conversation with Randy. As stated in the Official's Report to League President that I filed:

> Chelios then stated, "It wasn't right to make this a personal thing." I paused in my conversation to Mr. Lacey and not looking to incite or dignify the comments made by Chelios, I simply said, "I am going to leave your area, Chris." He said, "Ya, you shouldn't be here anyway." I said, "I was simply talking to a friend." Chelios said, "You don't have any friends." I summoned Supervisor Will Norris and Chicago coach Darryl Sutter and advised both of them of the exact details of this incident in front of linesmen Ron Finn and Andy McElman. I instructed Will Norris to try and contact Brian Burke by telephone, which

he attempted unsuccessfully. I viewed Chelios' opening comment as threatening and his conduct both inappropriate and unprofessional.

While the quotes I attributed to Chris in the report were accurate, there was one that I left out for his own good. He told me he was going to shoot a puck at my head if he got the chance that night. Before I walked away, I said, "You better not finish getting dressed, because you might not be playing." It was then that I summoned league supervisor Will Norris and had him bring Hawks coach Darryl Sutter to our room. When Suds learned what Chris had said he was going to do to me, he rolled his eyes, uttered a profanity, and asked me what I wanted to do. I left the decision up to Sutter, but told him if he dressed Cheli and a puck came within five feet of me, he was going to miss 20 games. Darryl thanked me and said he would talk to him. Chelios dressed, and didn't even look at me throughout the entire game. He never even passed the puck near me, let alone shoot it in my direction. As far as I was concerned, the incident was over. As a matter of fact, beyond that year I developed an excellent working relationship with the Iron Man. Chris has had an amazing career, and his longevity was a tribute to his work ethic and skill.

I did actually take a puck in the head in Chicago, but not until four years later, and it was off the stick of Tony Amonte. I'm sure it was purely coincidental that Chris Chelios was still on the team. Brian Sutter, the eldest of the famous brothers, was behind the Blackhawks bench this time.

It was during a game against the Pittsburgh Penguins, and it was televised on ESPN. The Hawks were on a power play and Tony had set up in his own end, along the wall at the top of the faceoff circle, after the Pens had dumped the puck in. Since there was no forechecker on the play, I stopped five feet up ice from Tony, near the blue line. Both of us, I assumed, were anticipating the Chicago defenceman making a clean pass to Tony to start the play up ice. As the hard pass was fired to Amonte, his intentions obviously changed at the very last second, from taking the pass to angling his stick and deflecting the puck upward into my face! My elbow came up a fraction of a second too late to defend against the incoming projectile, and the puck broke my nose, fractured my front tooth, and cut my lip for seven stitches. Since there was no Blackhawk player up ice to take Tony's offering, I always found his decision to deflect the puck at the last second an unusual one.

It was midway through the third period and the Hawks were down by a goal. I couldn't continue because when I blew the whistle, blood sprayed out the whistle hole. I went over to Brian Sutter and said we would have to stop the game until I got sewn up. In keeping with the Sutter family tradition, Brian shook his head in disgust and said, "Fuck, Kerry, hurry up and get back. We're pressing!" After a quick stitch-up job in the medical room, I was back out for the end of the game but had to blow the whistle out of the side of my mouth.

I'd love to work a game between a whole team of Sutters (six brothers played over 5,000 games in the NHL and collectively won six Stanley Cups) against the Hunter boys (three brothers who accumulated four Stanley Cups). These guys would do anything to win and even fought each other when playing on opposing teams. I'd declare the last man standing the winner. I absolutely love those guys—each and every one of them.

When I arrived in the NHL, the Chicago Blackhawks were a proud franchise with a fan base that extended well beyond the limits of the Windy City. Arthur Wirtz and James E. Norris bought the Blackhawks in 1952 and set about rebuilding the team. Throughout the decade, they added Bobby Hull, Stan Mikita,

Pierre Pilote, goalie Glenn Hall, and Ted Lindsay, and won the Stanley Cup in 1961. They reached the finals again in 1962, 1965, 1971, 1973, and 1992. Arthur Wirtz's son Bill took over as president of the team in 1966 and held that position until his death in 2007. For 18 years, Mr. Wirtz was chairman of the NHL's board of governors and oversaw the merger with the World Hockey Association.

Bill Wirtz was often known as "Dollar Bill" because of the popular belief that he took a miserly approach to player salaries. Bill also alienated fans by refusing to televise the Hawks' home games—he felt it would negatively impact attendance if fans could watch the game on TV. In 1998, the Blackhawks' string of 28 consecutive playoff appearances came to an end, and they missed the post-season in nine of the next 10 seasons. At the lowest point, the team played to a half-full arena, and ESPN named the Blackhawks the worst franchise in all of professional sports. The mood was so ugly that, after Wirtz's death, while general manager Dale Tallon delivered a pre-game eulogy at the United Center, fans jeered him. But the fact remains that Chicago would not have even had the team if not for the Wirtz family's ownership. And on at least two occasions, I was in the company of Mr. Wirtz in his capacity as chairman of the board, and saw him both as a shrewd businessman as well as someone who really loved and cared about the game.

In my second year in the league, there was more than a growing concern that player violence and disrespect against on-ice officials had escalated beyond anything that could be tolerated by the members of the NHL Officials' Association. Referee Andy Van Hellemond was the most high-profile target of player abuse, having been crosschecked in the back by Barclay Plager of the St.

Louis Blues and then punched in the chest by Paul Holmgren of the Philadelphia Flyers. Van Hellemond, along with Dave Newell, president of the NHLOA, and legal counsel Jim Beatty, pulled NHL president John Ziegler away from the annual office Christmas party in Montreal on December 23, 1981, in an attempt to convey how serious our concerns were. It was felt that if stronger suspensions were imposed, players would refrain from what had been taking place. The league seemed to prefer the status quo.

So, Beatty wrote a letter to the NHL, which he released to the media, advising that, because the officials feared that their safety was not being adequately provided for—as the league was obligated to do under the collective bargaining agreement—we would begin "working to rule." The letter clarified what that meant: if a fight broke out, the referee and two linesmen would retreat to the safety of the officials' crease by the penalty box. When the combatants had finished fighting, they were to make their way to the penalty box and take their respective seats, at which time the referee would assess the appropriate penalties. I had a game in Winnipeg on the weekend the work-to-rule campaign began, and Jets tough guy Jim Kyte got into a fight behind the Winnipeg net. I immediately blew my whistle to stop play, and my colleagues and I went to the officials' crease and waited. As the two players continued to trade punches, we could see them both looking for the officials to step in. When that didn't happen, they stopped fighting, picked up their gloves and sticks, and, obeying the commands of my waving arm and whistle, took their places in the penalty box for five minutes.

By the time that weekend was over, the NHL agreed to act, and, to the satisfaction of the NHLOA, and through the courageous efforts of President Dave Newell, a "blue-ribbon committee" was created to discuss and implement changes. The panel consisted of team general managers, coaches, referees, NHL executives, and Alan Eagleson, executive director of the NHL Players' Association.

This group was given the task of fashioning a rule change to take effect, subject to the board of governors' approval, at the beginning of the 1982–83 season. Before the current season finished and the panel got to craft the new rule, Van Hellemond was punched again. This time, Terry O'Reilly of the Boston Bruins hit him with a wicked right cross to the side of his head during a playoff game against the Quebec Nordiques on April 25. O'Reilly was suspended by the NHL for the first 10 games of the next season and fined $500.

After its deliberations, the blue-ribbon committee put forward a tough policy known as Rule 67. This rule called for an automatic 20-game suspension for any player who "deliberately strikes, or who deliberately applies physical force in any manner against an official." It also specified an automatic three-game suspension for any player who "physically demeans" an official or who "deliberately applies physical force" to an official while being restrained during a fight with an opposing player. In both of these cases, the penalty and automatic suspension were to be imposed by the referee immediately after the game, and the player had *no right of appeal!* The thinking must have been that, with consequences as dire as these, there would never be another case of physical abuse against an official. That, however, was very wishful thinking.

The night before Halloween 1983, Tom Lysiak was playing for Chicago against Hartford. Linesman Ron Foyt had waved him out of the faceoff circle several times that night and, frustrated, he deliberately tripped Foyt after the puck was dropped. Dave Newell happened to be the referee of that game, and, under the rule he helped draft, suspended Lysiak for 20 games. All hell broke loose. Lysiak went to court and got a temporary injunction and scored a goal in the Hawks' next game in Detroit. Ultimately, the suspension stuck. Lysiak was never the same player. Unfortunately, Ron Foyt was terminated at the end of the following season, in what many of us considered a case of retribution over the Lysiak affair. The band of brothers, the underpaid and underappreciated officials, had stood firm. While the league saw us as becoming militant, we sought protection against player abuse that was getting out of control. It would not be the last time that Dave Newell and the officials' association would have to stand strong against the courts and the league.

Prior to the start of the 1984–85 season, all the referees were invited to Bill Wirtz's farm in an attempt to ease tensions that had resulted from the Lysiak–Foyt affair. The next time I saw Mr. Wirtz was in 1998 at the Winter Olympic Games in Nagano, Japan. I was seated with Kathy in the NHL's VIP section; I had been assigned as the standby referee for the gold-medal game between Czechoslovakia and Russia. The VIP section was situated at centre ice in a very steep-stepped balcony. We were in the front row with a low railing in front of us. I stepped out to allow Mr. and Mrs. Wirtz into their seats, and Mr. Wirtz caught his foot and appeared to teeter on the brink of falling over the rail. I immediately grabbed him by his belt and yanked him backward into his seat. Most appreciative of my quick reaction, and a little embarrassed by his stumble, Bill offered me his thanks. Fortunately, his seat was right beside mine.

Our conversation led to Bill asking who I thought would win. I told him the Czech team was the best I had seen through the games that I had worked in these Olympics. He said, "I'm glad you said that, because I placed my money on them in Vegas. I made the mistake of losing Dominik Hasek once, and I'm sure not going to bet against him again!" Hasek shut out Russia 1–0 to win the gold, and Mr. Wirtz got some return on his initial investment in the Dominator.

While I loved working in the old building, the fans of Chicago have Bill Wirtz (and Jerry Reinsdorf, owner of the Chicago Bulls)

to thank for the beautiful new United Center, which opened in 1994. Long gone are the rough-and-tumble days of Chicago Stadium: my shoes no longer stick to the concrete, nor do I walk past the beer kegs to access my dressing room. Something, however, has a very similar flavour to my early years in Chicago. Under the direction of Bill Wirtz's son Rocky, changes have been made and fans have returned in droves, and they're as vocal and boisterous as ever. A new winning tradition has been established. Rocky Wirtz hired marketing guru John McDonough from the Chicago Cubs to serve as president of the team, Stan Bowman replaced Dale Tallon as general manager, and the coaching experience of Joel Quenneville replaced Hawk fan-favourite Denis Savard, who remains in the organization as a community ambassador—along with Blackhawks legends Bobby Hull, Stan Mikita, and Tony Esposito.

Stan's father, Scotty Bowman, was hired as senior advisor of hockey operations. Scotty's tremendous contribution to every organization he has worked for is well documented. His understanding of the game and all its facets is unparalleled. Maybe surprisingly to some, Scotty's thirst for hockey knowledge is also unquenchable. Whenever I worked a game in his building, he would seek me out to ask a question. Usually, when a coach does this, it pertains to a call I had made the last time I had officiated a game involving his team. Not Scotty; he would ask about some play he had seen in one of the three games he had watched on TV the evening or two before, which included a late-night West Coast game. Scotty's fingerprints are all over the Blackhawks organization.

In 2009–10, Chicago has all the ingredients for a championship-calibre team. The core of young players are surrounded by such quality veterans as John Madden, Patrick Sharp, and Marián Hossa. Their top defence pair of Duncan Keith and Brent Seabrook, combined with Brian Campbell, comprise a top three as good as any in the league. The two young Blackhawks superstars,

Jonathan Toews and Patrick Kane, have come of age and both have the ability to take over a game. Toews reminds me so much of Steve Yzerman, it's uncanny. He hasn't quite developed the "edge" or "look" yet, but I know he's working on it. I recognized very early in the season that Jonathan would become a more "vocal and active" leader in his role as a 22-year-old captain.

On October 12, 2009, their rival the Calgary Flames were the guests at the United Center when they scored five goals in a span of just 4:30 midway through the first period to grab a commanding 5–0 lead and silence the usually raucous Madhouse crowd. John Madden got one back for the Hawks just before the teams went to the dressing room at the end of the first period. The momentum shifted and the crowd reignited when Patrick Kane scored at 7:37 of the second period, and assisted on two other Hawks goals and brought them within one goal of the Flames. Sandwiched between Kane's goal and one by Dustin Byfuglien, however, was a goalie interference penalty to the Hawks' Troy Brouwer when he charged hard to the Calgary goal and knocked Flames goalie Miikka Kiprusoff into the net. Fearing their comeback effort might be thwarted by the penalty, the young captain, Jonathan Toews, protested the obvious call vociferously with an attitude I had not seen from him since he had arrived in the league. He got a little fatherly attitude back when I said, "Son, I was calling that a penalty in this league when you were in diapers, so I think you better be a little more respectful and pick your spots when and how to complain."

The very next stoppage in play Jonathan came to me and apologized for his conduct and admitted he had crossed the line. This young star, mature beyond his years, has not only earned the respect of all of his teammates, but on this particular night from the most senior referee in the NHL. The Chicago Blackhawks came from behind to tie this game as they also scored five consecutive goals and then won it 26 seconds into overtime on defenceman

Brent Seabrook's goal. It demonstrated to me, very early in the season, just how poised this Hawks team was to make a run at the Cup.

I watched the Blackhawks toy with Edmonton on January 26 in Rexall Place. The Hawks owned the puck, and I couldn't help but think of it as a game of keep-away on a frozen pond. Kane, in particular, skated throughout the entire Oiler zone, from blue line to goal line, and no one could get the puck away from him. The Hawks reminded me that night of the Oilers of the early '80s. At the end of the game, as I made my way off the ice, Hawks coach Joel Quenneville walked alongside me. I pointed up to the rafters, where all the Oiler greats' retired jerseys hung, including Gretzky's, Messier's, Kurri's, Anderson's, and Coffey's. I asked Quenneville, "When you were playing, do you remember chasing those guys around the ice when they were still kids?"

"That's why they're up there," Joel replied with a grin.

I said that it was now the Oilers' turn, along with everybody else in the league, to chase *his* group of young stars. He acknowledged they are fun to coach, and I acknowledged they are fun to watch.

After my final game at the United Center, Quenneville would be chasing *me*—out of the building into the parking lot.

The line of fans waiting to get into the United Center for this afternoon's game was as long as the one that circled the entire block for the 10 a.m. Mass at Holy Name Cathedral in downtown Chicago. The Blackhawks were looking to clinch first place in the Central Division, while the visiting Calgary Flames were fighting for their playoff lives. The pressure on one team, at least, was relieved when it was announced that Philadelphia had beaten Detroit, 4–3, handing the division crown and a preferred playoff

seed to the Hawks. But you wouldn't have known it; the Blackhawks looked like the more desperate team, as if they were the
ones clawing for a spot in the post-season tournament. I got the
sense of a team that is turning on the afterburners at just the right
time.

The announced crowd of 21,537 (9.2 percent higher than the
official capacity of 19,717), gearing up for a long playoff run, was
using this game as a tune-up for when the "real season" began
just over a week later. The outcome was in little doubt as Tomas
Kopecky put Chicago ahead just 2:56 into the game. The Hawks
snuffed out the Flames' hopes as Troy Brouwer scored a back-
breaker with just 56 seconds left in the first period. When Patrick
Kane put the Blackhawks ahead 3–0 at 15:32 of the second period, I could see the shoulders of the Calgary players and coaching
staff sag. Ian White put the Flames on the board a minute later,
but Chicago wouldn't slow down. Dustin Byfuglien scored for the
Hawks late in the third period to put the cap on a convincing 4–1
win.

I was just relieved that big guy they call "Buf" shot the puck
at the net and not at me, as he had in a previous game. On that
night, he was about to carry the puck into the attacking zone and
decided he would dump the puck in hard and get off the ice for a
line change. His head was down the whole time, looking at his
skates and the puck. I anticipated a dump-in and moved a good
15 feet off the side boards as I backed to the top of the end zone
faceoff circle to allow Buf to ring the puck in around the boards.
Instead, he pounded it right at me without looking and hit me in
the thigh. It really stung and left a huge bruise. I just raised my
two hands to him in a confused gesture as if to suggest, *What the
hell are you doing?* At the first stoppage I went over to the Hawks'
bench and said, "Buf, the rink is 85 feet wide. I occupy two feet of
it, which leaves you with 83 feet of available space to shoot the
puck. Can you advise me where the safest place would be for me

to stand when you shoot it?" With his head half down and an embarrassed look on his face, Dustin Byfuglien said, "Your safest place would probably be by the net."

Leaving United Center ice for the last time, I paused to take one final look as the crowd remained on their feet and cheers continued to erupt, even after the Blackhawk players had left the ice. While the fans hung around, I had no time to linger. I had to shower quickly and rush off to the airport on this Easter-Sunday afternoon to catch a flight home. I said some final goodbyes before joining my crew in the parking lot. Just as I was getting into the rented SUV, I saw Joel Quenneville running out of the building, shouting my name. I found it rather unusual for a winning coach to be yelling in the parking lot, but after 30 years I don't take anything for granted. As I greeted Joel, he gave me a big hug and said, "They told me inside that you had left. I'm glad I didn't miss you. I just want to congratulate you on a fantastic career. You have been tremendous for the game and it will miss you." I was so touched that Joel would make this kind of special effort for me. I knew he would be delivering an emotional post-game address to his players for clinching first place in the Central Division; followed by media interviews he would have had to accommodate, yet he sprinted out of the building to bid me farewell. While the game will certainly survive without me, I will miss interacting with people such as Joel Quenneville, the fans cheering through the national anthem, and the big ship's horn over my head, sounding every time the Chicago Blackhawks score another goal.

While this book was being edited, Game Six of the Stanley Cup final took place at the Wachovia Center in Philadelphia. At 4:06 of overtime, with the score tied at three, Patrick Kane shot the puck from an impossible angle, it eluded Flyer goaltender Michael Leighton . . . and promptly disappeared under the protective fabric that lines the base of the net.

For a brief moment, Kane seemed to be the only person in the world who knew what had happened. The goal judge didn't turn on the red light, and referee Kelly Sutherland, who was forced out of position while avoiding player traffic, didn't point to indicate the puck was in the net. The clock continued to tick as Kane made a beeline toward goalie Antti Niemi. Finally, after a few seconds of confusion, the whistle blew, and after a brief review it was official: the Chicago Blackhawks had claimed the Stanley Cup for the first time since 1961.

ON BROADWAY: NEW YORK RANGERS

The house lights were down, and it was darker inside the arena than it was outside among the neon lights of New York City. The national anthem was being belted out with gusto by long-time soloist John Amirante as the New York Rangers and their archrivals, the Islanders, stood eyeing each other from their blue-line trenches. They were waiting for the puck to drop to begin Game Three of the 1981 Stanley Cup semifinals.

The contrast between the teams couldn't have been greater. The Islanders, the defending champions, had finished the regular season atop the NHL standings with 110 points. In the playoffs to date, they had won 9 of 11 games (they would ultimately go 15–3 to claim their second of four consecutive Cup titles). The 13th-place Rangers were, at the time, in a major dry spell bordering on a dust-bowl drought. They hadn't hoisted the Cup since 1940. Coach Fred Shero was fired after an abysmal 4–13–3 start, but they not only rebounded to make the playoffs, they upset fourth-place Los Angeles and second-place St. Louis. It seemed as though their luck had run out against the Islanders, though. They'd dropped 5–2 and 7–3 decisions on Long Island, and the series was shaping up to be a rout.

As the anthem reached its climax that night, so did the frenzy of the fans, and for an instant, the battle being described through song seemed to come to life. *And the rocket's red glare*—SMACK!—*The bombs bursting in air*—SPLAT! The ice was being pelted with a puzzling volley of squishy missiles. The lights came up and Billy Smith, goaltender for the Islanders and one of the players most hated by the Rangers faithful, was squatting in his cage, surrounded by giant sea bass heads that had been launched into the Islanders' end with the precision that only riotous fans can muster when the target is the visiting team.

This strong (and strong-smelling) statement was in part an homage to the old days of the Original Six, when a Detroit fan would throw an octopus onto the ice during the Stanley Cup playoffs to represent the number of games needed to bring home the Cup. The Rangers faithful must also have been making a less-than-cordial reference to the fisheries of Long Island Sound as they turned the ice into an inverted ocean.

The passion, and sometimes extremism, of hockey fans, especially those from New York, can be both exhilarating and dangerous. The locals have welcomed me with open arms, and they have called to issue threats against my life and insults against my family. Not long after our move to the States, Kathy took three of our young girls to a pre-season game the Rangers were playing on Long Island. As fans tend to do, the two sitting directly in front of my family, a guy and his girlfriend, clad in their Rangers jerseys, were cursing very colourfully at my officiating. Our middle daughter, Jessica, who was 10 at the time, became very frightened and started to cry at what she thought was their hatred for her dad. Kathy, being the loving mother that she is, leaned down to the girlfriend of the fan, advised her that the referee's family was sitting behind them and that while cheering was fine, their language was scaring her little girl. Kathy politely asked the girlfriend if she would mind telling him to tone it down. In response, the big, foul-mouthed buffoon turned in Kathy's direction and said, "Lady, if you don't like it, take them to the fucking Muppet Show!" That wasn't exactly the response Kathy was looking for. Then two big Islanders fans sitting in the row behind her rushed to the defence of my wife and children, shouting back, "Hey, asshole, didn't you hear what the lady said? You're scaring her kids." As the verbal battle escalated between rival fans, the mother hen, now caught in the middle, collected her brood and quickly moved off before a Pier 6 brawl broke out.

Despite episodes like that one, I keep coming back, and New York remained one of my favourite cities to referee in. It's not just Madison Square Garden, the calibre of play, or the energy of the fans, although that doesn't hurt. I love the city itself, for the opportunities and experiences it affords me and my family when I bring them here. That's why I've chosen to have two of my milestone games with the Rangers. Few places beat Manhattan for energy and flair.

In 1985, this passion unfortunately manifested itself in a call to my hotel room at 3:30 in the morning. It was my fifth year in the league, and those of you who remember my work on the ice back then might ask why it took someone so long to utter the threat, or even why he didn't make good on it. It's easy to joke about now, but on that frigid morning of February 26, I was just plain pissed off. The Rangers, coached by Craig Patrick, had been soundly trounced, 12–5, by the Winnipeg Jets the night before in a game that was unremarkable for anything other than the fact his team had taken the night off. Nothing controversial happened during the game, nor did the penalty stats suggest anything out of the ordinary. It was just an embarrassing blowout loss the Rangers suffered to a non-conference team they would only see three times all year.

Following the game, linesmen Ryan Bozak, Ron "the Bear" Asselstine, and I unpacked our equipment in our room at the New York Penta Hotel, across the street from the Garden, and scooted out the side door to join the boss, director of officiating John McCauley, for a few cold ones at the Blarney Rock. With all the great restaurants and bars in New York City, the Blarney Rock happened to be the officials' choice for post-game libation, not because it was a high-class establishment but because it was convenient (on Thirty-third Street, literally out the side door of the Penta) and the bartenders looked after us very well. The regular crowd that filed in after Rangers games never bothered any of us, and it was usually a friendly and safe environment. This bar was, unfortunately, the place where McCauley's career as an official had come to an end six years earlier. An out-of-towner from Kapuskasing, Ontario, sucker-punched him for a harmless comment after the Soviet National Team trounced a collection of NHL All-Stars in the third and final game of the 1979 Challenge Cup. John suffered permanently blurred vision from the punch, which multiple surgeries were unable to correct. It was then that he took on a management role as an officiating supervisor and ultimately as director of officiating.

We all had the next day off, so we relaxed as good conversation flowed as freely and abundantly as the beer. The four of us retired late, and it wasn't until 3:30 a.m. that I fell asleep in the city that never does. Shortly thereafter, I was jolted awake when the phone rang and a guy with a thick New York accent told me he had been at the Rangers game and was in the lobby. He said he had a knife and was going to kill me, first by cutting my balls off when I checked out! I immediately called security and told them to rush to the house phones to look for the "slasher." In one of my less intelligent moves, I then rushed down to the empty lobby, looking to confront my attacker. As the elevator doors opened, I was met by hotel security and informed that the call had come from an outside line and not via the house phones.

I returned to my room, but was so ticked off that I couldn't get back to sleep. I thought if I was up, McCauley should be too, so I called his room and told him of the threat. After listening patiently, John asked what time I was departing and then told me to go back to sleep. At 8:30, I paused and surveyed the large lobby of the Penta Hotel with a mix of angst and caution before getting out of the elevator. Standing guard behind three pillars, I could see Stickle, Bozak, and McCauley. They held their posts until I checked out, and then we formed a column and marched out of the hotel to grab a cab to the airport. All of my body parts remained intact.

The zeal that Rangers fans demonstrated was mirrored on the ice by the players, especially when it involved games with the Islanders. The physical battles were obvious, but the battles were also fought with words. There was none better at this form of warfare than pesky little forward Ray Ferraro. Ray would wait for the linesmen to arrive on the scene of a scrum, then fire off his best volley of insults. One night at Madison Square Garden, around Halloween, Tie Domi, who was playing for the Rangers then, was on the receiving end of one of Ray's best barbs. Physically, Tie did not exactly fit the mould of an NHL "heavyweight." He was short and stocky, with no neck and a rather large head. As tempers flared and verbal assaults were traded, Ferraro, from his position of safety, shouted, "Domi, with a fuckin' head like that, you should be sitting on someone's porch!" I had to stifle a laugh. Tie did not find the insult the least bit humorous and needed to be restrained by the linesmen from ripping Ferraro's head off to hang on the rear-view mirror of his car.

To their credit, Rangers fans suffered from the same frustration as the players and deserved full marks for loyalty. The championship drought finally ended when the team acquired a rainmaker by the name of Mark Messier, one of the greatest leaders the game has ever known.

The Rangers met the New Jersey Devils in the Eastern Conference final in 1993–94 and took a 2–1 lead in the series, then dropped back-to-back games and were on the verge of elimination heading into Game Six in New Jersey. But on the day of the game, Messier, the Rangers captain, boldly predicted his team would win.

At the end of the second period, I made a bold prediction of my own, shared only with my linesmen, Pat Dapuzzo and Gerard Gauthier, in the privacy of the officials' dressing room. I said, "Stick a fork in them—this Ranger team is done." The first two periods had been all New Jersey. Goalie Martin Brodeur looked unbeatable until Alex Kovalev found a minor chink in his armour with just 1:41 left in the second period. I didn't think the Rangers would solve him beyond that, nor did I believe they had enough left in the tank to pull off a road win. To make matters worse, they would begin the third period on the penalty kill, as Esa Tikkanen was in the box for kneeing Stéphane Richer.

It would be the last time I ever doubted the words of Mark Messier. He took the game on his back and tied the score by sliding a backhander past Brodeur just 2:48 into the third. We had a new game going! Mess then scored the go-ahead goal by pouncing on a rebound at 12:12, and the Rangers didn't look back from that point on. With 2:49 on the clock, Glenn Anderson of the Rangers two-handed Bernie Nicholls and took a slashing penalty. Fifty-six seconds later, Messier won a faceoff in the Rangers' zone, to the right of Mike Richter. Messier drew the puck back to his defenceman at the bottom of the faceoff circle, who moved the puck behind the goal to the other corner. John MacLean of the Devils got there first and tried to centre a pass in front of the net, but it went past the intended target and right onto Messier's stick in the slot. Mess turned with the puck and fired a shot right into the heart of the Devils' unguarded cage. Mark Messier made good on his "called shot" by scoring his first hat trick as a New York Ranger (a natural one, at that) to force Game Seven two nights later at Madison Square Garden. The feat has been described as one of the greatest individual efforts in the history of the game. It certainly made a believer out of me—and only 20 minutes before, I had all but written them off.

The Rangers won the seventh game and advanced to the Stanley Cup final against Vancouver on the strength of Stéphane Matteau's goal in double overtime. But my season was about to come to an abrupt end. Even though I was rated the league's number-one referee under its evaluation process, I had been very active as a member of the executive of the NHL Officials' Association during our strike against the league that season. Among other media support for our group, I had garnered headlines in a piece that went across the AP wire where I accused Commissioner Bettman of placing a gag order on players and coaches which restricted them from voicing displeasure for the work of the replacement officials. Immediately following this I was invited to appear on ABC News with Peter Jennings. The officials strike was coincidentally settled in a secret meeting that was held just as I was putting on my tie to drive to New York to meet with Jennings. I advised the producer of the show that we had reached a tentative agreement with the league and I would be unable to go on the air that evening. He extended an invitation for me to be part of their show to do a nice post-strike follow-up once we returned to the ice. When ABC contacted the league and requested permission for me to

appear, the NHL denied access to me but suggested Terry Gregson instead. The producer called me and said they were cancelling
the nice piece they planned to do because ABC would not be told
by the NHL or anyone else who they could use on air. All of this
obviously did not endear me to the commissioner. I fully understand that some form of retaliation can arise following labour
disputes like the one that we were embroiled in with the NHL. I
believe I was perceived as the enemy. While I might suggest that I
was a "casualty of the war" and that practices of this sort aren't
appropriate, I don't hold a grudge against the commissioner. He
has tremendous power within the game and he isn't opposed to
wielding it.

At the end of the conference finals, I received a telephone call
from the assistant director of officiating, Wally Harris, advising
me that I was done for the year. He told me I should be proud of
the fact that I had done such a good job for the NHLOA during
the strike—too good a job, as he put it. The order had come down
from Commissioner Bettman that under no circumstance was
Kerry Fraser to work the Stanley Cup final. It was just one example of the politics that can be found in all forms of business. You
can't fight city hall, although it wouldn't be the last time I tried.

As I sat at home with the final about to begin, the names of
the officials working the series were announced. I received a call
of support from an unusual source: my old "landlord," Mike
Keenan, who was now coach of the New York Rangers. He told
me that he and "Collie" (Colin Campbell, his assistant coach at
the time and present-day senior VP of hockey operations, my ultimate boss) wished to express their upset over the league's decision
not to use me to work in the final and that Mark Messier was also
very upset with the decision. According to Mike, Mess had told
him that "Kerry Fraser is the best referee in the National Hockey
League, bar none, and that it was an injustice to the game that he
wasn't chosen for the finals!" I took some consolation in these

sentiments while watching from the sidelines with the rest of the hockey world as the Rangers won the Stanley Cup in one of the most exciting finals of the modern day.

The mutual respect that I was so privileged to develop and share with Mark Messier, Wayne Gretzky, Ray Bourque, and so many other of the game's greatest players is something I will hold on to long after my final call has been made. When I took to the ice to work games involving legends such as these, I always received a friendly tap as they took their very first turn around the ice during the warm-up. It seemed as though they would seek me out in these moments to let me know they were confident that a fair game would be called and they were glad to see me.

The National Hockey League recognizes milestones for officials as well as players. The standard that every referee aspired to reach was 1,000 games. If you lasted that long, there was no doubt you'd had a great career. (Over the years, the benchmark for linesmen increased to 1,500 games, since they start their career directly in the NHL and do not log the time in the minor-pro ranks that referees put in.) Some thought and consultation go into where these milestone games will take place, as well as the choice of officials who will work alongside the one being honoured. In a pre-game on-ice ceremony, with family members assembled on the red carpet, a league vice-president or member of the officiating department management team presents the official with an Inuit soapstone carving when he reaches 1,000 games. In my case, an extra-long red carpet was required to accommodate Kathy, our seven kids, and my mother and father as they joined me to mark my 1,000th game on Friday, December 6, 1996.

Working with me on that special night were Pierre Champoux and Gerard Gauthier. I chose two "Original Six" teams (the Toronto

Maple Leafs and New York Rangers) at Madison Square Garden. It was extra special for me that the NHL's supervisor of officials, and my friend and former colleague Dave Newell (also a member of the 1,000-game club), was the one who presented me with the carving. A week later, I returned to Madison Square Garden for another game, and afterward there was a knock at the dressing-room door. Tommy Horvath, a dear friend who works the Rangers' home games as an equipment and room attendant, walked in and said, "Gretz asked me to give you this." It was one of Wayne's Easton silver-tip sticks, with this inscription on the blade: TO KERRY, CONGRATULATIONS ON YOUR 1000TH GAME, WAYNE GRETZKY 99.

On Saturday, March 30, 2003, in Chicago, I set a new record for the most NHL regular-season games worked by a referee (1,476), eclipsing the old mark set by Andy Van Hellemond. Eight months later, November 30, for my 1,500th game, Bill Daly, the deputy commissioner of the National Hockey League, presented me with a Tiffany crystal in a pre-game ceremony, again at Madison Square Garden and with the same two teams, Leafs and Rangers, looking on. We were now working under the two-referee system and I was honoured to share the chores with my son-in-law Harry Dumas, as well as linesmen Ray Scapinello and Pat Dapuzzo.

Unbeknownst to me, Kathy commissioned an outstanding local artist by the name of Phoebe Darlington to do a pencil sketch measuring four feet by three feet. I was at the centre of the piece, surrounded by legendary players with whom I'd shared the ice. Kathy had a very difficult time settling on which great players she wished to depict; there were so many, but she could only include four. She chose Mario Lemieux of the Pittsburgh Penguins, Wayne Gretzky (as an Edmonton Oiler), Guy Lafleur of the Montreal Canadiens, and Mark Messier (as a New York Ranger) to adorn each corner. In the centre, I appear in profile, with the 9/11 patch on the sleeve of my jersey, forever in remembrance. Also depicted is my father, around the time he played in the International Hockey League, holding my hand as a little guy and teaching me to skate. My dad passed on September 2, 2001, just nine days before the attacks on the World Trade Center and the Pentagon, and United Flight 93 was downed in a Pennsylvania field by heroes in the form of passengers. Sharing space beside Dad is my mentor and former boss, John McCauley. Touching my chin and shedding rays of light downward upon the deceased is the Holy Spirit. Various special game pucks are displayed, like the 1985 Stanley Cup final (my first), the 1998 Winter Olympics in Nagano, Japan, the 1996 World Cup of Hockey, and the 2000 All-Star Game in Toronto.

Kathy asked Mark Messier to present this beautiful piece of artwork to me on behalf of the Fraser family. Due to television time constraints, Kathy was told that Mark would have to present it at a post-game reception she was hosting in the Garden Club. When word got to Mark about Kathy's special request, he insisted on presenting it on the ice before the game, and he did. Who would argue with the Moose? I was blown away when Mess skated toward us and directed me to one side of the draped artwork. As we unveiled it, I was brought to tears. At the end of the game, Mark further honoured me by asking if we could sign and exchange sweaters that we wore in the game that evening.

At the end of the 2003–04 season, I was assigned to the Rangers' last game, at home against Buffalo. There was speculation that this might also be Mark Messier's last game, even though he wouldn't confirm it to the media. But when I saw the emotions that Mark displayed that night, I felt confident that the buzz was correct: this would be Messier's final game in the National Hockey League. As he skated past and tapped me on the pants, there was something very different about him. Normally, in moments like this, our eyes would meet momentarily and I could always see a boyishness in the man they called Moose. "The Look" that had instilled the fear of God in so many opponents would soften as he prepared to join in a kid's game of shinny, and he'd flash a blazing smile that told it all. Mark Messier just loved to play the game. Tonight, his eyes were misty and that impish twinkle was harder to detect.

After the national anthem was sung and Mark and I stood alone at centre ice awaiting the Buffalo centreman, Mess held that famous pose with his stick across the top of his shin pads, looked over to where his family was sitting, and fixed a gaze upon them for as long as his ragged emotions would allow. This gladiator then turned his tear-filled eyes upward toward me and uttered a sentence I will never forget: "Kerry, I wouldn't have wanted anyone else here but you!" The ultimate compliment that this great ice general paid to me before his final game will be etched in my heart and mind forever. It was *my* honour to be there.

Mark's family was seated along the glass near the penalty box, and a new "assistant coach," Mark's 17-year-old son Lyon, stood behind the bench. Dressed meticulously in a suit, Lyon stood as stiff as a statue for fear of being noticed and removed from the bench by the referee. He didn't have to worry: there was no way that was going to happen—although, during a TV timeout, I went over to Rangers coach Tom Renney and said that if this "new assistant coach" of his opened his mouth one more time, I was giving them a bench penalty. Poor Lyon just about had a heart attack, until the bench broke out laughing. Mess gave me a smile and a wink, and mouthed the words "thank you."

During the game, Mark scored the 694th and final goal of his career. The Rangers fans, in appreciation of all that he had done for them, especially for ending the 54-year Stanley Cup drought, rose to their feet and chanted, "God bless Mess!"

On April 7, 2010, I entered my dressing room at Madison Square Garden an hour and a half before game time. A parting gift had been placed on my chair. It was a bag from Tiffany & Company, which held a sterling silver apple. Engraved on one side was the New York Rangers emblem; on the other side, below my name, was the inscription:

> THANK YOU FOR THIRTY THREE YEARS OF
> EXCEPTIONAL DEDICATION TO THE NHL.
> YOUR FRIENDS AT THE NEW YORK RANGERS.

I was touched by the words and generosity of Rangers general manager Glen Sather, special assistant Mark Messier, and their staff in my last visit to the Garden. As I read this inscription, the faces of all the great Rangers players, coaches, and staff flashed in my mind's eye, reminding me of the memories we shared during the years that are etched on the gift I now hold in my hand.

My emotions are still raw when I take to the ice, with the Toronto Maple Leafs once again in the Big Apple. This is a game that the Rangers absolutely must win if they have any hope of making the playoffs. They could then control their own destiny against the Philadelphia Flyers in this same building two nights later and in Philadelphia on the final Sunday of the regular season.

Before dropping the puck at centre ice to start the game, I looked for my family seated in the crowd, just as Mark Messier had done six years earlier. Even though I knew they couldn't hear me as my misty eyes connected with theirs, I mouthed the same words that Mess offered to me: "I wouldn't have wanted anyone else here but you!

A SHORT STOP
IN NEVER-NEVER LAND:
BOSTON WINTER CLASSIC

I awoke before the 7:00 a.m. alarm sounded in our darkened suite at the Marriott Marquis Times Square and quickly turned it off so as not to disturb Kathy, who slept peacefully beside me. A smile etched on her angelic face gave me cause to believe that her subconscious was replaying the wonderful evening spent with some of our children for my last visit to Madison Square Garden. The sweet slumber was much needed. I wasn't the only one grinding it out as the end of my final season nears. Kathy accompanied me on some of my last visits to the Original Six NHL cities while also planning and preparing the festivities that would begin when I returned home from Boston.

By this time, my brother Rick, his wife, Karen, and my mother, Barb, would already have left Sarnia to make the eleven-hour drive to our home in southern New Jersey. Kathy would be home in time to greet them. Our son Matthew, his wife, Kristy, and our little granddaughters, two-and-a-half-year-old Madyn and eight-month-old Daryn, would be hitting the road tomorrow morning, as soon as Matt's work schedule, as a firefighter in London, Ontario, allowed. Kathy and I were so excited at the thought of getting our children (all seven) together again under our roof. Adding to our joy, all five grandchildren would be with us too. Madyn and Daryn would be meeting their cousins Harrison (age eight), Brady (soon to be six), and baby Kiera (six months) for the first time. They live two doors up from "Mama" and "Papa," with our oldest daughter, Marcie, and her husband, Harry.

Meanwhile, I had one more road game to officiate, in one of my favourite cities, not just in the NHL but the whole United States. Much as I love the city and its people, Boston is also the site of my most memorable game—and of all places, in a ballpark!

I quietly repacked my officiating equipment, which I had spread out to dry in the living room of the suite last night—including my undergarments, which hung from the chandelier over the dining room table. Hockey officials don't have the luxury of equipment managers to pack, dry, and launder their gear. If I am lucky enough to get a hotel room with a balcony, or, as in this case, a large suite, I am spared the odours that make me feel like I'm sleeping in a dressing room.

I was booked on the 8:30 Acela train out of Penn Station, located under Madison Square Garden. Kathy was awake by now, and after we chatted briefly about the night before, I kissed her goodbye and grabbed a cab.

Since we moved to New Jersey, I pretty much drove to games in Washington, Philadelphia, and the New York area so that I could come straight home afterward. When I worked in Boston, I usually flew with US Airways out of Philadelphia. I had forgotten how pleasant train travel in the Northeast Corridor can be—once you finally get on it, that is. The Thursday-morning rush hour is already in full swing, and Penn Station is the subterranean domain of commuters caught up in the New York rat race rushing and pushing to get to street level or make subway connections. As the train pulled out of Penn Station, I couldn't help but think fondly of all the memories that had been made just a few floors "upstairs" on the MSG ice.

Riding the rails is an extremely pleasant and relaxing experience. The telephone poles seemed to fly past my window as quickly as the games and years of my on-ice career. As the train sped along, I continued to find myself not looking ahead to my final game in the TD Garden, but focusing on days past—to a time when my approaching workplace was Boston Garden, where the home team enjoyed a well-deserved reputation that was captured perfectly in their nickname: the Big Bad Bruins. Their loyal and boisterous fans never wanted the tradition to end. The Garden was an intimidating building with steep balconies that seemed to hang right over the ice, giving the impression that the fans were right on top of you; some nights it even felt like they shared the ice with you. One night, a crazy fan literally did.

The guy lost his mind over a call he thought Bill McCreary should have made, climbed over the glass, and started to jog toward him. McCreary was standing on the goal line with his back to his unannounced attacker, waiting for the puck to be dropped. As the would-be assailant approached McCreary, linesman Ron Asselstine, who once had a tryout with the Montreal Alouettes of the Canadian Football League and was known as the Bear, saw what was taking place. He worked up a full head of steam and speared the guy with his helmet, right between the shoulder blades, driving and carrying him into the end boards all in one hard pop. The guy never knew what hit him as he went headfirst into the boards. The rink attendants opened a gate and Asselstine tossed the guy through the door to waiting security officers. Without question it was the best hit of the season in that building, and in Boston, that was saying something.

Like the Boston fans, coach Don Cherry was a blue-collar, lunch-bucket kind of guy. He was no longer the coach in 1980–81, my first season in the NHL, but he had made his mark on the organization. There could be as much appreciation for Terry O'Reilly or Stan Jonathan's penalty minutes as Rick Middleton's 103 points or all that Brad Park brought every night. Wayne Cashman was as much a hero for his grit and ability to scare the hell out of opposing players (and me) as Ray Bourque was for his end-to-end rushes and wicked slapshots.

It was a pleasure and honour to see, up close, the gentlemanly skill of Jean Ratelle in his 21st and final season in the league. Mr. Ratelle (I say with deep respect), who amassed 1,267 points in 1,281 games, was cut from the same bolt of cloth as Jean Béliveau. They both have an aura of elegance about them.

One regret I must admit to having is that I never refereed a game involving the greatest player in Bruins history, and without a doubt, one of the greatest players the game has ever known. Robert Gordon Orr, in my humble opinion, changed the game like no other. He revolutionized the defence position and could take over a game at will. He wasn't regarded as a Big Bad Bruin, even though he was never a slouch in the penalty-minute department, but he stood alone as the finest offensive defencemen to ever play the game. He was the only defencemen ever to win the NHL scoring title, and he did it twice. His knee problems, sadly, cut short his career, forcing him to retire in 1976 at the age of 28. I was 24 at the time and still four years from my NHL debut.

Our paths would cross, however, and each time they did, it filled me with such awe to be in the presence of this hockey legend. During the 1990 Stanley Cup final, when Mark Messier's Oilers defeated the Bruins, I took my dad, Hilt, with me to Boston. We had our own morning skate at the Garden and played some pond hockey. Bobby stopped by to say hello. Once he showed up, my dad left the ice and the game. I'll never forget how kind and gracious Bobby Orr was to my dad as they sat on the Bruins bench together and chatted. My father spoke of that meeting often until the day he died in 2001.

I felt that same sense of awe most recently, watching Orr stand with another legend whom I did have the privilege to referee, Bobby Clarke, for the ceremonial faceoff at the Winter Classic on New Year's Day, 2010.

One of the great lessons off the ice that I've learned in this business is that when we are given the opportunity to touch people's lives we should take it. In the same vein, I have been touched by many in my career. One of the most special was by Nate Greenberg, the Bruins' former director of public relations. Nate joined the Bruins in 1973, and in 1988 became the assistant to the president. He was there with Orr, Espo, Cashman, Johnny "Pie" McKenzie, and the rest of a group of characters who played hard on and off the ice. Their antics must surely have presented a challenge for a PR person given the task of making sure the public saw the organization in its best light. Win, lose, or draw, good calls or bad, Nate was always the same friendly face who would stop by after the game to say hi and wish you well. The Bruins lost a gem when he retired a couple of years ago, and I am proud not only to have known him, but to call him my friend.

When it comes to public relations, the annual Winter Classic is one of the most intelligent things the NHL has ever done. About the only thing that could top it would be to take head shots out of the game. I don't know who thought of it, but I am sure there was a long line of folks with thumbs pointed toward their chests until someone at the top put his name on it, but whoever it was, good for you—and better for the fans, players, officials, and, most important, the game. This event has taken on a life of its own, and has followed the pattern set by the Super Bowl in terms of the way the hype begins to build well before the actual game is played. For the game at Fenway Park in 2010, hotels in the city and surrounding area were booked up, and it was hard to get a table at the better eateries in Boston. The Boston Red Sox also benefited from the chance to rent out their facility at a time of year when the only thing that might have been thrown on that historic field was snowballs, by the custodial staff and security guards.

Once the rink was built by NHL guru Dan "Iceman" Craig, high school and college teams staged games and practices on this hallowed ground, as did anyone who could afford the hefty hourly rental fee. Skating parties and city events planned through the office of Mayor Thomas Menino were a great way to market all that Boston had to offer during the festive season. Hockey fans old and new (and it's always a great thing when new fans catch the hockey bug) couldn't wait to share a beer and a braut with Red Sox fans and see if a Bruin or Flyer could shoot one off the Green Monster.

After 30 years in the hockey business, which, prior to the game at Fenway, included more than 2,100 games in the NHL, two All-Star Games, a dozen Stanley Cup finals, the World Cup of Hockey, the Winter Olympic Games, and opening the 2008–09 season in Prague, Czechoslovakia, I have to admit that I caught the Winter Classic fever, too. This wasn't an ordinary event where I would just show up and go to work. This was way more than just another regular-season game that meant two points for someone.

Two years ago, when I negotiated a succession-planning agreement with Terry Gregson and Stephen Walkom, who was then the NHL's senior VP of officiating, one of my "demands" was to be able to work the Winter Classic of my choice. I knew how special this event would turn out to be, and I wanted to be a part of it. When Walkom reneged and assigned Bill McCreary and Tim Peel to work the 2009 game at Wrigley Field in Chicago, my only recourse was to accept the 2010 game, at a location that had yet to be determined. I couldn't believe my good fortune when Fenway was chosen.

I wasn't the only one who was excited about the trip to Boston for this extravaganza. Most of our children were able to make it to Boston, and Kara said she'd even bring her own tea to the party. Accommodation was booked well in advance at the historic Marriott Custom House, near the wharf and Faneuil Hall. We set up camp the day after Christmas and prepared to take in all that the wonderful city of Boston had to offer.

I had to leave briefly for a game in Ottawa between the Senators and Montreal Canadiens on December 28, then flew back into Boston the following day to rejoin my family. It was a bitterly cold day as Kathy, Kara, and I walked through Boston Common on our way to Fenway to pick up our credentials. The wind felt like it was eating our faces, so we ducked into Filene's, made some unfashionable but smart purchases, and then grabbed a taxi in Copley Square to take us the rest of the way to Fenway.

As we entered an old residential area, it appeared that the only ballpark in this confined space would be a sandlot. Pulling up to the old brick structure, I was reminded of what Roger Clemens said when he arrived in Boston for the first time in 1984 and told the cab driver at Logan Airport to take him to Fenway Park. As the taxi pulled up in front of the stadium, Clemens told the driver, "No, Fenway Park. It's a baseball stadium. . . . This is a warehouse." It wasn't until he saw the light towers that he realized it was a ballpark. I now understood his confusion. My perspective would change in a couple of days.

Before we got a chance to skate in centre field, I had a Bruins game to work on Wednesday, December 30, as the Atlanta

Thrashers visited TD Garden. The Bruins won 4–0, limiting the Thrashers to just 18 shots on Tuukka Rask while combining for 30 on Johan Hedberg and Ondrej Pavelec. The Bruins put on a defensive clinic.

When I witnessed this shutout recorded by Boston, I couldn't help but wonder about the effect that assistant coach Craig Ramsay has had on this team. His defensive prowess as a Selke Trophy winner in Buffalo has obviously carried over from his playing days in the '80s, to his coaching over the past 15 years in the NHL. As a player Craig was very methodical, utilizing angles to cut down the ice space of his opponents, always "thinking" the game instead of just playing it. As a coach, Rammer is the consummate teacher to young and old players alike and I can't help but think that his quiet but studious influence has already made its mark on Boston.

After the Thrashers game, Terry Gregson, who replaced Walkom as senior VP of officiating when the latter returned to refereeing, informed us that our time slot for a family-and-friends skate on the ice at Fenway was scheduled for between 9 and 10 a.m. So the next morning, New Year's Eve Day, my small army of 20 assembled early at the press gate. My gang excitedly joined the other officials' families and friends to fill in the paperwork, signing waivers before being allowed to enter Fenway. Between Chris Rooney's large family and mine (Chris was the other referee assigned to the Winter Classic), it was suggested there were enough of us to play a game.

After only a few steps past the press gate turnstile, I had the sense I was walking into a mausoleum. Entering through a green door (everything was green) in a plywood wall, we were transported into another world of vendors' booths and an underside of the bleachers that displayed construction from the stadium's opening in 1912. We were ushered through a gate where I imagined gentlemen with straw hats and spats and ladies with frilled dresses and parasols must have entered back in the day. As I walked beyond the darkness of this dimly lit corridor, the world of 1912 meshed with the Winter Classic of 2010 and exploded in the bright sunlight and crisp air. I stood, frozen in my tracks. Not by the cold, but by the sheer awe I felt in this intimately historic setting. Looking through the backstop behind home plate and scanning the field, I felt as though I was looking at a lithograph. The Green Monster, with Fisk Foul Pole atop it, Pesky's Pole down the right field line, and "the Triangle," which encroached centre field at its deepest part, all seemed within my grasp. And then, as though it had been air-dropped into this hallowed ground, stood the rink. It rose up from the ground and awaited our arrival to glide and play and pay our respects to the two historic sports leagues that joined forces to ring in the new year in such a spectacular fashion. I looked at my children as their eyes widened and their jaws dropped. Everyone was spellbound in that instant.

The frozen moment quickly gave way to excited energy as the inviting ice surface, freshly flooded and made pristine by the superstar talent of Dan Craig and his all-star staff selected from various arenas around the league, waited. The ice looked like a piece of artwork that was too perfect to blemish with the slashing of skate blades, but no one could resist. Our "field of dreams" beckoned us as we walked through our make-believe cornfield and the open players' bench door. Stepping onto the artificial ice that seemed as natural as Whitey Stapleton's outdoor rink back home in Sarnia, we were all transported back in time to a place that held special memories for each of us. In that magical moment, we all became kids again.

When our hour of play had concluded, I gathered my troops and headed back to the Marriott to feed the army made ravenous by the fresh air and exercise. It started to snow quite heavily after brunch, resulting in a scene befitting our Canadian heritage. That afternoon, the snow was too inviting to watch from the window, so we all decided to go for a walk through the streets of Boston and take in the beauty of this historic city. Our oldest daughter, Marcie, a 35-year-old mother of three, was the first to make a snowball and pitch it straight at the back of my head. Everyone, including me, burst out laughing, and before we knew it, the Fraser family was hurling snowballs back and forth, right in front of the aquarium on the waterfront. Our grandsons, Harrison and Brady, found themselves in the middle of an adult battle and laughed with glee as they popped one off Papa's chest. The tour guide operators and the line of out-of-towners waiting to board a trolley must have thought the Hatfields and McCoys had just arrived. What an afternoon!

Back at the hotel, we all sipped coffee or hot chocolate and decided we had better get ready for New Year's Eve. Silently, I had already started to prepare for the game the next afternoon. I was filled with joy at the thought of spending the evening with my family, but was especially excited that they were here to share this memorable game with me.

Because of the size of our group, not to mention varying tastes, we split up for dinner, then gathered back at the hotel, with its large clock tower and walk-around balcony from which the entire city can be seen. We huddled together by the rail at midnight, overlooking the river basin, with Logan Airport off in the distance. From here, we had the best seat in the city to take in the fireworks that were being launched off a number of barges, and illuminating the clear night sky. It was an unforgettable display that began at midnight, as we all embraced as a loving family and looked forward to a new year with much hope for all.

After a good night's sleep, I awoke in game mode. I would have to leave my family for the ballpark (strange not to say *rink*) well in advance of my normal pre-game arrival time, due to the sheer size of the crowds and the many street activities that were taking place around Fenway. I was advised to take the T, the underground metro. Dragging my equipment bag through the snow that hadn't stopped until early this morning, I boarded the already jammed T car at 9 a.m. (Kathy and the kids would follow on their own later.) At the stop for Fenway Park, I moved with the crowd up the stairs and squinted like a groundhog as I stepped into the bright sunlight on this glorious New Year's Day. The scene surrounding Fenway was incredible. The streets were jammed with mobs of people. They weren't stragglers from the New Year's Eve celebrations; these were hockey fans participating in and savouring every special moment. I fought my way through the crowd and heard many calls from fans to "call 'em fair" and to "be good to us today, Fraser." All were in a joyous and festive mood.

Walking through that same little green door I had used for the family skate the day before, I now clearly knew that I was in a ballpark. The space under the stands bustled with activity as vendors and hawkers stocked their stands. The smell of beer, grilled onions, and bratwurst wafted in clouds of billowing smoke that hung in the air.

It was time to seek the shelter of the umpires' room and prepare physically and mentally for the game. A smorgasbord of hot chicken noodle soup, fresh fruit, and sandwiches had been set out for after the game. Hot chocolate and coffee were at the ready should we need to warm up between periods—in case Jack Frost came out to play. We were provided with special undergarments, gloves, and hooded masks that are used in the NFL. All I would need was the underwear to keep me warm.

Each of us tried to prepare for the game according to his normal routines of stretching and biking, even though it was impossible to see anything about this game as normal or routine. Before we put on our skates, the officiating crew—referee Chris Rooney and linesmen Lyle Seitz (also retiring at the end the season) and Brian Murphy—were summoned to home plate for a ceremonial exchange of lineups. Bruins coach Claude Julien sported a fedora as a homage to Toe Blake, who led the Montreal Canadiens to eight Stanley Cups between 1955 and 1968. His assistant coach, Craig Ramsay, looked like famous Dallas Cowboys coach Tom Landry in his fedora. After the lineups were given to the "umpires"/ referees, I asked both coaches if they wanted me to go over the ground rules and mentioned that the Green Monster was in play. The intertwining of baseball and hockey made me feel blessed to be standing in this spot. Before walking out of the umpires' room, I had touched the pictures that hung on the wall of the first two umpires inducted into the National Baseball Hall of Fame in Cooperstown, New York: Bill Klem, known as the "father of baseball umpires," who worked in 18 World Series; and Tom Connolly, known for standing firm against the toughest players of the game in defence of the rules. As I touched their pictures, I carried them in my thoughts to home plate, along with my very dear friend, retired umpire and umpiring supervisor Marty Springstead. I was walking on their turf now, and home plate at Fenway Park, where I was about to stand for the very first time, was their sacred ground.

The warm-up now over, we returned to our borrowed dressing room, laced up our skates, and vowed to one another to enjoy the moment. To get to the ice, we had to traverse a corner of the visiting team's locker room, and proceed down a tunnel to the dugout and ultimately the field. I saw a different form of excitement on the Flyers' faces as I strolled by. They also knew this was a special moment that they would remember long after their playing days were done. I walked down three steps and found myself in a narrow, dimly lit tunnel leading to the dugout. I quickly realized I was walking where so many legends had been before: Babe Ruth, Lou Gehrig, Ted Williams, Carl Yastrzemski, Carlton Fisk, Roger Clemens, and more. I touched the sides of the walls, knowing that so many baseball heroes had brushed against them. At first, there was an eerie silence until I made it up the steps of the dugout and the park came alive. People were standing, cheering wildly as we stepped into the jammed park and the daylight. They weren't cheering for us; rather, they cheered because we represented an omen that the arrival of the teams was imminent. Walking to the rink and removing my skate guards before stepping onto the ice, I was greeted by old friend Bobby Clarke. I found it easier to recognize him with his teeth in today than in the early '80s, when I started my career.

I ripped around the ice with youthful enthusiasm and tried to scour the stands in search of Kathy and the children. For a moment, I had forgotten that I was now in a baseball stadium, and locating fans in the seats from deep at shortstop or in shallow centre field was not an easy task. But for a fleeting second, I thought I heard my sometimes overenthusiastic daughter Jessica screaming, "Go Fraser!"

I was drunk on the taste of the crisp air and the sunshine that reflected off the polished ice. Although the temperature was 40 degrees Fahrenheit when we arrived on the ice, the wind against my face felt frigid as I sped along. I noticed my eyes were watering; since I don't skate quite as fast as I used to, I thought perhaps I was just caught up in the emotion of it all and they were real tears. Either way, I glided along and danced on this frozen river a little longer, then gave way to the teams, stood by the penalty box, and drank it all in. Between the players' benches, two diminutive ex-goaltenders turned television analysts, Darren Pang and Glenn Healy, stood ready to broadcast. The smell of bratwurst wafted over their heads.

Bobby Clarke and Bobby Orr lined up at centre ice for a ceremonial faceoff. I dearly wanted to drop the puck between these two legends, but that honour was reserved, deservedly so, for U.S. Army staff sergeant Ryan R. LaFrance, who had served multiple tours in Afghanistan and Iraq.

Looking at the lineup sheets, I couldn't help but think there was an omission on the Bruins' side of the ledger. Where was Raymond Bourque, the man I think of as the face of the Boston

Bruins? Many times during his playing career, Ray would approach me quietly after the national anthem and say, "Kerry, if we win the draw back to me, be sure to step back because I'm going to pound one at their net." After he issued that warning to me one night, I got tangled up momentarily with the opposing centre and did not retreat as quickly as Ray—or I—desired. Ray wound up to let it go, then, seeing my eyes widening in fear with the realization that I was in his line of fire, he held up, double-pumped, and waited until the coast was clear.

Boston native James Taylor sang "The Star-Spangled Banner," while Daniel Powter performed "O Canada" beautifully as well. The starting six for each team was ready to go, but I had not yet been given the signal to drop the puck. The officiating crew and I stood at centre ice, waiting and listening for what we had been told would be an air force flyover. But the air above Fenway Park was still. Anticipation turned to discomfort when nothing happened immediately. Then, from beyond the Green Monster, a hulking dark shadow appeared in the shape of a giant black bat. The stealth bomber, true to its name, appeared ominously, passed over, and was gone. I was informed it was two states from us as we waited and closed the distance in a matter of seconds.

We officials performed our own ritual, one we had initiated after we returned from the lockout season, during which one of our dear friends and colleagues, linesman Stéphane Provost, died in a traffic accident. Each of us touched our heart, our shoulder, and our fists as we remembered our fallen comrade. All was ready. My colleagues assumed their positions, and I called the two starting centremen to centre ice for the faceoff. I then touched my heart for Kathy and the kids, raised my whistle hand to the scorekeeper, offered a quiet "Play Ball," and snapped the puck to the ice as the game got under way.

It was such a unique feeling to be outdoors again as we all returned to our hockey roots and felt the surge of boyishness that I know I had long forgotten. It returned, as suddenly as the stealth that had flown overhead, as soon as I dropped the puck. The sensation was invigorating and caused me to question whether I had perhaps discovered the NHL equivalent to the fountain of youth. If that was so, why would I ever want to retire? At 12:01 of the first period, Daniel Carcillo of the Flyers and Shawn Thornton of the Bruins exchanged some good punches. I really like both of those guys and have a great deal of respect for the way they come to play every night. At the end of the scoreless first period, I went into the umpires' room, grabbed my cellphone, and hastily sent a text to Kathy, asking her where she was sitting and telling her I felt "just like a kid again." I signed it "Peter Pan."

At 4:42 of the second period, Danny Syvret stepped into the slot from his point position and scored the first goal of the game on Bruins goalie Tim Thomas, who had gotten himself tied up with pesky forward Scott Hartnell and put himself in a poor position. The way Thomas and Flyers goalie Michael Leighton were playing, it looked as if that goal might just be the game winner. Leighton had not allowed a goal for 154 minutes and 7 seconds when former Flyer Mark Recchi scored on a power play with just 2:18 left in the third period to force "extra innings."

The Flyers entered the overtime killing a late tripping penalty to Daniel Brière, and the play was end to end. The sellout crowd of 38,112, most of whom stood throughout the game, were all standing and cheering at this point. Jeff Carter had a great opportunity on a two-on-one rush and missed the open side of the net, then Boston picked up the puck and capitalized on their rush up ice as Marco Sturm put the game away at 1:57 of overtime. The only way the ending could have been better scripted would be if the game had gone to a shootout.

Back in the warmth of the umpires' room, each of us savoured the memory of what we had just experienced—moments that would be locked into our minds and hearts for the rest of our days. While it was one game out of the 2,165 of my career, I will never be able to say that it was just another game. I can say without reservation that the 2010 Winter Classic at Fenway Park was the most special game—and sporting event of any kind—that I have ever experienced in my life.

Kathy, our children, our grandsons, and other family members came down to the umpires' room to share in the joy and celebration that we all felt at being part of this historic and special event. All Kathy had to do was take one look at the smile etched on my face to know that the man she loves and calls "the Wayne Gretzky of refereeing" had taken a trip to Never-Never Land and returned a better man for it.

On the way home that night, I received a telephone call from Marty Springstead in Florida. Marty had watched the game on NBC and heard Hockey Hall of Fame broadcaster Mike Emrick say some very nice things about me, as well as the quotes I provided him before the game about Fenway and the baseball legends I had thought of. Marty was overtaken with emotion at the thought that we, as old friends, had shared the experience of officiating in a place that was so dear to him and had provided him with many memories over his distinguished career. Two men, who had reached the top of their professions as officials in our respective sports, reconnected in that special moment where the ice met the outfield of Fenway Park.

The train jolted to a stop at Boston's South Station, and I was similarly jolted from my dreams of the Winter Classic—my "Never-Never Land"—to the present reality that my Peter Pan days were now over. I was forced to focus on the night's game, my final one in Boston. The old Garden may be long gone, but as I entered our dressing room in TD Garden, I was greeted by a link to the past:

Eddie Sandford, the official scorer in Boston since I arrived in the league, and a legendary former player with the Bruins, Red Wings, and Blackhawks, brought in the lineup sheets. Since the inception of the two-referee system, the junior referee is handed the sheets to take to the ice for safekeeping. On this night, Ed broke with protocol and, as he had done many times when I was the sole referee, handed them to me. It was a nostalgic moment for both of us.

The Bruins won the game, 3–1, which kept them in the three-way race with Philadelphia and the New York Rangers for the final playoff spots in the Eastern Conference. As it turned out, the Bruins did qualify for the post-season, earning the sixth seed and facing these same Buffalo Sabres in the first round. The game I worked offered a glimpse of the way the matchup would shake out: the Bruins won in six games, almost all of which were decided by just one or two goals. Boston then met their Winter Classic opponents, the Flyers, and held a 3–0 lead in Game Seven at TD Garden, only to lose the game and series 4–3.

In the third period of the game, it was rewarding to receive private acknowledgement and well wishes from players who knew it was the last time we would share NHL ice together. Buffalo goalkeeper Patrick Lalime called me to his goal crease after the last commercial timeout to tell me how I had made the game better over the many years he had been watching me, first as a youngster growing up and then as an NHL player. Patrick said it had been his honour to be on the ice with me in the NHL. I was deeply touched. Patrick broke into the NHL with Pittsburgh in 1996–97; then, after three years in the minors, moved on to Ottawa, where he enjoyed an excellent run, in 1999. In all those years, I couldn't recall either of us saying more than a few words to the other, beyond "Watch my crease, please." A few minutes later, big Zdeno Chára struck up a similar conversation. The difference was that Big Z, who stands six-nine, had to bend over at the waist to reach the level of my ear. He too commended me on my career and said the game was going to miss me very much. At the end of the game, I was a little embarrassed as Mark Recchi came over and gave me a big hug. At least in Mark's case I could look him in the eye! Now 42 years old, Rex has been a real warrior, a leader on and off the ice, and his work ethic and passion for the game serve as an example for young players to follow. In addition to his skill, those intangible qualities are the reason he's still in the league and so effective after 21 seasons. What a champion!

Back in the dressing room, as I removed my sweater, skates, and gear for the last time in this building, Eddie Sandford entered to have me sign the game sheets. This 82-year-old legend, arguably the Bruins' best player on the team that went to the Stanley Cup final in 1952–53 (the year I was born), was choked with emotion as he handed me the pen and paperwork that he always prepared so meticulously and had handed me hundreds of times before. Instead of the crushing handshake he usually sent me off with, tonight we embraced in friendship and mutual respect built over 30 years of working together. Both of us recognized it was the end of an era.

Now that I had said goodbye to Eddie Sandford, as well as my memories of the great players and games and the friends I had made in this city over the years, it was time to go home. My family awaited my arrival to celebrate the end of my officiating career. The countdown had come down to a single game: Sunday afternoon in Philadelphia, between the Rangers and Flyers.

LETTING GO

Two days ago, as I settled into my seat for the flight from Boston to Philadelphia, heading home, the harsh reality hit me: this will be my final game as a referee in the National Hockey League. The ride ends here! Holding on to the thought, I find myself struggling with all the uncertainty that letting go would entail. Letting go of a job and a game that I love, one that has dominated my entire adult life, seems impossible. The question of what comes next for a retired referee, who might be best known for his beautifully coiffed hair that never moves, leaves me feeling empty. Suddenly, I found myself considering difficult questions: Who is Kerry Fraser? *What* is Kerry Fraser?

The answers haven't come, and they'll have to wait a little longer. Right now, the most pressing issue is that I need to start this crucial hockey game. The opposing centres, Jeff Carter of the Flyers and Artem Anisimov of the Rangers, have lined up and put their sticks on the ice, but the puck refuses to leave my right hand. It's as if the puck has come to represent the job and game that I love, and it's impossible for me to release it. But I have no choice, my grip on the rubber disc loosens and it floats downward and lands softly between the violently slashing sticks. Instantly, it is as if someone has turned up the volume on the crowd noise, which until now has been drowned out by my thundering heart and internal monologue.

Neither player wins the draw cleanly, a possible by product of my reluctance to offer it in my usual snap-to-the-ice fashion. The puck finds its way to the stick of Flyers defenceman Braydon Coburn, and for one last time I am able to say "Game on!"

Both teams' seasons have come down to this, the 82nd and last game of the season. The winner goes to the Stanley Cup playoffs; the loser's season ends today. I wonder if, as each player laid his head on the pillow last night, he had any thoughts of a point here or there that had been squandered. Was there a recollection of something he could have done in just one of the previous 81 games to add to his team's point total? I recall officiating games involving both teams where I saw late leads given up that cost them a point. The Flyers held the lead for most of the Winter Classic before surrendering a late goal to Mark Recchi and losing in overtime. Jeff Carter and Mike Richards had had good chances to turn the decision the other way. Just two nights ago, these same two teams met in Madison Square Garden, and Marián Gáborik's goal with just over three minutes left in the third period gave the Rangers a 4–3 victory. Had that been a Flyers goal, today's game would have been worthless. In Toronto, on March 27, New York took a 2–0 lead into the first intermission, only to lose 3–2 in overtime, giving up a point *they* could have desperately used today.

Of course, it would be counterproductive to dwell on those things. All that matters now for these teams is the task at hand. As the legendary baseball pitcher Satchel Paige said, "Don't look back. Something might be gaining on you." With all that is riding on the result of the game, it is vital for the players and game officials alike to remain in the moment and not be snared by the temptation to reflect on a missed opportunity or call. I believe there are two key ingredients that will play a role in the outcome of the game this afternoon: the first is which team wants it the most and is prepared to sacrifice in all areas of the game; the second, and possibly most critical, is goaltending. It all boils down to who stops the puck. I don't envy the pressure that Henrik Lundqvist of the Rangers and Brian Boucher of the Flyers must be feeling.

It strikes me as somewhat odd that Ranger coach John Tortorella has started his fourth line of Artem Anisimov, Brandon Prust, and Jody Shelley. Peter Laviolette of the Flyers has countered with the powerful grouping of Jeff Carter, Scott Hartnell, and Daniel Brière. But it doesn't take long for Tortorella's confidence in his crash-and-bang line to be rewarded. Shelley sets himself up perfectly in front of Boucher and redirects a blast from the point by defenceman Michal Rozsíval for a 1–0 lead just 3:27 into the first period. The goal is Shelley's second of the year; his first was scored two nights ago in the 4–3 win over the Flyers. I guess you could say that Jody saves his goals for big games.

Lundqvist is called upon early to make multiple saves as the Flyers, who seem to be the team with more energy in the early going, generate many golden scoring opportunities. They say it's good to be lucky and lucky to be good, and Henrik has a little bit of luck going his way when Mike Richards, Matt Carle, and Simon Gagné all rip shots past him that hit nothing but the iron crossbar. At the end of the first period, he has stopped all 18 shots the Flyers fire at him, compared with the four that his teammates manage against Boucher. But the only stat that matters at this stage is Jody Shelley's lone goal.

The players want to play, so Kelly and I let them. We don't impose ourselves unnecessarily. It's not until 6:49 of the first period that Kelly calls the first penalty, against Brandon Dubinsky for tripping. The only other call of the period is at 11:33, when I whistle Brière for a similar infraction. Each game has a unique heartbeat, and if you interfere with that by overcalling the game, it flatlines. You also risk generating a negative flow of emotions directed toward the officials.

At each commercial timeout, I duck into the Flyers' penalty box, where our commercial co-ordinator, Scott Adams, has another of my nine game jerseys at the ready. I sit low on a chair in a corner of the box and discreetly switch jerseys. Midway through the second period, I find myself sharing the space with Daniel Brière, who is serving a coincidental roughing minor (Rozsíval is in the Rangers' box). Needless to say, his appeal for parole is to no avail.

Once I've changed, Kelly and I take a few moments to compare notes on how the game has progressed since the previous timeout. Most often, though, I am left with my thoughts of other games and experiences in this building—and across the parking lot at the Spectrum, the original home of the Broad Street Bullies.

My very first game at the Spectrum was not actually as a referee. In April 1975, I was sitting at home on a rare Sunday morning off, having just returned from an American Hockey League game the night before, when the phone rang at 8 a.m. On the other end of the line was NHL referee-in-chief Scotty Morrison, who asked me to get to Philadelphia right away for the game that night. Linesman Claude Béchard had hurt his back the night before in New York, and I was apparently the only NHL-contracted official available to join linesman Leon Stickle and referee Wally Harris.

The Broad Street Bullies, who would beat the Buffalo Sabres four games to two that year to win the Stanley Cup for the second consecutive year, were playing the Atlanta Flames that night. The Spectrum was an intimidating place to enter for the first time. I wasn't just intimidated by the thought of throwing Bobby Clarke out of a faceoff (which wasn't going to happen), but by working with these two veteran officials, even though they did their very best to make me feel welcome. Leon was a loose and funny guy. He would tell a joke and laugh loudly before he even got to the punchline; just a great guy to be around.

Things went pretty well in the game; by the middle of the third period, the Flyers were ahead 5–2 and there had been only one fight that didn't amount to much. The Flames had shown little interest in going 15 rounds with any of the Bullies that night, which made for a good first visit for me. Stickle handed me the puck for a faceoff in the Atlanta zone and told me to wait before I dropped it because there was a TV commercial timeout. I asked how I would know when the break was over, and Stick (or "Tickle with an S," as he would often say) told me he would let me know. I told Clarke and the Flames centre to hold on, and they waited patiently as I stood and awaited further instructions from the senior linesman. Finally, Wally Harris skated over and said, "Can I ask what the hell you're waiting for to drop that puck?" I said I was waiting for the commercial to end. Wally looked at me as if I had two heads and said, "You dumb-ass, the game isn't even televised! Drop the puck and let's get the hell out of here before they [the Flyers] wake up!" Then, he added, "And don't listen to Stickle anymore."

I laugh quietly to myself at the memory. This game *is* being televised, and now the commercial break is over and it's back to work. At the end of the first period, Jody Shelley has a nick on the bridge of his nose and says Mike Richards high-sticked him as they both went to their benches for a line change. None of us saw it, and Shelley is more upset at Richards than with us as the period ends, causing words to be exchanged between the two on the way to their dressing rooms. At the start of the second period, I approach

Shelley and tell him the officiating crew discussed the line change and none of us saw what had taken place; after apologizing for the oversight, I suggest that he let it go. I tell him he's playing great, and recall instances from my 30-year career when the team that won the Cup did so on the backs of their fourth-line players. In particular, I mention Randy McKay and Mike Peluso's major contribution to one of the New Jersey Devils' Cup victories. I close by warning him to stay disciplined and not to screw it up—I can tell that he's very focused today, and I just want to make sure that he stays that way. A focused Jody Shelley and his linemates, coming out hard for their first shift of the second period, are rewarded with two good scoring chances off the Flyers' turnovers they force.

There are certain players who have a feel for the pulse of both the game and their team. A team leader like Philadelphia's Ian Laperrière knows exactly when to light the fire. Down a goal, and with the Rangers' fourth line coming out hard at the start of the period, Laperrière lines up for a faceoff in the neutral zone opposite Aaron Voros, who's always a willing combatant. When the puck is dropped, so are the gloves, and the hometown crowd scores the fight a win for Lappy. Whatever the outcome, Laperrière has accomplished what he set out to do. On his way to the penalty box, he pumps his fists as the crowd erupts in cheers to energize their heroes. He has lit the fire again.

Now seated in the penalty box following the fight, Laperrière puts his sweater back on after adjusting his equipment. I sit on the chair beside him, taking my own sweater off and putting on a fresh one. With a puzzled look, he asks what I am doing. I tell him of my plan to wear nine in this, my final game. On the spot, Lappy asks me if he can buy one. I laugh, but he says, "No, I'm really serious. I want one of your jerseys." When I tell them they are for my kids, he asks if I would adopt him! I have seen Ian Laperrière perform over many seasons since his rookie year in 1994. He's a true warrior and has been a spiritual leader of every hockey club he has been on. He does whatever it takes to get the job done, and has earned the respect of players and officials all around the NHL. I am going to miss interactions like these with quality guys like Lappy.

Stepping out of the penalty box, I almost trip over one of the ice girls as they scrape the ice near the blue line. I have a flashback to lying on my back and looking up into the face of Flyers athletic therapist Jim McCrossin from a similar vantage point, at the Spectrum in 1982–83.

The Flyers' guests that evening were the Calgary Flames, and I found out the hard way that Calgary defenceman Richie Dunn could hit the bull's eye with his shot. The Flyers had attempted a pass out of their zone, and Dunn stepped out of nowhere to intercept it. I was chasing the play out of the Flyers' zone on the same side that Richie was on. Since he was under some pressure—about to be levelled by a check—he wound up and took his best slapper to pound the puck back into the Flyers' end. The problem was, I was only 20 feet away, and directly in his sights. *Pow!* I thought I had been hit by a cannonball as the shot drove me backwards, shattering my protective cup. Down I went, lying on my back with the feeling (or lack thereof) that my manhood had been damaged beyond repair. I didn't just see stars, I caught a glimpse of the entire universe!

Usually, the treatment for a contusion is to rub the injured area, but neither Jim McCrossin nor I was about to do that. Eventually, I returned to my feet and Richie offered an apology. By now, I was able to smile, and I told him—in a voice two octaves higher than usual—that I was just glad it was he who shot the puck and not Lanny McDonald or Kevin LaVallee, who could really wire it. I've always found that when it hurts that much, it's always better to try to laugh.

Neither team is laughing today, though. The Flyers are pouring it on offensively, and the Rangers' slim lead is holding up purely on the strength of Henrik Lundqvist's exceptional play in goal. At 11:29 of the second period, the Flyers' other tough guy (and resident actor) Daniel Carcillo draws a penalty against P.A. Parenteau. Parenteau placed his stick near Carcillo's feet, he felt the pressure, and went with the contact, snaking his leg on the way down to make sure Kelly sees he has been tripped. Daniel Carcillo is a good kid. He's a solid player with both skill and toughness, and he has become extremely effective. He'll learn the hard way, especially as a tough guy, that it's better to try to fight through some pressure than to use it to draw a foul and embarrass the ref and the game.

Watching him fall from my vantage point a considerable distance away, I am reminded of the conversation Rangers coach John Tortorella initiated with me when I first stepped onto the ice prior to the start of the game. "I don't want you to think this is gamesmanship," Torts said, "but I want you to be aware that Carcillo falls down very easy for them, and he tried to draw fouls the other night in our building." I said that I had seen that game, and my colleagues and I had addressed the subject in a meeting earlier. "Okay," John said, "I just wanted you to be aware." That must be why I see him now, behind his bench, ready to pull the hairs out of his beard. In honour of my final game, all of the on-ice officials are wearing number two, so Torts must be wondering which "Fraser" to yell at. The Rangers kill the penalty, but not before Lundqvist makes a great save on a one-timer from the stick of Chris Pronger.

Pronger really comes up big when the game is on the line. He was an even more intimidating presence a few years ago, when the rules still allowed for stickwork in front of the net. When Chris arrived in the NHL, we applied a liberal standard when a team was killing a penalty. A player almost had to put his stick clean through an opponent before we would put his team two men short. When Chris played in St. Louis, he came to learn that I didn't subscribe to that approach to a degree that satisfied him. But he came around to my way of thinking, and as an intelligent player, he understood what he could get away with—and with whom. Now, with 23.9 seconds left in this second period, the puck is cleared along the side boards from behind the Rangers' net by Michal Rozsíval. High up the boards, Jody Shelley turns to receive the puck. Just as he touches it, Pronger steps up from his blueline position and levels Shelley with a monster hit. While Jody may not be seeing as many stars as I did after Richie Dunn's slapshot, I believe a couple of little birdies tweeted around his head for a moment.

In the dressing room during the second intermission, my colleagues and I review and update our mental checklist once again. I have always maintained that a referee's latest game is the one everyone remembers most. And, when asked which game was the most important one I've ever worked, I have always answered, "My next one." Since there won't be a next one for me, how I finish this game could make the difference as to how I will ultimately be remembered. My 30 years could come down to the next 20 minutes. I exit the dressing room with the burning desire to give my personal best one last time to a game that I love.

Stepping onto the blank sheet of ice, I'm transported across the parking lot once again to an empty building that awaits the wrecking ball. Those were the days of the "Philadelphia flu," when every player who wore the distinctive black-and-orange crest on their sweater automatically became a little bigger and more menacing. The personnel changed over the years, but the face, the team, and the organization had not changed since 1969, the Flyers' third year in the NHL. That distinction belonged to their captain, Bobby Clarke, who was as fearless as he was toothless. His team could be as tough on referees as they were on their opponents, and Clarkie could chew up (and chew out) many an official with the few teeth that remained.

As a cocky young referee with my name on my back rather than a number, my objective was to quickly establish throughout the league that I was a referee who could be counted on to be fair and would not be intimidated. I also realized early on that I would need to develop relationships within the game, opening lines of communication and letting players know exactly how far they could go. The best place to start with every team is with their leader, and there was no doubt that in Philadelphia, that player was Bobby Clarke. While there were times that I had to bare my own fangs in dealings with Bob, I always did my best to communicate in a professional manner and counter disrespect, when it came my way, with respect. Sometimes, this was a tall order. Although I dealt with Clarke in the last four years of his career, I don't think it can be said that he had mellowed with age. You would be hard pressed to find a tougher competitor anywhere, right up to the last time he broke his stick over someone's ankle. Bobby Clarke was an intelligent hockey man; he knew the game and he knew how to win. I like to think that, during our time on the ice together, we established mutual respect rather quickly. When I'm working in Philadelphia, I can't help but think of Bobby Clarke. To this day, his face is as recognizable as any in the history of the game—with or without his teeth.

I skate one more lap around the ice before the teams arrive for the start of the third period. I join my fellow officials at centre ice, where Kelly Sutherland offers me the puck to drop at centre ice one last time. I decline his kind offering, not as a rejection of his respect and friendship, but rather as a sign of my own. I step back and paraphrase the memorable and meaningful words from Lieutenant Colonel John McCrae's 1915 poem "In Flanders Fields," which adorned the Montreal Canadiens' dressing room in the old Forum (and now the Hockey Hall of Fame in Toronto): "To you from failing hands I throw the torch; be yours to hold it high." It's my turn to pass the torch to this fine young man whom I first met when he was a 17-year-old boy in the mid-'80s at the Western Hockey League School of Officiating in Calgary.

I watched him work throughout the week at that camp, and in the subsequent years that he continued to attend and learn. At the time, Kelly had obviously patterned some of his officiating mannerisms after mine. Heck, he even styled his hair like mine, though not quite as well! The other students even teased him that first year, because Kelly carried my hockey card in his wallet. The first time I saw Kelly work, I told Richard Doerksen, a vice-president of the WHL, that this Sutherland kid was a star, a can't-miss NHL prospect. He has long since arrived. I am so proud to be standing here today with Kelly, Darren Gibbs, and Don Henderson, all former students of mine at the WHL School of Officiating.

We assume our positions, and Kelly drops the puck as the third period gets under way. Although there is more desperation evident in the Flyers' attack right from the start of the period, they still can't find a weakness to exploit in Lundqvist's game—until, that is, Ranger rookie P.A. Parenteau takes a penalty for interference, for something he might have gotten away with in the American Hockey League. On the penalty kill, the Rangers turn over the puck in the neutral zone. Jeff Carter grabs it and leads a speedy attack that results in a direct shot on goal from in close. Lundqvist makes the first save, then gets caught off balance as Matt Carle jumps in from his defence position and taps the puck past the fallen Rangers' goalie to tie the game at 13:06.

Carter's determination on the play reminds me of Eric Lindros, who always drove hard to the net and would not be denied a goal when one was needed. There was much fanfare throughout the hockey world when Lindros finally agreed to play in the NHL, after the Quebec Nordiques made the deal that landed Eric in Philadelphia.

I was assigned to Lindros's very first game as a Philadelphia Flyer. There was so much interest surrounding him that my father flew in from Canada just to watch this new superstar play in his first game. I could see that he was a superior talent in that very first game. Rather than make a move to go around a player, he took the "bull in the china shop" approach, preferring to go over or through an opponent. I knew it would take its toll. He had some wonderful years, and was a joy to watch. In the end, Eric Lindros was truly a great talent that, unfortunately was unable to reach maturity before injury claimed him.

As the centre on the famed Legion of Doom Line with John LeClair and Mikael Renberg, Lindros was part of one of the most prolific scoring units of the time. Given their size, speed, and skill, this trio was very aptly named. Teams trying to find a way to neutralize them found it impossible. Lyle Odelein of the Canadiens thought he had the answer one night in Montreal in 1995, when he challenged the Big E to a fight. Things didn't go too well for Odie, though, after the game, he threatened to get Lindros in the rematch game back in Philadelphia a couple of nights later. Brian Burke was the VP of hockey operations and had me reassigned to that game. Burkie and his assistant, Dave Nonis, attended the game in case Odelein made good on his threat. I was prepared to bring the hammer down if necessary to keep the game safe and under control.

For the opening faceoff, I fired the puck down so hard that it scooted through my feet and just behind me. I rotated my upper body, both to find the puck and to move away from it, when Le-Clair came racing out of his starting blocks from the wing position to get the loose puck, hammering me right in the middle of my back. Two of the discs in my back were herniated upon impact. I was doubled over and could not straighten up. I backed up toward the penalty box, and one of the linesmen blew the whistle to stop play. Still bent in half (I measured about two and a half feet tall in this position), I was guided off the ice by Jim McCrossin, the Flyers' trainer. The game, one to which I had been assigned for a specific purpose, was only a dozen seconds old and I was being dragged off the ice, unable to stand up.

The doctors were waiting for me in the medical room. They got me partially undressed, and Michael Wienik, a doctor of osteopathy from Temple University, manipulated me to the point where I was able to stand erect. The problem was that now I couldn't bend over! Burkie and Nonis, both of whom are outstanding people as well as great hockey minds, were in the room and very concerned. Burkie asked me what I wanted to do. I said we didn't have an alternative; I was going out to finish what he brought me here to do. But first, I needed their help to get dressed. Since I couldn't sit or bend over, I had to stand while they dressed me. I wish I had had a camera as Brian Burke hitched up my pants.

Brian and Dave then bent down and each laced up one of my skates. Burkie commented that the size of my feet reminded him of lacing up his boys' skates the week before. I couldn't resist giving Brian Burke a little tap on the top of his head while he was down there tying my skates. He said, "Kerry, if you ever tell anybody about this, I'll fire you." (I guess retirement beats "fire-ment.") I was helped to the ice, and the game continued. At every stoppage for a commercial, I went to the referee's crease, lay on the ice, and stretched my back every way I could. Between periods, I was unable to sit, and Dr. Wienik continued to work on me.

Fortunately, Lyle Odelein never made good on the threat he issued. I finished the game and shuffled my feet like a 90-year-old man as I left the arena that night. I ended up flat on my back on the floor for two nights, unable to sleep. It was definitely the worst sustained pain that I ever felt. After four weeks of therapy that wasn't helping, I got a spinal block that had me moving and back on the ice just in time for the playoffs. The Legion of Doom certainly inflicted some pain that night.

Interestingly enough, as I arrived at the Wachovia Center this afternoon, I received a congratulatory text message from John Le-Clair that was very much appreciated. LeClair is one of the all-time nice guys in this business and a real class act. I know one thing: I can always count on him to have my back, a fact that I'm reminded of every time I pick up one of my grandkids.

Fortunately for Jeff Carter and the current Philadelphia Flyers, he prefers to move around opponents as opposed to going through them. If Jeff takes care of himself, I can see him plying his trade for many years to come. Having set up the tying goal this afternoon, he has inspired his Flyers' teammates to mount an even more ferocious attack against Henrik Lundqvist, who stops everything the Flyers throw at him.

In the final 30 seconds of the period, the Flyers are buzzing all around the Rangers' end zone. With 14.6 seconds remaining, Daniel Carcillo follows his shot to the net despite Lundqvist having already frozen it, causing me to kill the play. Rangers defenceman Marc Staal engages Carcillo at the side of the Rangers' net. Fire is streaming from Carcillo's eyes as both players bring their hands up toward each other's chest and face. This is the tipping point for Carcillo, where a glove to his face could instinctively result in a retaliatory punch—and a penalty. As I blow the whistle and kill the play, I anticipate a hot spot in front of the net. I move quickly from behind the net, arriving behind Carcillo just as he appears ready to throw a punch. I decide to fully take on my role as an "enforcer." I grab Daniel by the sweater and spin him toward me, skating him quickly toward the corner and away from the scrum.

Carcillo snaps his head toward me. He thinks I'm a Ranger, and is ready to let fly with a barrage of punches. Realizing who has grabbed him, Daniel, still fired up, says, "You're lucky it was you that grabbed me." I respond, "No, *you're* lucky it was me that grabbed you. You do not want to take a penalty at this time." I pat Carcillo on the chest with my open hand and calm him; the team player in him quickly returns, and he regains his focus. My last call in regulation time turns out to be one that I prevented.

The third period ends with the score tied at one. This nail-biter is heading to overtime.

But overtime doesn't resolve anything. The Rangers play it conservatively, doing nothing to risk making a mistake that could result in a Flyers goal. At one point, they seem to be content to let the clock run out, as they pass the puck back into their own end. Whatever the outcome, one thing has already been settled in my mind: I would be hard pressed to remember a better display of goalkeeping than the one Henrik Lundqvist is putting on today. After 65 minutes, Lundqvist and his Rangers teammates have been outshot 47–25 by the Flyers. This guy is an All-World player!

With the score still tied, there will be a shootout. Kelly stations himself at the Rangers' end, while I prepare to make the calls at Brian Boucher's goal line. Philadelphia's Danny Brière scores first on a nifty move, while Erik Christensen of the Rangers is foiled by a Boucher blocker save. After Lundqvist stops Mike Richards's shot, P.A. Parenteau has the puck hop off his stick momentarily, before he regains control and catches Boucher off guard, sneaking a shot past him.

Claude Giroux now approaches Lundqvist slowly and makes a slight move to freeze the Rangers' backstop. With enough daylight showing through the five-hole, he finds the back of the net with his shot. The Flyers hold a 2–1 lead in the shootout with the Rangers' third shooter, Olli Jokinen, ready to bring his 40-percent success rate down on Flyer goalie Brian Boucher. I check to make sure Boucher is ready. He gives just a slight nod of the head, and his gaze communicates an intensity of focus that he does not wish to break. His eyes are now set firmly on the puck that sits on the centre-ice faceoff dot as Jokinen circles in the distance, at his own goal line. I blow my whistle loudly and point to him to take his shot. He builds speed, then winds up. Brian Boucher teases Olli with an open five-hole, and he takes the bait and goes for the gap. Just as quickly, Boucher seals it off—save! I wave my arms, signalling NO GOAL! The Philadelphia Flyers have won the game and will move on to the Stanley Cup playoffs. And I have now made my *"final call"* as an NHL referee.

As the Flyers vault over the boards to tackle their new hero in his goal crease, I can't help but think of Lundqvist skating off alone at the other end. While the Flyers clearly outplayed the Rangers and deserved the win, the Rangers' goalie deserved a better fate for his outstanding performance. His dejected teammates, with the exception of a few, filter off their bench into their dressing room. I stand near the penalty box outside the blue line closest to the Flyers' end, waiting for their celebration to wind down so that I can skate to the Zamboni entrance to my dressing room. New York centre Vinny Prospal climbs over the boards from his bench with the heaviness that a crushing loss can display and skates toward me. He then takes off his right glove and extends his hand. As I shake it, Vinny wraps his other arm around me, and, embracing me, utters the words, "Congratulations on a great career; you are the best." Others—Marián Gáborik, Artem Anisi-mov, Chris Drury, and the player who might be the most disappointed of them all, Olli Jokinen, offer a congratulatory embrace as well. I can't tell you how meaningful it is to have these players recognize me in this way after suffering such a devastating defeat.

As the Flyers make their way off the ice to continue the celebration in their dressing room, I am approached first by Brian Boucher, who embraces me, then Ian Laperrière, Mike Richards, and Jeff Carter, who offer their congratulations. Just as I am about to skate off the ice, I hear an excited voice beckon me back. It is Flyers coach Peter Laviolette. He hugs me and offers some very complimentary remarks and hopes that we can remain in touch with one another. In spite of the differing emotions that each team was experiencing, there is a common sentiment in the way all of them approached me. I feel humbled, and feel that my journey is now complete. The most important thing I ever wanted to achieve in my career was to be respected for a job well done and make a positive difference to the game. The heartfelt outpouring of respect I am now receiving is the greatest reward I could have hoped for.

After congratulations are extended by each of the other officials, the telephone line from the Toronto war room rings. It's Mike Murphy, senior vice president of hockey operations. Mike is a good man and says he wishes to thank me for all the great years of service, as well as the excellent work each of us has done today. In closing, he says "they" will be in touch next week. (As this book goes to press, I'm still waiting for "them" to get in touch with me. Still, I appreciated his call to the dressing room.) I'm quite sure they were heaving a big sigh of relief when our game finished without incident or controversy.

After showering and dressing, I am paid a visit by an unexpected guest: Ed Snider, chairman of Comcast Spectacor and co-founder of the Philadelphia Flyers. Since his company owns the building, I guess he doesn't really need permission to enter. Back in the days when he brought the Flyers franchise to Philadelphia, this passionate owner's occasional visits to the officials' dressing room were not, as in this case, to congratulate a referee on anything. It is truly a surprise and pleasure to have Mr. Snider make a special trip to my dressing room to congratulate me and to thank me on behalf of the Flyers organization for, as he puts it, my outstanding service to the game. I introduce him to my colleagues, and he is most gracious with his time. Mr. Snider makes each of the guys feel appreciated for their contributions to the game as well. I invite Ed to join my family and friends at a reception up the hall at the Lexus Club.

Instinctively, I sign the game sheet presented to me by Augie Conte, the official scorer in Philadelphia, as I've done so many times before. Augie asks me to sign an extra copy for him as a keepsake of our long tenure together and our friendship. I notice a tear forming in his eye. I am struck once again by the reality that I can't delay the inevitable. There are no more destinations marked in my day planner or a schedule to keep. All this adds to the uncertainty and apprehension as to what I will do next. For the moment, the only appointment I have to keep is in the Lexus Club, where 100 people are gathered to toast me and offer their best wishes. Have my 30 years in the NHL come down to this final hour in the Wachovia Center, my last place of work? (Just one of 30 offices I have worked out of this season.) Am I truly being swept out with the popcorn boxes, empty beer cups, and other refuse discarded by the patrons?

Of course, before I join the party up the hall, I have one last detail to attend to—my hair! Standing in front of the mirror in my dressing room, brush in one hand and a bottle of Paul Mitchell hairspray in the other, I am stopped in my tracks, spellbound by the piercing gaze of the face looking back at me. I examine the image as closely as I ever have before, searching for some revelation of a new direction. On the surface, my face exposes signs of age and scars from battle wounds, the perfect hair is now traced with hints of grey, and my eyes are wearing a glaze of fatigue from the many miles travelled and battles that have been fought—some won, but many lost. It is not vanity that causes me to study my reflection in the smudged glass in this moment, but to find the answers to those elusive questions. Who is Kerry Fraser? What is Kerry Fraser? None are forthcoming. Perhaps I need to delve more deeply and enter that space where hurt and love are held simultaneously and can meld together to confuse the mind. But the wall is up, one I am unable to penetrate in this room, alone with my thoughts and shallow reflection.

NHL security representative John Malandra snaps me out of my frozen pose in front of the mirror and advises me that Kathy and my guests are anxious for me to arrive. It's time to go. I take one last fleeting glance at my reflection before heading out the door. The connection is broken—or has it just been made?

With each step of the walk from the dressing room, I continue to ponder the man in the mirror. Passing by the vacant Flyers locker room, I wave to Rock Oratorio and Mike "Huggy" Craytor as they finish hanging the players' equipment that, thanks to the shootout win, will be used again in a couple of days, up the turnpike in Newark, New Jersey.

As I approach the empty visitors' locker room, I am pleasantly surprised to see NHL deputy commissioner Bill Daly standing in the hall. He is waiting for me. Bill was in Washington this afternoon to present the Presidents' Trophy to the Capitals, who, despite losing to Boston in a shootout, finished first in the overall standings. He made a special trip to Philadelphia, even though he missed the game, to stop by and congratulate me on my final game. It would have been so much easier for Bill to continue up the turnpike to join his wife, Gloria, and their new baby at home. Instead, he took this detour and has been waiting for me. I invite Bill to come and join my family and friends up the hall. He protests that he doesn't want to crash my party, so I ask him if he didn't hear me say the gathering included my *friends*, and I would be honoured if he, as my friend, would join me there. Walking up the hall together, Bill and I reminisce about many of the good times we have shared—and even a few that weren't so good.

As Bill and I continue up the hall, I am greeted by the ushers and hallway attendants I have seen many times over the years. They have remained at their posts just long enough to wish me well before they punch out. With each hand I shake and warm smile I receive, I am brought one step closer to communion with the man in the mirror I left in the dressing room a few short minutes ago.

As I walk into the party at the Lexus Club, I finally confront the depth of my reflection face to face. The wall is down at last, and I can see clearly into my heart, where I find the answers to the questions that have eluded me. My first answer comes in the misty eyes of my dear wife and soulmate, Kathy, whose tight embrace sends a statement that I had been away from her far too long and our time had now come. I get more insight from the adoring eyes and loving words that each of my children offers me. They all connect with me in a very distinct and special way in our moments together. It is as though they are telling me, "It's okay, Dad, that you had to be away so often. We understand, we love you so much, and are so proud of you!" The next generation greets me with the innocence and tenderness that melts the heart of every proud grandparent as they jump into my arms and squeeze me tightly around the neck.

As I look beyond my family, I see more than a hundred friends greeting my entrance into the room with applause. Perhaps even more important, they are applauding the newly acquired blessing of time, knowing that Kathy and I will be able to be more active participants in their lives as friends. Yes, I have found the answer to my questions. It has only taken 30 years or more, but my search is over!

I have finally arrived at my destination. It's time to let go.

ACKNOWLEDGEMENTS

Whenever I read a book, I am often guilty, like most everyone I'm sure, of simply skimming this section, perhaps looking for a familiar name or just passing over the acknowledgements entirely. Who ever really reads a seemingly endless *thank-you* list posted by the author, other than those who expect to be gratified for some form of contribution?

Trust me, from now on I will read every line and every name that the author deems worthy of his or her appreciation. I now understand that without the time, talent, and support of many special individuals, even a seasoned author's creation would never go to publication. I sincerely hope you read this to the end and join with me in acknowledging the special people who made this project possible. If you like the book, you have them to thank—if you hate it, then blame me for missing my final call because it truly wasn't their fault!

The first toot of the whistle goes to my biggest critic and adversary when I arrived in the NHL as a referee, but who ultimately became my friend, the Hockey Maven Stan Fischler, who inspired me to read and write as a young boy through the many books he wrote about my hockey heroes. (I can't wait for Stan to critique me as an *author*.) First an apology to the many English teachers I frustrated by taking up space in their class as I day-dreamed about making it to the NHL. More important, thanks to all of you for occasionally bringing my mind off the ice rink and back to some form of creative thinking that proved invaluable to writing this book; especially Mr. Ken Ayers (grade 7) and Mr. Jim Capes (grades 9–10).

I haven't read the *authors' rule book*, if there is such a thing, but I quickly learned a great call an author can make is to team up with the right publisher. On the depth chart it is akin to acquiring that key player to provide a chance to win the Stanley Cup. I am most grateful to Alan Kreda for scouting and providing the intro-duction to my first draft choice overall, Jordan Fenn of Fenn Pub-lishing / Key Porter Books. A man of unshakable character, integ-rity, and knowledge in his field, Jordan and I established a solid professional business relationship in our very first meeting. I am equally as grateful to have developed a personal friendship with Jordan as well. A standing ovation to Fenn Publishing's team of All-Stars led by editor Jane Warren; her assistant, Diana Mara-goni; freelance editor/hockey historian Lloyd Davis; the mystery man I only encountered through an electronic source, but in my book is clearly the winner of Hart Trophy as MVP, Martin Gould, art director, for supporting the stories in picture form; and to Sheila Douglas, assistant to the publisher, for answering my many questions. This book would not have got into your hands if not for the energy and talent of the sales team led by Tom Best, VP of marketing at Fenn, along with publicist Lisa Mior. To all of you at Fenn Publishing I offer sincere thanks for guiding me through my rookie season.

I am deeply indebted to my father, Hilt, and my mother, Barb, for providing a loving home to shelter and nurture the varied tal-ents my brother, Rick, and I acquired. They introduced us to and coached us in the game of hockey where both of us were able to earn a living. To my valued and respected friends over the years from the NHL, beginning with Frank Udvari for discovering me, Scotty Morrison for giving me a chance to succeed, and John Mc-Cauley for his undying friendship and mentoring; to Mr. Clarence Campbell, John Zeigler, Gil Stein and Brian O'Neil, Bill Daly and Brian Burke for whom I developed the greatest respect. Thanks to every team owner (past and present) that provided the ice for me to skate on, the officiating supervisors that coached me, my colleagues on the ice that I broke a sweat with and who stood beside me through many challenges and rewards the game had to offer; to Benny Ercolani, league statistician, and to all the unsung heroes in the NHL offices that I am proud to call my friends; to every NHL security representative that provided me protection and friendship; and to team management (general managers, coaches, scouts, and trainers) that security sometimes protected me from, but most often for your professional support and conduct. The loudest cheers go to all the players that I encountered during my career. Each of you ultimately made this book possible. You are the game in the present as well as in the historical form, and it has been my distinct honour to skate on your frozen pond. Finally in this category I must recognize the hockey fans; even those that love to hate me! Without you this great game would be a relatively meaningless game of shinny. You hold us and the game accountable through your voice.

The very *best* of accolades I have saved for Kathy, who is my partner in all things and my soulmate. She not only supported me through my career but also in the writing of this book. As Kathy listened, she drew the best stories from my vast archive of memories, made key suggestions, provided research, and became my home editor, always bringing me back to center ice. When I worked around the clock in often failed attempts to meet the publisher's deadline, Kathy coached me and cheered me on when the task seemed overwhelming for a rookie author. I flat out could not have completed this book without her.

I want to thank each one of our children and grandchildren for their love, support, and understanding when I was locked away writing for days at a time. I would also like to thank our youngest daughter, Kara, for her assistance and input. Kara is the true writer of the family and once she completes her studies at Mount St. Mary's University in Emmitsburg, Maryland, as an English major, you will be reading one bestseller after another by Miss Kara Fraser.

And now a message to you, the reader. I sincerely thank you for picking up this book. It has been a labour of love for me from start to finish. I hope that you enjoy the book and I look forward to your comments and reviews. Hopefully, we will get the chance to meet in person as I visit a city near you. In the end you, the reader, will make *The Final Call*.